The Pubs of the Royal Forest of Dean

The Pubs of
the Royal Forest
of Dean

by

Heather Hurley

Logaston Press

LOGASTON PRESS
Little Logaston Woonton Almeley
Herefordshire HR3 6QH

First published by Logaston Press 2004
Copyright © Heather Hurley 2004

ISBN 1 904396 22 4

Set in Times New Roman by Logaston Press
and printed in Great Britain by
Bell & Bain Ltd, Glasgow

Contents

This book is dedicated to Jon Hurley for his continued support in seeking the past and present pubs, inns and taverns.

Sources of Illustrations

(t-top, b-bottom, m-middle, r-right, l-left)

Gloucestershire Record Office (includes references)
20 (D637 11/5/L2), 21 (D637 1/5/B2), 23, 37m, 49, 54, 58, 60, 61m, 63b, 66b, 68t, 69t, 70t, 78b, 94, 95ml, 96t, 232, 267, 269, 272m, 285, 287, 289, 290, 291, 294tl, 296, 298, 299t, 299b, 303b, 304t (D2242 11/2/1), 83br (D1405/2/84), 86t (D1405/2/84), 91 (D7042/8), 114t, 114b (637/1/42), 117t (D4496/83), 117b (D4496/84), 120, 127b, 129b (D3921 V1/26), 123 (D637/V3), 138t (D637/11/5/B2), 185b (GPS110/11), 222b (Q/Y6/3/1), 222t (DC/H8)

Christine Thomas (The Harris Collection)
27, 146b, 153, 223t, 223b, 224b, 228t, 229t, 230, 232b, 234t, 235b, 236, 237, 238t, 244t, 246

Cinderford Library
93, 195t, 197, 213

Monmouth Museum
138m

Herefordshire Record Office
24t, 30, 297, 303t

Hereford City Library
83

Bristol Library
257b

Dean Heritage Centre
17, 124t, 202, 210tr, 215t

Wilf Merrett
178, 180, 200, 210tl, 265b, 272t

Anne Lloyd
198b, 199tl

Ruth Hirst
149t, 155, 156t

Alan McClean
87t, 87m, 90

Maurice Bent
72b, 79

Neil Parkhurst
275

Ian Pope
24b

Amanda Wooley
22

Ian Jenkins
24b

Acknowledgments

This is another volume in the Logaston series on the social history of pubs; in this book they are situated in the Forest of Dean and its neighbourhood. The preparation of this work would not have been possible without the co-operation of many people who have spent time and effort in providing infor-mation and illustrations. Thanks are due to the late Ray Allen, for informa-tion on Forest of Dean pubs; David Campion, brewery deeds; Geoff Gwatkin, parish boundary maps; Jon Hurley, newspaper cuttings and wine information; Avril Kear, Forest of Dean knowledge; Alan McLean, Lydbrook history; Doug Mclean and John Saunders, Forest books; Dave Watts, Freeminer Brewery; and Cyril Hart, books and archives.

The majority of the research was carried out at the Gloucestershire Record Office and the Local Studies Centre at Cinderford Library with other material obtained from the Gloucestershire Collection at the Gloucestershire County Library, the Herefordshire Record Office, Hereford Library, Ross on Wye Library, Wiltshire and Swindon Record Office and Whitbread Archive. My grateful thanks to the friendly and helpful staff who were always willing to assist. Other sources of information have been gathered from articles written by John Belcher in the *Forester*, Bob Smyth in the *Wye Valley and Forest of Dean Review*, the numerous newscuttings filed at Cinderford Library and individual publicans. Not forgetting the support, encouragement and help from Andy Johnson and Ron Shoesmith of Logaston Press.

The sources of the illustrations used in this book are listed opposite. Others are from the author's collection.

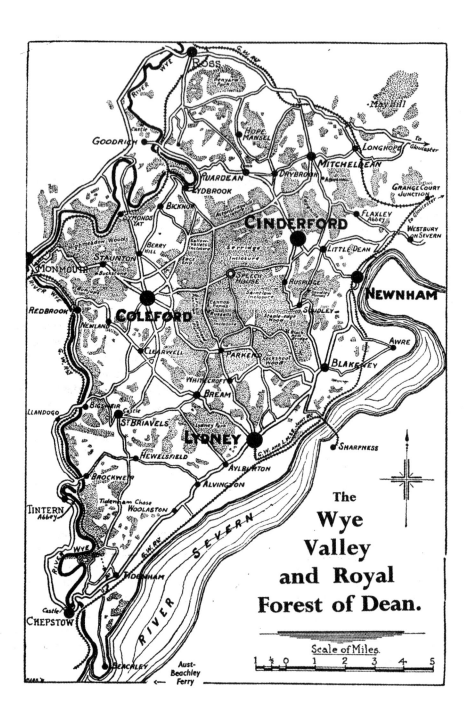

The
**Wye
Valley
and Royal
Forest of Dean.**

Scale of Miles.

Introduction

Preparing the introduction for a book such as this is the final task following the hours of researching, investigating and writing, and the only desire is to see the finished product in print. Time has been well spent in revealing the history of roadside inns, old-etablished taverns, street corner public houses, country-house hotels and the modest beer and cider houses.

This book includes all the readily available information about the past and present pubs of the Forest of Dean and its neighbourhood. It is a fascinating area lying between the rivers Wye and Severn, and stretches from the Herefordshire boundary to the outskirts of the city of Gloucester.

Here are the stories of the people and places associated with the old coaching inns which provided food and shelter to travellers; the ancient alehouses where only beer and ale were served; the town taverns where wine was also sold; and the numerous beer and cider houses that sprung up during the 19th century.

The sequence of chapters and contents changed and evolved over the two year period it took to research and write about the pubs of the Forest. The book has been planned to describe the inns, pubs and beer houses along the main routes, in the towns and villages, at many tiny settlements and former industrial sites and in isolated and scenic places along the banks of the two rivers. In order to locate old pub sites it has been necessary to wander along long lanes and footpaths, amble along stretches of the sullen Severn and the meandering Wye, and to explore the depths of the Forest.

The first two chapters cover the origin and development of inns, taverns and public houses, and the effects of varying legislation throughout the centuries. The importance of cider-making, brewing, malting and the expansion of the wine and spirit trade in the Forest of Dean is covered from early times to the present day.

Pubs have been altered and changed, opened and closed, built and rebuilt through the ages, and apart from serving as important social centres when there were few alternatives, many were used as magistrates' courts, sale rooms, doctors' surgeries, meeting places for friendly societies, and are still used as venues for auction sales, dart matches and quiz nights. In the 21st century pubs are closing at an alarming rate, so use them instead of losing them, and the traditional English pub will continue.

Heather Hurley,
Hoarwithy, August 2004

CHAPTER ONE

Inns, Taverns & Beer Houses

Early references to ale-sellers and ale-houses are sparse and cryptic, and it is only with the thirteenth century that we obtain clear evidence of the spread of ale-retailing across the kingdom. Even then it it doubtful whether many ale-sellers, variously described as brewsters, bribsters, bucksters, regrators [local dealers] of ale, and (in the case of women) ale-wives or pole-wives, ran recognisable ale-houses, at least outside towns. By the fifteenth century, however, popular drinking houses were starting to appear in considerable numbers, acquiring several of the key functions one associates with the fully fledged ale-house of the Tudor and Stuart periods.

(Peter Clarke, 1983)

Ever since man realised that fermented grain, fruit and honey produced alcoholic beverages, communal drinking places were established in settlements and along the highways. In the Bronze Age mead was made from hemp and honey, and from fermented lime and honey flavoured with meadowsweet. It is thought that a strong cocktail was produced from hemp and cannabis mixed with alcohol. In the Iron Age a brew was made from emmer wheat, a type of cider produced from crab apples and wine was imported from the Roman world in amphoræ, two-handled storage jars.

The Iron Age population of the Forest of Dean, although geographically isolated by the rivers Severn and Wye, were able to trade, but were self-sufficient to a great degree with their rich resources of iron-ore, timber and stone, and fish and animals to hunt. The better known hill-forts were at Lydney, Soudley, Lancaut, Symonds Yat and Littledean, where the inhabitants ate a diet of wheat and barley and drank a type of beer made from grain. This concoction was probably drunk communally during festivals. When the Roman settlement at *Ariconium* (Weston under Penyard) was founded late in the 1st century A.D., as a modest administrative centre and iron working site for the 10th legion, a drink 'made from barley' was often drunk instead of wine, but a Greek physician wrote it 'produces headaches, is a compound of bad juices, and does harm to to the muscles'.

1

At *Ariconium* and other nearby Roman sites, fragments of amphoræ were associated with olive oil and not wine, although it is known that the Romans poured a layer of olive oil on top of their wine containers to seal them. Throughout the Roman Empire a staple drink was produced by brewing and fermenting the fruit of vines and adding honey and spices. The Roman temple at Lydney contained a *mansio* — a guesthouse dedicated to Nodens — where pilgrims could stay and drink locally produced alcoholic cordials.

After establishing a garrison base at Gloucester around 50A.D., the Romans crossed the Severn and headed into the Forest to secure its iron resources. Transportation and communications were soon improved as they developed at least four major routes partly along existing ways which were upgraded to provide roads from Gloucester to Monmouth, Gloucester to Chepstow, Newnham to Monmouth, and Mitcheldean to Lydney along the Dean Road. Along these routes the predecessors of the inns were established for the benefit of travellers and traders for rest and refreshment.

The break-up of the Roman Empire in England took place following the withdrawal of the Roman troops shortly after 410A.D. During the Dark Ages, Saxon invaders crossed the Severn and settled in the Awre area, where Saxon place-names are traced. Between 784 and 796 King Offa marked the boundary between England and Wales with the great dyke that still bears his name. Frederick Hackwood in his *Inns, Ales and Drinking Customs* of *c.*1904 wrote:

> Our Saxon forefathers were notoriously addicted to the use of ale and mead, and regarded drunkenness as rather honourable than otherwise; for the man who could withstand the intoxicating effects of strong drink longest was the most admired and the one most respected among them.

In 853 the King of Mercia gave Lydney to Ethelred of Wessex, who conveyed the property to the monks of Glastonbury, and the manor known as Tidenham was granted to the Abbott of Bath. At the monasteries brewing and wine making took place, and the office of Cellarer was an enviable position. Religious houses offered accommodation to travellers, and according to Frederick Hawkwood 'there were three kinds of establishment open to the public, the Ale-house, the Wine-house and the Inn' during the Anglo-Saxon period.

Before 1066 the Forest of Dean was a large area of wood and waste that was reserved for royal hunting. In the 13th century the Forest stretched from the Wye to the Severn and extended from Ross to Newent and Gloucester, but since then it has shrunk in size. In the 12th century a royal castle was built on a commanding position above the Wye at St. Briavals, which became the administrative centre of the Forest. There were also castles built at Lydney,

A 14th-century inn

English Bicknor and Newnham, which were conveniently placed for hunting and were visited by several royal monarchs. The medieval travellers stayed in inns offering little comfort — a bed in a shared room and a meal 'chiefly meat, a little bread, and some beer'. Hawkwood adds:

The beds ... could not be considered dear at a penny a head in London, and sometimes less in the country, servants being generally charged at half these rates. The modern traveller might think them dear at any price when it is stated that they were invariably overrun with fleas, bugs, and other vermin.

In addition to the inns where wayfarers slept at nights there were lesser establishments along the highway, and nearly always at the road crossings — mere calling-places known as ale-houses. These could always be seen a long way off if the weary traveller but raised his eyes to look ahead for the one common sign which distinguished them all. From above the front door of every ale-house projected a long, horizontal pole, on the top of which was a thick bush. In the towns it became necessary to regulate the length and height of these signs, as not infrequently they were affixed so low as to endanger the heads of horsemen riding along the narrow thoroughfares of a crowded city. An Act of 1375 retricted them to a maximum of 7 feet above the public road.

From the 13th century there was a gradual increase in the sale of wine, ale selling was an important economic activity in town and village and rough cider was produced in great quantities. A separation began to emerge between taverns selling ale and wine, alehouses selling only ale, and the wayside inn or hostel which apart from serving food and drink also

The bush hung out some distance across the road

3

provided accommodation. Once the influence of the church began to wane and merchants started to travel, inns and alehouses became a common feature in the countryside, at crossroads, beside river crossings, near industrial activity and in the growing urban areas.

Although there had been previous attempts at curtailing the number of drinking houses, the first formal licensing law came at the end of the 15th century. This empowered Justices of the Peace to obtain sureties for good behaviour from the landlords and, if necessary, to close alehouses. Some 50 years later the Justices obtained the power, which they still retain, to both licence and suppress alehouses — hence 'licensed premises'.

A 14th-century tavern with a cellar for storage

Legislation continued and 1553 saw an Act of Parliament that curtailed the number of 'taverns', and thus limited the sale of wine. Indeed, the Act also prohibited the sale of French wines. The limits on taverns provide an indication of the size and importance of the towns at that time—London was allowed 40; York, nine; and Bristol, six. Gloucester was limited to four, the same as Exeter, Chester, Norwich and Hull. This did not mean that the population of the country was being deprived of places in which to drink — there were approximately 44 alehouses for every tavern in the latter part of the 16th century! This was equivalent to more than one drinking establishment for every 200 persons, a far higher ratio than exists today. These early alehouses were probably little different to the timber-framed and thatched houses that surrounded them. The larger ones would have had sheds at the rear where brewing was carried out and possibly cellars in which to protect their brew from temperature variations.

Taverns, being of a higher status, were probably of a superior construction. This may well be the reason why the more important towns and cities in the country tend to be well-endowed with substantial stone cellars of a late medieval date. They were obviously designed for public use and usually had well-constructed vaulted roofs and entries leading directly from the streets.

During the settled years of Elizabeth's reign the 'inn first enters its great days'. In the market towns of Coleford, Newnham, Lydney and Littledean, and along the great highways from Gloucester to South Wales, inns and taverns were meeting and trading places as described by André Simon:

A 16th-century brewer

> In all the better-class taverns there were a number of private rooms either on the street level or on the first floor; sometimes even on the second floor. The regular patrons of each tavern had the priviledge of meeting in one or the other of those private rooms. There they could discuss in private, politics and religion, if so was their wish, and that at a time when political and religious opinions were not only extreme but highly dangerous. In the privacy of the room that was theirs for the evening, they could argue to their heart's content, drink toasts that were not loyal, tell tales that would not bear repeating, and generally enjoy each other's company.

During the greater part of Elizabeth's reign, wine was abundant and inexpensive. When a pullet cost 2s., a quart of wine sold from the cask was purchased for 4d. There are numerous references to wines in Shakespeare's works, such as 'A man cannot make him laugh; — but that's no marvel; he drinks no wine' *(Henry 1V Part 2)*. The brewers were busy producing two sorts of beer: the 'double' selling at 4s. a barrel and 'the other sort of beare of the best kynde at 7s. 6d.'

5

16 **99**

Whereas by the Laws and Statutes of This Realm

NOTICE

IS HEREBY GIVEN TO ALL

INN KEEPERS, ALEHOUSE KEEPERS, SUTLERS, VICTUALLERS

and other Retailers of

ALE and BEER,

AND EVERY OTHER PERSON or PERSONS KEEPING A PUBLIC HOUSE
IN ANY
CITY, TOWN CORPORATE, BOROUGH, MARKET TOWN, VILLAGE, HAMLET, PARISH,
PART or PLACE IN THE *Kingdom of England*

That, as from the **24**th *day of* JUNE, **1700**

THEY SHALL BE REQUIRED TO RETAIL and SELL THEIR ALE & BEER

by the **FULL ALE QUART** OR **PINT**

According to the Laid Standard

IN VESSELS DULY MARKED *with* W.R *and* CROWN

be they made of

WOOD, GLASS, HORN, LEATHER OR PEWTER etc.

Any Person Retailing Ale or Beer to a TRAVELLER *or* WAYFARER *in Vessels not signed and marked as aforesaid will be liable to a* **PENALTY** *not exceeding*

FORTY SHILLINGS

FOR EVERY SUCH OFFENCE

By Act of Parliament ~ at WESTMINSTER
In the Reign of Our Sovereign ~ WILLIAM III by the Grace of God, King,
Defender of the Faith &c

By 1700 it became a legal requirement that vessels in which ale and beer were served should be accurate and marked

There is little or no documentary evidence of inns in the heart of the Forest of Dean during the 16th century, but it is probable that some were established when the Forest's resources of coal, iron and timber were becoming increasingly important and easier to transport on road and river. Certainly by the 17th century there were a number of well established inns in the towns of Lydney, Mitcheldean and Coleford, and serving the Severn at Awre, Newnham and Tidenham.

Various attempts were made during the Civil War to levy duty on both the manufacture and the sale of beer and ale—attempts which were consolidated following that war and still apply to this day. This was when beer was brewed in three different qualities: strong, table, and small, and each variety attracted a different rate of duty. It was not until the late 19th century that the duty levied became based on the original gravity of the beer. The specific gravity (density) of the liquor before fermentation gives an indication of the amount of sugars present and therefore the likely alcoholic content of the final brew. Prior to the use of a hydrometer other methods were used to judge the strength of the beer, one of which was for the examining officer to don a pair of leather breeches, pour some of the beer to be tested upon a stone step and then to sit on it. If, at the end of a specified time, he found that he was stuck to the step, then the beer was deemed to be strong!

After the turmoil of the Civil War a revolution in road travel began, so town and wayside inns played a more important role, as Richardson describes:

> The large houses flourished on the influx of new custom and on their new-found importance as stages in a regular coaching system; and the amenities they offered must have been a substantial comfort to the shaken passenger deposited there after an arduous day's journeying. From the mass of contemporary evidence available, it would seem that landlords were now genuinely eager to do their best for travellers. The rooms were well furnished at the larger inns, which catered for regular as well as chance custom, the supply of food and drink was generous, the stables were roomy, and the ostlers, waiters and serving-maids generally civil and obliging.

Inn signs had developed from the Middle Ages when the tavern, inn or alehouse needed to identify themselves in a visual manner to a population that was mainly illiterate The earlier signs chosen usually represented an association with a religious house, a local family, a trade, or a place. The occasional Crown sign often indicated an establishment dating from the Restoration, but as it showed loyalty to the reigning monarch some disappeared during Cromwell's period of power. In the Forest of Dean

7

popular inn signs included the George, representing one or other of the kings of that name; the New Inn, which was once new and often replaced an earlier establishment; whilst equally used were the Rising Sun, the Red Lion and the Nag's Head.

During the 18th century more pack horses, cumbersome wagons, traders' carts, carriages and droves of livestock were using the inadequate and narrow roads leading through the Forest and accidants happened such as one reported in the *Gloucester Journal* in 1785, when two servants of John Scudamore clashed with the Rev. Mr. Morris of Monmouth on the turnpike road near Gloucester. The latter threatened prosecution, but 'showed compassion' when they 'humbly asked his pardon' and published a full apology in the paper.

The method adopted nationwide to cope with similar problems was the setting up of Turnpike Trusts to improve the roads. The system was established in 1663 to improve the New Great North Road, but it was not until the 1750s that it had spread throughout the country. The effects were observed by the *Gloucester Journal* in 1796 when a Mitcheldean innkeeper announced 'that the new road through his Majesty's Forest of Dean, leading from Mitcheldean to Coleford and Monmouth, which is the high road from Gloucester to South Wales, is already greatly improved, and in a short time will be equal to any in this part of the country'.

With the increase in travel and transport along the mail and coach routes, modest ale-houses blossomed into larger coaching inns and post-houses, offering rest and refreshment to the weary traveller. The stableyards presented a busy scene, with impatient horses waiting to be changed, harnessed or stabled. Neighbouring activities included a smithy to replace loose or cast shoes, wagon loads of hay and fodder being delivered, gallons of water being manually pumped and piles of manure heaped onto the 'dung pit'. Facilities of coaching inns were available at Mitcheldean, Coleford, Lydney, Newnham and Gloucester.

In 1780 an Attorney at Law, Mr. Cotterell, stayed at the 'Booth Hall Gloster' for three days. His bill for meals and drinks for himself and friends or business colleagues totalled £4 9s. 11d. Each day breakfast, bread and cheese, dinner and supper were served together with ample measures of beer, toddy, punch, wine, and Madeira. According to T.A. Layton's 1959 *Encyclopaedia of Wines and Spirits*, a toddy 'is a hot beverage made of whisky or brandy or other spirituous liquors, plus hot water, and flavoured with lemons'. Punch 'is a beverage composed of wine or spirits with hot water, milk or tea, and flavoured with sugar, lemon, some spices or cordial'. It was served hot, with rum and lime being the most popular spirit and fruit. The 16th-century Booth Hall was replaced in 1816 by the Shire Hall.

However, in 1781 the Hon. John Byng was not impressed with the Beaufort Arms at Monmouth, 'I arriv'd here this evening, rather tired, and am now sitting in a mean room at this bad inn; which may be the best here. The stables are new and good, that's a comfort; for if my horse does not fare and sleep well, well there wou'd be an end of my travel'.

Arriving at Gloucester on an 'intolerable bad' road, Byng wrote 'the first person met in Picadilly cou'd tell more of the country, than I cou'd learn in the Bell Inn'. However he was delighted with the road back to Monmouth 'mounted upon such a clever horse, that if at the end of 40 miles, I do but shake my whip, or close my legs, he instantly curvets from playfullness, distaining to trip on any stone' and he found the landlord 'tolerably intelligent'.

On his second tour to South Wales in 1787 Byng stayed at a public house near Gloucester 'where already a gentleman of the country had stop'd for the same cause; when down we sat together to dinner, on eggs and bacon with bread and cheese, for it was past 3 o'clock'. He continued in his diary 'No turnpike road is so bad as the last six miles to Gloster, narrow, wet, and stoney; and only mended with black iron ore, dangerous to man, and horse', but found 'Our road was very good and pleasant, thro Huntley, and thro narrow, wooded lanes by the villages of Lea'.

In an old Gloucestershire inn, the *Rules of the House* in the 18th century have survived and provide an insight into the travellers of a bygone age:

> Fourpence a Night for a Bed:
> Sixpence including Supper.
> No more than THREE to Sleep in a Bed.
> No Ale allowed Upstairs;
> No Smoking in Bed;
> No Boots to be worn in Bed.
> No Dogs or Monkeys Upstairs.
> No Gambling or Fighting.
> No Razor Grinders and the Like
> To sleep in the Attic.

A vivid impression of 18th-century travellers arriving at an inn is supplied by Richardson:

> The tired traveller arriving at one of the large solid inns of the later eighteenth century would generally have been justified in expecting the highest degree of 'comfort and elegance'. If the coach was timed to stop for half an hour to change horses and enable the passengers to dine, the waiters would be standing at the door in readiness to assist him with his hat, shawl and coat. The landlord and landlady would be waiting in the hall, where there would be a good display of cold meats, game pies,

cheeses and pastries on view in a special glazed cupboard. The coffee-room or dining parlour would reveal an immense central table, round or rectangular, laid in readiness for the meal, with good plated cutlery and spotless table-linen. Some inns could boast a special dining-room for coach passengers, while the upstairs bedrooms, each with its curtained four-poster and good plain furniture, often of mahogany, including a mirror, a washing-table and a wig-stand, were still generally known by individual names such as the Moon, Star, Crescent or Paragon.

Although there was a duty on beer, spirits were exempt and towards the end of the 17th century, and well into the 18th, there was what Monckton, in his *History of the English Public House*, described as 'one of the biggest orgies of over-indulgence our island history has ever seen'. Every small alehouse in the country was in a position to sell cheap brandy and, in particular, gin. The result was that consumption of spirits, sold in taverns, inns, alehouses, brandy shops, dram shops, and by street hawkers, increased from half-a-million gallons in 1684 to over eight million gallons in 1743 — an increase of well over one gallon per person per year! This was the 'Gin Era' a period of drunkenness, misery and total wretchedness so well depicted by Hogarth. The various 'Gin Acts' that followed, together with increased duties and a strengthening of the powers of the Justices, rapidly changed this trend. But it was not until 1751 that the sale of spirits was successfully brought under the control of the Justices with licences issued to those already possessing an alehouse licence, and by 1758 excise duty was paid on less than two million gallons per year.

From the end of the 18th century and into the early years of the

The Apprentice's Monitor.

O R,

INDENTURES

IN VERSE

Shewing what they are bound to do.

Proper to be hung up in all Shops.

EACH young Apprentice, when he's bound to Trade,
This folemn vow to God and Man has made,
To do with joy his Mafter's juft commands,
Nor truft his fecrets into other hands.
He muft no damage to his fubftance do,
And fee that others do not wrong him too.
His Mafter's goods he fhall not wafte nor lend,
But all his property with care defend.
He fhall not buy nor fell without his leave,
Nor lie, nor injure, nor at all deceive,
Taverns and ALE-HOUSES he fhall not haunt,
Thofe fnares to Youth, thofe fcenes of vice and want,
At CARDS and DICE he fhall not dare to play,
But fly from fuch temptations far away.

O Youth! remember thou to this art BOUND.
See that no breach of this in thee be found.

The 19th-century apprentice had to foreswear all drinking-houses!

next, came the great coaching era. Apart from the traditional stage-coachmen, fashionable men drove their own lavish vehicles, drawn by quality horses. A breakfast was often served to private parties in a separate parlour of the inn, such as that taken by Lord Nelson and his companions at Ross in 1802, and at the Kymin Pavilion overlooking the Wye and the town of Monmouth. During the early 19th century Charles Heath, bookseller and antiquarian from Monmouth, wrote in detail about Lord Nelson's visits in his *Excursion Down the Wye*, but this volume contains much more interesting material of Heath's own excursions during the early 19th century. At Lea 'is a respectable Inn, should the traveller be disposed to take advantage of its hospitality'. He found the inn a 'House fitted up in the most elegant manner, and visitors will meet with every accommodation, from its present occupier'. Travelling from Chepstow to St. Briavels, Heath noted a 'Public House' where 'the visitor will have his horse taken care of, while he notices the scenes on the Wye', and at St. Briavels he observed 'The Castle is now a public house', and added 'the traveller may pass a little time very pleasantly, in surveying these ruins, with the attendant scenery, here noticed; and, being half-way between Chepstow and Monmouth, in the village will meet with a clean room, and his horses taken care of, at either of the two public houses, which adjoin the side of the road'. At Newland, Heath was impressed with the 'valuable meadow land, interspersed with rich orcharding and fruit trees, producing the best kind of cider and perry'. In this same book, published in 1828, Heath provides a contemporary description of the Forest of Dean:

> The whole Forest, of more than 23,520 acres, which is extra parochial, is divided into six walks, or parts, known by their respective Lodges ... to each of which there is a Keeper, with a salary of twenty pounds per annum, paid out of the Exchequer, beside a house and ground for their further encouragement.
>
> The privileges of the Forest are very extensive, — the free miners claim a right of digging iron ore, and coal; also to cut timber necessary to carry on their works. A gold mine was discovered in the year 1700, at a village called Taynton, on the northern borders of the Forest, of which a lease was granted to some refiners, who extracted some gold from the ore, but did not continue the work, the quantity of gold being so small as not to answer the expence of separation.

In 1821 William Cobbett published his *Rural Rides*, and when travelling from Herefordshire to the Forest of Dean, he wrote;

> No wonder that this is a country of cider and perry, but what a shame it is, that here, at any rate, the owners and cultivators of the soil, not content with these, should, for mere fashion's sake, waste their substance on wine and spirit! They really deserve the contempt of mankind and the curse of

their children — The wooded hill mentioned before, winds away to the left, and carries the eye on to the Forest of Dean ... At Gloucester (as there were no meals on the road) we furnished ourselves with nuts and apples, which, first a handfull of nuts and then an apple, are, I can assure the reader, excellent and most wholesome fare.

By the 19th century the Friendly Societies were well established in the Forest of Dean towns and villages, including Blakeney, Cinderford, Drybrook, Lydbrook and Soudley. Most meetings were held in pubs, but some societies formed by miners met at chapels. The Forest Friendly Societies date from 1760 when they were founded to provide a payment in sickness, injury or old age, to members who paid a regular subscription. Popular lodge names appear to have been Odd Fellow, Heart of Oak and the Ancient Order of Foresters.

Another occurrence during the 19th century was the rise of the Temperance Movement to encourage less drunkenness, due to the fact that many criminal offences were found to be drink related. The movement started in England around 1820, from American influences. In 1831 the British and Foreign Temperance Society was formed, and the church took up the cause in 1862.

In the 1870s the evangelists held services and served coffee at a building in Woodcroft, in an attempt to combat drunkenness amongst the Irish labourers employed in building the Wye Valley Railway, and in 1877 the opening of a temperance hotel in Cinderford was disrupted by a band organised by a local publican. At Bream in 1902 Temperance Sunday was held at the Primitive Methodist Chapel, where the preacher 'delivered two very powerful sermons, dealing with drink as a curse and total abstinence as the cure'. Due to the First World War, the temperance movement lost impetus and influence, but in some areas was reactivated in the 1920s.

Maybe the Temperance Movement had some effect on the number of licences granted and renewed in the Forest of Dean. In 1882 the *Dean Forest Mercury* reported that the Superintendent of the Forest District stated that in his opinion no fresh licences are necessary because 'the number of spirit, beer and grocer licences in the district are 67 spirit houses, 49 beer houses to be consumed on the premises, 20 off and 11 grocer licences'.

Apart from earlier attempts to regulate the marking of drinking vessels to show the capacity, it was during the 19th century that most of the legislation that affects the present-day consumption and sale of alcoholic drink was enacted. The Alehouse Act of 1828 meant that the licensee no longer had to find sureties for his behaviour. However, he was bound to use the legal, stamped measures, not to adulterate his drinks, and not to permit drunkenness on his premises. The Beerhouse Acts of 1830, 1834 and 1840 followed — the first allowed premises to open for the sale of beer, but not spirits, on payment of a simple excise licence; the second differentiated between 'on' and 'off' licences and made 'on' licences more difficult to obtain; whilst the third ensured that licences were issued only to the occupier of the premises. Throughout the country as a whole there was a proliferation of beer-houses following the first Act, many in the country areas.

Beer houses were often small and poky, located in alleys or down lanes, and frequently kept in back rooms. The customers were generally those who could not afford the higher prices of the publican's taproom, where the miners, colliers and foresters could meet, play games, find jobs and seek lodgings.

At that time there were few restrictions on licensing hours. As a whole, the only non-permitted hours were during Divine Services on Sundays, Christmas Day and Good Friday. Beer houses could only open between 4a.m. and 10p.m. The 1872 Licensing Act tidied up and tightened the complex legislation, but at the beginning of the 20th century public houses were, in general, still allowed to open for some 20 hours each day.

When the tramroads and railways rapidly took over from road travel, many wayside inns closed due to lack of business, but changes in licensing laws led to the opening of pit town and forest beer houses, where the beer retailer often doubled up as a shopkeeper, blacksmith, quarryman, butcher, mason or some other trade in order to make a living. As the industrial population grew during the late 19th century, 'successive governments sought to regulate the sale of beer, cider and spirits for the sake of public health — and even more importantly an active workforce', wrote Ray Allen in the *Wye Valley Review.*

Towards the end of the 19th century and in the early years of the following one, considerable efforts were made to close down inns, pubs and beer houses by refusing to renew licences, although these buildings were centres of civic and social life, providing a venue for recreation and leisure, and a place for magistrates courts and club meetings. According to Ray Allen:

> The story of individual Forest pubs is set within this wider framework of periodic Parliamentary Acts imposing licensing hours, attempts to reduce the number of licensed properties, and the centuries-old battle of constabulary against drunkeness and ensuing disturbance.

After the Second World War there were several minor Acts, which culminated in the 1961 Act that provided for 'restaurant' and 'residential' licences. It also gave the customers' grace — the ten minutes of 'drinking-up time'. A late 20th-century Act restored the situation to more or less what it was at the beginning of the century by allowing inns to stay open throughout the day if they so wished, most commonly any times between 11a.m. and 11p.m., with a somewhat shorter 'window of opportunity' on Sundays. A new millennium has brought new thought and it is most probable that restrictions upon public houses will be further reduced leading to the possibility of 24-hour opening once again.

Commenting on the 2002 Licensing Bill the *Daily Telegraph* reported that 'ministers presented the proposal as a law and order measure, saying that it would reduce the drunken disorder caused when all pubs close at 11pm. Residents will be given a powerful voice in deciding licence applications and the police will be given powers to close pubs for up to 24 hours if that is neccessary to protect the public'. The following year the *Forester* reported that the police 'closed two Forest pubs', refused a 'licence application' and stated that their 'main concern in Forest pubs and off-licences were under-age and after-hours drinking'. The same bill is attempting 'to tidy up the situation on who needs entertainment licences. In the past, many pubs and clubs have not needed licences because they have never had more than two musicans appearing at the same time'. This could lead to the loss of a pub tradition in and around the Forest of Dean.

> When you have lost your inns drown your empty selves,
> For you will have lost the last of England.
>
> (Hilare Belloc)

CHAPTER TWO

Brewers, Cider Makers & Wine Merchants

During the Tudor and Stuart periods when there was a limited range of drinks, cider, perry and mead were popular alcoholic beverages in the West country. A chronicler in 1601 observed that drinkers in Gloucestershire and Worcestershire were accustomed to 'be refreshed with great store of cider and perry', and in 1630 cider was praised as 'a drink both pleasant and healthy'. From around 1700 there was a greater choice of drinks including the 'West Country Tipple' of cider, which due to improved transportation was available nationwide.

Cider was also renowned for its medicinal powers. In 1664, John Evelyn wrote 'Generally all strong and pleasant cider excites and cleanses the Stomach, strengthens Digestion, and infallibly frees the Kidnies and Bladder from breeding the Gravel Stone'. Remarkable properties indeed!

Defoe wrote in 1726 'so very good, so fine and so cheap ... great quantities of this cider are sent to London, even by lane carriage tho' so very remote, which is an evidence of the goodness of it beyond contradiction'.

Captain James Cook also carried cider on his ships, as a scurvy preventive, during his second voyage of exploration from New Zealand to Tahiti. By 1800, cider was considered to be a 'cure for a wide range of ills, including vomiting, gout, ailments of the urinary tract and rheumatic diseases, and to be an effective and cleansing surgical dressing'.

In 1755 Robert Pyrke, a merchant, built a new quay at Newnham to ship cider and coal. At his quay in 1780 a Gloucester auctioneer offered for sale 'The Brig Martha' and 'The Trow Farmer', followed the next day with the sale of 'A large Quantity of Stire and choice Cyders; to the Amount of 100 Hogsheads; Squash Pear and other Perry, strong Beer, etc. by the Cask and in Bottles', together with 'a Quantity of Glass Bottles and Hampers, 200 Cyder Casks, 200 empty dry Casks' and 'a very good Malt-Mill' amongst many other items. In George Turner's account of rural Gloucestershire in 1794, he wrote:

> In my own remembrance, wine was seldom produced, but at superior tables, and then only occasionally. The principal gentlemen of the county rivalled each other in their cyders: but now, the case is altered; and cyder, and perry, are seldom produced but at dinner, and then only for a draught, as small beer [i.e. watered cyder]: after the cloth is taken away you must treat with foreign wines, or incur the imputation of not making your friends welcome.

Two years later William Marshall author of the *Rural Economy of Gloucestershire* wrote about the evils of cider drinking:

> Drinking a gallon-bottle-full, at a draught, is said to be no uncommon feat: a mere boyish trick, which will not bear to be bragged of. But to drain a two-gallon bottle, without taking it from the lips, as a laborer of the vale is said to have done, by way of being even with master, who had paid him short in *money* — is spoken of as an exploit, which carried the art of draining a wooden bottle to its full pitch. Two gallons of cider, however, are not a stomach-full. Another man of the vale undertook, for a trifling wager, to drink twenty pints, one immediately after another. He got down nineteen (as the story is gravely told) but these filling the cask to the bung, the twentieth could not of course get admittance.
>
> But the quantity drunk, in this extempore way, by the men, is trifling, compared with that which their masters will swallow, at a sitting. Four well seasoned yeomen, (some of them well known in *this* vale) having raised their courage with the juice of the apple, resolved to have a fresh hogshead tapped; and, setting foot to foot, emptied it at one sitting.

Cider was sometimes produced as a cash crop, but was usually made to be used by the farmer's family and labourers. Cider is made from bitter-sweet apples, which are richer in sugar but rather unpleasant to the taste as they contain a lot of tannin. After crushing the apples and pressing to extract the juice, farm cider was produced without the addition of cultured

A mobile cider press

Cider making at Blakeney in the early 20th century

yeast, as the fermentation relied upon the natural yeasts in the apples to produce a still, cloudy, acidic, invigorating and thirst-quenching drink. This was much appreciated during the heat of the next summer when the farmer would provide bread, cheese, and cider for those helping with the hay-making, a practice that continued into the 20th century. These delights of making hay, along with others, are described by Laurie Lee in his best-selling book *Cider with Rosie*.

During the 18th and early 19th centuries cider was being produced in the traditional method on farms and at country houses. Westbury-on-Severn contained extensive orchards where nearly every farmer made cider, which gave Westbury a reputation for 'quality cider'. Advertisements in local newspapers of that period show the importance of the cider trade: 'Three Hogsheads of good Family Cider' for sale at Gloucester in 1822, and 'Twenty Hogshead of Cider of superior quality, some of which is exceedingly fine and rich, and fit for Bottling' for sale at Hereford in 1836. The hogshead is a cider and wine measure equivalent to 110 gallons.

From the late 19th century cider started to be produced on a more commercial basis in some parts of the country, but in the Forest of Dean area there is little evidence to suggest that this happened. At Hagloe near Blakeney, a former beer retailer turned to fruit farming and cider making in the 1890s, and at Woolaston 'cider-apple-growing' remained an important crop on most farms. During the first quarter of the 20th century Sydney Willetts was making cider together with Schweppes Ltd. at Bledisloe in Blakeney. A farm at Littledean expanded its cider production to supply cider and perry to pubs in the area, but this enterprise eventually failed.

In his *Country Diary*, Eric Radley recalls that the 'best perry pears all grow within sight of Yarkleton Hill', better known as May Hill, a prominent landmark with its circle of pines and marking the boundary between the shires of Gloucester and Hereford. He wrote:

> Consider for a moment the following: Fox Whelp, which originated in the Forest; Barland and Newbridge; good varieties for amenity. Forest Styre, Hagloe Crab, and Blakeney Bark which came from Taunton and produced so sharp-tasting a drink that it is 'sufficient to take away the flesh from the inside of the mouth'. Then there were Startle Cock and Huff Cap, the latter's perry being strong enough to lift a man's headgear.
>
> The most widespread variety today is the Blakeney Red, which has become the basis of the considerable industry producing and marketing the drink labelled 'Babycham'.

At Taurus Crafts in Lydney a new shop called Random Shot was reported in the *Forester* as a 'new outlet' for selling 'a wide range of bottle conditioned beers, locally produced wines and traditional ciders', and in 2003 the *Wye Valley Review's* reporter, Bob Smyth, featured Yewgreen Farm in Brockweir where cider and perry is made and sold in bottles at local stores. It is heartening to read in the *Daily Telegraph* in January 2004 the following report:

> With names such as Hens Turds apple and the Bloody Bastard pear it is perhaps little wonder that ancient varieties of British fruit are struggling to survive. But a rescue project by the Environment Agency is saving some of the more colourful elements of our fruit-growing heritage from extinction. For the past two years the agency has been restoring 10 historic orchards in Gloucestershire. The venture will enable the reintroduction of a host of critically endangered local varieties.

However, with a long tradition of malting and brewing it appears that beer was the preferred drink in the Forest of Dean. From the early 17th century cottagers in Dean were brewing ale on a small scale at the time that John Taylor published his *Famous Historie of the most part of Drinks*. This pamphlet included the description of ale, beer, cider, perry, and meade, as well as metheglin, a spiced meade originating from Wales; sack, an old English name for sherry; and braggot, a popular spiced ale sweetened with honey.

The 1811 *Book of Trades* states:

THE BREWER

The art of brewing is of very high antiquity, but in no country has it been carried to greater perfection than in our own. The different counties are, many of them, celebrated for their peculiar ales, and London porter is famous in almost all parts of the civilized world. Different as these several sorts of liquor are, they are nevertheless composed of the same materials variously prepared.

Malt liquor, in general, is composed of water, malt, hops, and a little yeast: and the great art is to find out the proper proportions of each ingredients, to what degree of heat the water must be raised before it is poured on the malt and how best to work it afterwards.

There are two kinds of malt, distinguished by the colour; these are called brown and pale malt, and they depend on the degree of heat that is used in drying. The malt which is dried by a very gentle heat differs in its colour but little from the barley; but if exposed to a higher temperature, it acquires a deeper hue, till at length it becomes of a dark brown.

When the malt is made, it must be coarsely ground in a mill, or, what seems to be still better, bruised between rollers; it is then fit for the brewer, in whose hands the process of making beer is completed.

By this date, in large city breweries, the process of mashing no longer used human labour — the machinery was kept moving by means of steam

A mid-18th-century brewhouse

19

engines, but the method used in the small brew houses in Gloucestershire would doubtless have been as follows:

> Boil twelve gallons of water, put it into a tub with about two gallons of cold water, let it stand until the steam is sufficiently off to reflect your face with ease to yourself: put in the malt, stir it well up, and let it stand three hours. This will produce about seven gallons: after this, mash again with about twelve gallons of water more, and let it stand about two hours, stirring it well, and frequently, boil the first gently in the mean time, after being run off from the grains for nearly three quarters of an hour with three quarters of a pound of hops, strain it, boil the other in the same manner: mix it with the first, let it now stand till it is about blood warm or as warm as new milk then put in a quarter of a pint of yeast, work the whole if possible in one vessel let it stand till next afternoon, then run it in perfectly clean barrels: it ought to work after tunning, a week or ten days: in a few weeks it will be fit for use.

Reading Thomas Rudge's *Report on the Forest Pits* in 1807 it is understandable that the miners working in vile conditions needed a good brew:

> The Pits of the Forest [of Dean] are numerous, not fewer perhaps that one hundred and fifty. Many of these are worked at a shallow depth ... There are, however, at this time three engines; and, from the pits connected with them, coal of good quality has already been raised; though in all, much sulphur is contained, which in burning emits unpleasant, if not unwholesome, vapours.

An envelope of 1846 addressed to the Redbrook Brewery

20

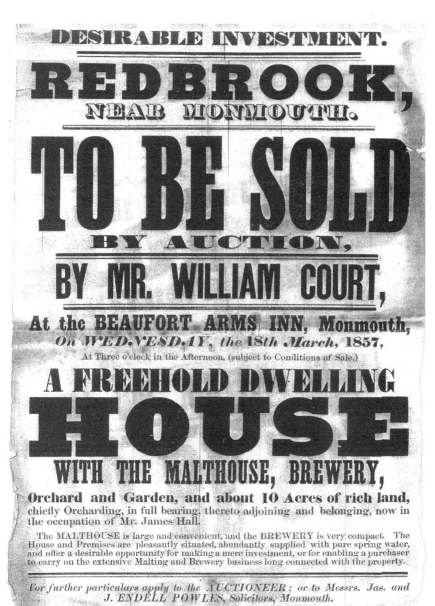

The sale of Redbrook Brewery in 1857

In the past inns undertook brewing and malting on the premises, but during the first half of the 19th century larger and more commercial enterprises were established. One of the earliest was the brewery at Redbrook. Established by Richard Sims in 1825, he placed the following advertisement in the *Monmouth Merlin* before retiring in 1835:

[He] begs to thank his friends and the Public for the patronage he has experienced, and also to inform them he is succeeded by his brother, Edward Sims, who he is sure will do his utmost to offer a malt beverage of the choicest flavour. Edward Sims, late of the firm of John and Edward Sims, of the Stroudwater Brewery having dissolved partnership with his brother on 25th day of March last, begs to inform the public that he has taken the Redbrook Brewery.

Although the documentation is unclear, it does appear that James Hall, a spirit merchant, maltster and brickmaker acquired the Redbrook Brewery a few years later, but due to Hall's death and debts incurred by the brick trade the brewery was 'To be Let or Sold' in 1855 with its 'commodious Malthouse, 'compact three-quarter Brewery' and 'constant supply of excellent water'. Two years later the property was still for sale, and the particulars offered the buyer 'a desirable opportunity for making a mere investment, or for enabling a purchaser to carry on the extensive Malting and Brewing business long connected with the property'. It was purchased by Thomas Burgham whose family ran and expanded the business and supplied at least 22 licensed premises either owned or tied to the Redbrook Brewery. In 1923 Ind Coope & Co. took over the brewery which was demolished in 1926 exposing a pleasing house. Other smaller malthouses and another brewery operated by John Ansley were recorded at Redbrook in the mid-19th century.

Mitcheldean was another place that enjoyed a long history of malting and brewing in order to supply its numerous inns. In 1839 there were eight maltsters in the town, a number that had rapidly declined when Thomas Wintle established his Forest Brewery in 1868 and adjacent malthouse in 1870. The business expanded into a huge enterprise, and after Thomas died in 1888, he was succeeded by his son, Francis, who had a reputation for paying 'poor wages' to his 60 employees. Mild and Bitter Ales and Stout were brewed and then dispatched by cask, and a limited amount was bottled by Francis's brother at Bill Mills at Weston under Penyard.

Francis Wintle retired from business in 1923 due to ill-health, and

Thomas Wintle

22

The Forest Steam Brewery
Mitcheldean, Glos.

Together with Seventy-two Licensed Properties,
also Shops, Cottages, etc

To be Sold by Auction, at the Bell Hotel, Gloucester,
on Tuesday, 6th March, 1923, at 3 o'clock precisely
(unless disposed of privately)

Solicitors :	Auctioneers :
Messrs. YEARSLEY & WADESON, Mitcheldean, Glos	Messrs. FLEURET, ADAMS & HAXELL, 22, Bloomsbury Square, London, W.C.1.

Sale of the Forest Steam Brewery in 1923

the Forest Steam Brewery which he had 'most successfully carried on, and his father before him, for nearly Sixty Years' was offered for sale together with 72 licensed properties. However, it appears that the Forest Brewery continued to operate until 1937 when 'it was resolved that the Company be wound up voluntarily and that the Liquidators be appointed ... and he was thereby appointed Liquidator for the purpose of such winding up'. The Cheltenham Original Brewery Company then took over Wintle's Brewery and 93 licensed premises situated in the counties of Gloucester, Hereford, Monmouth and Brecon.

Francis Wintle retired to live at Lea and the brewery at Mitcheldean closed, but the buildings were later re-used by Rank Xerox, and are now occupied by various small companies.

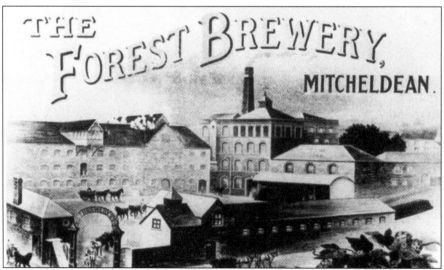

Advertisements for the Forest Steam brewery at Mitcheldean, c.1900

A George Wintle was recorded as a 'brewer' at Coleford in 1830 when Richard Nash and Mary Pearce were maltsters in the town. By 1833 John Trotter had converted a former skinhouse into a 'Brewhouse or Public Brewery with the Counting house, storehouse, furnaces, yard and appurtenances' situated in Spout Lane leading off Bank Street. The Trotters in 1842 were heavily involved with brewing, malting and hop dealing, but the brewery was later leased to a succession of brewers including Henry Salmon, Henry Courteen and Harry Clark, the last name associated with the brewery before it closed around the end of the 19th century. It was known as the Coleford Brewery in 1851 when Salmon was brewing 'Bright & Sparkling Ales, Old Beer and Porter — warranted pure, and brewed from the finest malt and hops'.

Beer is still a popular drink in Coleford, and its praises were versed by the Forest's own poet Keith Morgan in 1978:

> There byunt nothin' like good ale.
> There byunt nothin' like good ale.
> Thee cost kip thee tea an' coffee 'cause
> There byunt nothin' like good ale.
> Thee cost sup thee pint an' blind a bit
> An' argue all night a long,
> Thee cost laugh an' shout an' stamp thee vit   [vit : feet]
> And thee cost sing a song
> But when thee's be through wi' all o' that
> An' quietly wi' yer pint be sat,
> Thee's gotta nod thee yud an' say that
> There byunt nothin' like good ale.
> There byunt nothin' like good ale.

Keith Morgan (born 1942),
The 'azards o' chimuck szwippin' and other poems, Coleford, 1978

At Cinderford in 1856 John Smith was trading as a 'brewer and wine and spirit merchant', but the business was short-lived, and Cinderford waited over 150 years before another brewery was based in the town. The Freeminer Brewery was established in 1992 at Sling near Coleford; according to its printed history:

> The brewery was built with the simple aim of brewing the best real ales using the best ingredients; this tough but simple strategy has led to the brewery receiving international recognition for its quality ales, with customers in Canada, the USA, New Zealand and Europe as well as the British market ...
>
> All of the beers produced are given names which reflect the rich mining heritage of the region from which the brewery derives its name.

In December 2000 the brewery moved to its new home in Cinderford, another town with a strong mining and iron producing heritage, and near the site of the last deep shaft mine in the Forest, Northern United, which closed on Christmas eve 1965.

In 2003 the brewery produced ales and beers named Freeminer Bitter, Speculation Ale, Back Street Heroes, Resolution Pale Ale, Stay and Drink and Trafalgar 'brewed to a 19th-century recipe'. These traditional beers and real ales from the Freeminer Brewery together with those from the Wye Valley Brewery based in Herefordshire, are available in many Forest of Dean pubs.

At Blakeney a brewery had been established by the 1870s by Wilkinson Smith who brewed ale and porter. It became known as the Forest of Dean Steam Brewery around 1885 when it was operated by J.H. Hands who was followed by Samuel Evans. In 1897 the *Dean Forest Mercury* reported that the brewery at Blakeney, which had 'lately been purchased by Messrs. Arnold, Perrett and Co. from Mr. A. Burke, was closed on Monday evening, the Wickwar firm having resolved to supply their local customers from their stores at Lydney'.

During the 19th century Lydney had been associated with maltsters, hop dealers, and merchants dealing in ales, porter, wines and spirits, so it was perhaps an obvious location for the breweries of Arnold, Perrett, the Anglo Bavarian (based in Shepton Mallet) and Alton Court to dispatch their ales, beers and stout at the beginning of the 20th century.

From the Alton Court Brewery's offices and stores at Newerne in Lydney the following beverages were available in 1898 — Celebrated Mild and Bitter Ales in Cask or Bottle, Golden Crown, Golden Hop, Old Vatted Ales, Bottled Stout and Aerated Water at prices ranging from 10d. to 2s. a gallon.

At the beginning of the 20th century the Forest pubs were supplied with beer from other small breweries including Edward Thompson's Hillside Brewery at Ruardean, Lloyd and Yorath, Godsell & Sons, the Rock Brewery Co., and the breweries at Stroud and Nailsworth. It appears that these breweries were taken over either by West Country Breweries or Cheltenham Original Brewery, who in turn were acquired by Whitbread in 1963. In *Uncommon Brewer — the Story of Whitbread* written in 1992, the author, Barry Ritchie, remarks 'The relationship between breweries and the pubs they owned was complicated to the point where it was almost impossible to pinpoint exactly who benefited most from the links: the brewer, the tenant or the customer'. He also noted that:

ANGLO=BAVARIAN BREWERY

SHEPTON MALLET.

⇒ CASK PRICE LIST. ⇐

BITTER ALES.	PER KIL.	PER FKN.	PER PIN
No. 1. PALE ALE	30/-	15/-	7/6
No 2. ,, ,,	27/-	13/6	6/9
SPECIALITY AMBER ALE	21/-	10/6	5/3
FAMILY PALE ALE	18/-	9/-	4/6
MILD ALES.			
STRONG ALE	30/-	15/-	7/6
No. 1. MILD ALE	27/-	13/6	6/9
Mo. 2. ,, ,,	24/-	12/-	6/-
No. 3. ,, ,,	21/-	10/6	5/3
No. 4. ,, ,,	18/-	9/-	4/6
STOUT.			
No. 1. STOUT	27/-	13/6	6/9
No. 2. ,, (For Invalids)	24/-	12/-	6/-
No. 3 ,,	21/-	10/6	5/3

In 4½, 9, 18, 36 and 54 gallon Casks.

BOTTLED ALES AND STOUTS.

PRICES ON APPLICATION.

AGENCIES IN ALL TOWNS.

Offices and Stores: HIGH STREET, LYDNEY.

F. H. GOSLING, Manager.

The Anglo-Bavarian Brewery had offices and stores at Lydney.
A 1904 price list

By 1980 beer consumption in the U.K. had climbed to more than 40 million barrels, paralleling the growth in population and the rise in disposable income. Admittedly, there has been a fall in the last decade to more like 35 million barrels. That in itself, however, has come about partly because pubs have become only one of the places catering to public needs; its competition including wine bars, fast-food restaurants, steak houses, brasseries, cafés, clubs and hotels of all sorts, shapes and sizes.

In Roman times wine was imported in amphoræ, and in Saxon times imported and home produced wines were available, with few monasteries without vineyards. After 1066 wine was sold in most towns and during the reign of Henry I cost around 1d. a gallon. William of Malmsbury recorded that the vale of Gloucestershire was

> planted thicker with vineyards than any other province in England, and they produce grapes in the greatest abundance and of the sweetest taste. For the wine made in them does not twist the mouth by its tartness, and is little inferior to the sweetness of French wines.

The medieval merchants and monks drank wine, and a little was imbibed by the less fortunate at special occasions. In the *Canterbury Tales*, Chaucer portrays the mixed drinking company at The Tabard:

> Our Host gave us great welcome; everyone
> Was given a place and supper was begun.
> He served the finest victuals you could think,
> The wine was strong and we were glad to drink.

From the 12th century wine was imported from France to Chepstow, which enjoyed a long association with the wine trade, and from the 15th century French, German, and Portuguese wines were shipped in casks from Bristol along the Severn to Newnham. From the mid-17th century there was a growing taste for spirits which led to the popularity of gin and excessive drinking in the 18th century, when according to Hackwood:

> Everybody drank, and nobody drank moderately; the vice was common to all, rich and poor alike. At social parties no gentleman ever thought of leaving the table sober; the host would have considered it a slight on his hospitality. Even ladies and clergymen sometimes got drunk, and intoxication was so common a thing it passed without remark. The upper classes drank wine, and every man among them liked to boast himself a 'two-bottle man'; and even if he could not consume that quantity, he could at least drink till he fell beneath the table.
> The lower classes drank beer when they did not drink gin, and it was a common thing among working men to drink three or four quarts of strong, heavy ale each day of their lives. In 1761 an attempt to raise the price of ale to 3¹/₂d. a quart was successfully resisted by the public.

JOHN W. WATTS,

IMPORTER OF

WINE AND SPIRITS,

Ale, Porter, and

Cider Merchant,

COLEFORD.

- BASS'S -

BITTER, BURTON, AND LIGHT ALES OF OCTOBER
BREWINGS, IN ALL SIZE CASKS.

ALTON COURT FAMILY ALES

IN CASKS OF 4½ GALLONS, OR UPWARDS, NOW IN
SPLENDID CONDITION.

ALL THE CHOICEST BRANDS OF

WINES AND SPIRITS

Bottled in my own Cellars, and GUARANTEED ABSOLUTELY
PURE, at the Lowest Price commensurate with quality.

An 1894 advertisement for John W. Watts of Coleford who also supplied the produce of the Alton Court Brewery

Brewer's Covered Two-wheel Dray.

This Dray is constructed in a light, strong, and substantial manner, fitted with portable cover, hoops, and boards as shewn, and mounted on three springs, patent axle, and brass caps, and painted, lined, and varnished complete.

No. 1.	To carry up to 25 cwts.	..	..	..	£30	0	0
2.	,,	,,	30	,,	..	..	..	32	0	0
3.	,,	,,	35	,,	..	..	..	34	0	0

Best Waterproof Canvas Cover, with curtains back and front, £3 15 0 extra. Or if fitted with best India-rubber Cover and Curtains £5 0 0 extra.

Brewer's Spring Float.

This Float has been made so as to combine the greatest possible strength with lightness; and, being low on the ground, it is very convenient for loading; fitted with springs, patent cranked axle and brass caps, and skids for rolling up casks.

No. 1.	To carry up to 20 cwts. (say 4 barrels) wheels 4 ft. 6 in., tyres 2 in.	..	£25	0	0
2.	,,	,,	25	,,	,,	5	,,	,,	4	8	,,	2¼	..	27	0	0
3.	,,	,,	30	,,	,,	6	,,	,,	4	8	,,	2½	..	29	0	0

19th-century brewer's drays

At the beginning of the 19th century a Gloucester wine and spirit merchant sold pipes of 'Port Wine' and 'Old Dry Sherry' for £90, which is equivalent to about 2s. a bottle, whereas a pipe of 'Cape Madeira' was only £42, and a dozen bottles of sauterne, moselle, barsac and claret cost 75s. Spirits were sold by the gallon, including brandy for 26s. and rum for 14s. 6d. Some of these tasty drinks may have reached the homes of the wealthy and the more important coaching inns in the Forest of Dean, but there is little evidence of wine and spirit merchants trading in the Forest until the 1830s when James Hall was recorded at Redbrook. By the 1850s Knowles and Carn at Newnham, Richard Porter at Coleford and John Smith at Cinderford were all selling wines and spirits, and a decade later John Shingler was a wine merchant at Bream, J. Tamplin a spirit merchant at Lydney and James Dennis at Coleford. Towards the end of the 19th century W. Gilbey had agents in most Forest towns, and Cornelius Baynham and Alfred Jones were independent merchants at Mitcheldean and Newnham.

John Watts had established his wine and spirit business at Coleford around 1880, and in 1901 was advertising his firm as 'Wine and Spirits, Ale, Porter, and Cider Merchant' offering 'All the Choicest Brands of Wines and Spirits Bottled in my own Cellars, and Guaranteed Absolutely Pure, at the Lowest Price commensurate with quality'. The cost of wine nationwide was between 16s. and 31s. per dozen bottles depending on quality and country of origin, and 26s. for a quart flagon of burgundy or chablis. In 1921 the Watts family sold their licensed premises including the 'Wine and Spirit Merchants and Bottling Stores', which appears to have been taken over by S.J. Highley who was still trading in 1927 together with Mrs. Miller at Coleford. Otherwise the wine and spirit trade was based at Gloucester, Cheltenham, Stroud and Bristol, unlike today where wine and spirits are available from Forest supermarkets and smaller village stores.

> To exalt, enthrone, establish and defend,
> To welcome home mankind's mysterious friend:
> Wine, true begetter of all arts that be;
> Wine, privilege of the completely free;
> Wine the recorder; Wine the sagely strong;
> Wine, bright avenger of sly-dealing wrong—
> Awake, Ausonian Muse, and sing the vineyard song!
>
> (H. Belloc)

To cater for the more temperate drinker, the manufacturing of mineral water was an industry that started around the 1880s. In Gloucester there was T. Talbot & Co's 'High-Class Mineral Water', whilst at Bill Mills Alfred Wintle extended his business to manufacture mineral water and in 1892 purchased another aerated water business from Richard Williams & Sons in the Forest of Dean. 'Perneyley Water' was produced at Lydney, the 'Royal Forest of Dean Mineral Water' was made by George St. John at the Speech House, and at a later date 'Lydbrook Valley Springs' were 'Mineral Water Manufacturers' but fortunately dealt in 'Beer, Cider, Wines & Spirits' as well.

A. J. WINTLE & SONS,

MILLERS

AND

Mineral Water Manufacturers,

BOTTLERS OF

ALLSOPP'S ALES

AND

GUINNESS'S DUBLIN STOUT.

N.B.—A. J. W. & S. have just put in a complete Roller Mill, with all latest improvements, on Messrs. Robinson's System, at

BILL MILLS, nr. ROSS.

H. & S.

Wintle's had a new bottling plant at Bill Mills in 1891

CHAPTER THREE

From Gloucester to the Forest

The Forest of Dean lies between the rivers Wye and Severn in an almost detached part of west Gloucestershire. It has developed its own identity and character in a large area of woods and waste that was originally reserved for royal hunting and now survives as a principal Crown forest. In the past the Forest's natural landscape was spoilt by man exploiting its valuable raw materials of iron, timber, coal and stone. With its own laws and courts the Forest of Dean and its neighbourhood appears to have remained largely independent of the county and city of Gloucester.

Since Roman times man has lived and worked in the city of Gloucester, which grew on the banks of the Severn with two great roads leading westwards through the Forest of Dean to South Wales. With its riverside quays and fordable river crossings Gloucester grew and expanded over the centuries. The Normans established a castle and abbey and Gloucester became an important trading centre for iron goods, cloth and agricultural produce. Some buildings date from this period including the 12th-century cellar, known as the Monk's Bar, at the Fleece in Westgate Street. The Gloucester streets were then narrow and dark and 'within the walls crimes of violence were not uncommon; for every man carried a knife, and everyone drank ale, often to excess'.

During the medieval period wine and ale would have been consumed in the guest houses that were built in the abbey precinct and in the newly established inns such as the New Inn in Northgate Street. Still trading at the beginning of the 21st century, this building serves as a typical example of an inn built by the abbey around 1457 to accommodate pilgrims. These places would also have been used by the merchants and traders importing wine, salt and timber and exporting cloth and corn via the river Severn. Cattle from Wales were driven across the bridges and causeways into the city, and iron ore from the Forest of Dean was conveyed by packhorses along difficult and dangerous roads.

After Henry VIII's visit in 1535 Gloucester suffered many changes due to the Dissolution. St. Peter's Abbey church became a cathedral making Gloucester a city, and monastic property passed into private hands. In 1580 Gloucester achieved a greater status when Queen Elizabeth decreed it as a port which led to increased revenues for the city and the establishment of the 16th-century Bell Hotel in Southgate Street, which although refurbished at great expense in the 19th century has since been demolished.

During the Civil War the puritan city of Gloucester survived a siege when it was surrounded by 30,000 royalists. This was in 1643, the same year that Lord Herbert 'marched through Coleford and the Forest of Dean, for Gloucester, at the head of an army of 500 horse and 1500 foot'. They were delayed at Coleford by a troop of parliamentarians 'aided by a disorderly rabble of country people', which led to a serious affray, before marching to Gloucester. Another scare, which was announced by the Gloucester town crier in 1651, required the citizens to send ammunition, hay, hides and 'forty barrels of strong beere' and a cask of 'double beer' to Cromwell at Worcester. After his victory a celebration of a 'quart of sack' was drunk by the mayor of Gloucester and the captain who had conveyed the news from Worcester. The political change of 1660 was celebrated with 'all three conduits running with wine for many hours' to the sound of drums and trumpets.

With an increase in travel, trade and transport at the turn of the 18th century, the inner city streets of Gloucester were greatly improved to allow an easier access for coaches, carriages and waggons, and the roads leading from Gloucester to other major towns and cities were improved by the newly formed turnpike trusts. From as early as 1697 all important routes from Gloucester were gradually turnpiked including the roads to and through the Forest of Dean. The city and country inns benefited from better roads and began to advertise in the *Gloucester Journal*. In 1744 Thomas and Sarah Cole kept the Black Spread-Eagle in Lower Northgate Street, an inn which offered 'Stabling for above an hundred Horses, and a large Yard stock'd with Coal for the Use of the Hill-Country Waggons, and a parcel of very fine Hay in the Stables; and at Lady-Day next there will be fine Grazing Grounds for Depasturing Welch Cattle on their way to London', and John Heath in 1758 'fitted up the Golden-Hart, being a very commodious Inn, in the Southgate Street'.

Most inns brewed their own beer in adjacent brew houses before the larger industrial breweries were established from the late 18th century onwards. Although there are no known industrial breweries in Gloucester at this time, there was one started by Thomas Gardner in Cheltenham in 1760. This became known as the Cheltenham Original Brewery in 1888, which merged with the Stroud Brewery in 1959, and was taken over by Whitbread in 1966. It was not until 1868 that Thomas Wintle established his Forest Brewery at Mitcheldean, which expanded into a huge enterprise owning and running many of the pubs in the Forest of Dean and a few in Gloucester, until the business was taken over in 1937 by the Cheltenham Original Brewery and subsequently acquired by Whitbread in the 1960s.

The 19th century brought sweepng changes to Gloucester and the Forest of Dean where coal and iron mining, iron and tinplate workings, foundries, quarries and chemical works had reached their peak. They were served by a complex network of tramroads and railways leading to Gloucester, Ross, Monmouth and Chepstow. Gloucester expanded and its population grew as the railway encouraged more trade and created more industries. In 1814 the discovery of a spa led to the formation of a Spa Company and the Spa Hotel, which were unfortunately overshadowed by fashionable Cheltenham. By 1823 Gloucester's two breweries, two spirit dealers and seven wine and spirit merchants were supplying the gentry and numerous inns, taverns and public houses with a range of alcoholic beverages. The Bell, Ram and Booth Hall emerged as the principal coaching inns, and the Red Lion, Black Dog and Green Dragon catered for the carriers, along with the Swan and Falcon, New Swan and Saracen's Head which provided carriers to Mitcheldaen and Newnham in the Forest.

In 1927 the 'modern part of the city of Gloucester' was described in *Kelly's Directory* as being

> pleasantly seated on an eminence on the banks of the Severn; and from the Cross, where the principal streets intersect each other at right-angles, as in most cities of Roman origin, it has an easy descent every way towards the suburbs. All the streets are well paved, and the main streets and roads are lighted by electricity and the remainder with gas ... Tramways have been laid along some of the principal thoroughfares.
>
> There are seven banking establishments, breweries, maltings, railway carriage and wagon works in which a large number of hands are employed, steam, flour, saw and planing mills, engineering works, brass and iron foundries, a match factory and brickyards, and rope, sail, sack, brush and pin factories; boat and barge building are also carried on, and there are manufactories for agricultural implements and railway fittings, marble, slate, enamelled slate and chemical works, and a large trade is done in timber and corn.

At that date Arnold, Perrett, Godsell & Sons and Ind Coope all had stores, offices and brewery buildings in Gloucester, and there were several wine and spirit merchants trading in the city centre. In the second half of the 20th century many old buildings were demolished during redevelopments to provide a traffic free zone, a shopping arcade and outer ring roads, but the past can still be appreciated 'in the pattern of the streets and in the buildings, which survive from Roman, Saxon, medieval, and latter times'.

The route which now serves as the A40 from Gloucester to Huntley and Lea closely follows the line of a Roman road leading from *Glevum* (Gloucester) to *Ariconium* (at Weston under Penyard). It was established as an important thoroughfare by the 16th century, and became one of the first roads to be turnpiked by the Gloucester and Hereford Trust after the Road Act of 1726. From 1730 the two cities ran their own trusts and maintained an independent network of roads. In 1722 coaches carried passengers from Hereford and Ross along a rugged route to Gloucester, but in 1774 Thomas Pruen from Gloucester was able to run a post coach service from Hereford to Gloucester and on to London. In 1785 John Phillpotts from the Bell at Gloucester was 'conveying the MAIL from London to Gloucester, Hereford and all Parts of South Wales', and during the early 19th century coaches named the *Regulator*, the *Champion* and the *Rising Sun* were transporting passengers from the Booth Hall Inn and the City Arms Hotel in Gloucester to Ross, Hereford and Carmarthen. At that time the Gloucestershire roads were in such a bad condition that it was reported that a farmer 'without a powerful team, could neither convey his corn to market, or take advantage of various manures, which distant places had the means of affording'. Later Road Acts enabled the turnpike trustees to widen, realign and ease the gradient for horse-drawn vehicles.

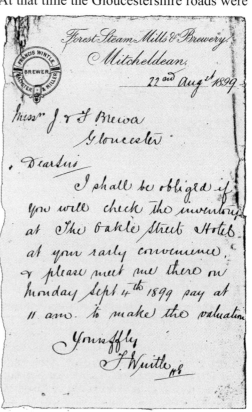

The modern day motorist travels from Gloucester to the Forest of Dean along the present A40 which crosses the river Severn over a bridge erected in the 1970s. This is the last of a succession of bridges built since medieval times, and replaces the Over Bridge constructed in 1830 by Thomas Telford. The earlier bridge is now preserved as an historic

Oakle Street valuation letter, 1899

36

monument and is used by walkers and cyclists seeking a quieter route in and out of Gloucester. On the opposite side of the fast dual-carriageway is the Toby Carvery, formerly called the Dog, which enjoys a long and fascinating history since its days as the Talbot Inn in the 18th century, but as it stands outside the area of this book its story will have to await another pub history.

From Over the main road passes Highnam Woods and the sign to Churcham's remote church before entering the district covered by this volume. Opposite Churcham School a country lane leads to Oakle Street, a straggling hamlet named after an 'oak clearing on Roman Road to Wales'. Beside the railway bridge stands the former **Oakle Street Hotel** which presumably opened after the 1851 South Wales Railway was taken over by GWR, who provided a station at Oakle Street sometime after 1863. The hotel was run by Mr. Wheeler in 1885 then by Mr. Haines as a tenant of the Forest Brewery in 1899. When the brewery offered for sale its 72 licensed properties in 1923, Mr. Goatman was the landlord of the 'imposing Modern Brick-built Premises situated outside Oakle Street Station on G.W. Railway'. In 1937 when Albert Mark Lane was running the **Oakle Street Hotel** it was

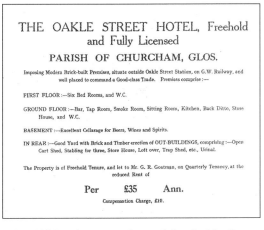

THE OAKLE STREET HOTEL, Freehold
and Fully Licensed

PARISH OF CHURCHAM, GLOS.

Imposing Modern Brick-built Premises, situate outside Oakle Street Station, on G.W. Railway, and well placed to command a Good-class Trade.   Premises comprise :—

FIRST FLOOR :—Six Bed Rooms, and W.C.

GROUND FLOOR :—Bar, Tap Room, Smoke Room, Sitting Room, Kitchen, Back Ditto, Store House, and W.C.

BASEMENT :—Excellent Cellarage for Beers, Wines and Spirits.

IN REAR :—Good Yard with Brick and Timber erection of OUT-BUILDINGS, comprising :—Open Cart Shed, Stabling for three, Store House, Loft over, Trap Shed, etc., Urinal.

The Property is of Freehold Tenure, and let to Mr. G. R. Goatman, on Quarterly Tenancy, at the reduced Rent of

Per   **£35**   Ann.

Compensation Charge, £10.

The 1923 sale particulars of the Oakle Street

purchased by the Cheltenham Original Brewery and was taken over by Whitbread in the 1960s.

It is said that when the station closed around 1964 the pub became known as the **Silent Whistle**, although by 1968 it was againbeing advertised as the **Oakle Street Hotel**. Then it was welcoming coaches and offering snacks and skittles; this was some considerable time before its closure some 30 years later.

CHURCHAM.—OAKLE STREET HOTEL.

ALL THAT messuage or Inn known as the Oakle Street Hotel situate at Churcham in the County of Gloucester and all outbuildings and appurtenances thereunto belonging comprising in rear yard with brick and timber erection of out-buildings comprising open cartshed stabling for three store house loft over trap shed etc. and urinal and all other outbuildings and appurtenances thereunto belonging TOGETHER with the site thereof and the land occupied therewith which said premises are now in the occupation of Albert Mark Lane as tenant.

Sale of the Oakle Street Hotel in 1937

The Oakle Street Hotel in retirement

From the Oakle Street sign the A40 continues through the large parish of Churcham, where 18th- and 19th-century farmers benefited from the

> fine and loamy clay, producing good crops of grass and corn; the arable in greater proportion than the pasture and fruit trees planted in the fields. The east side of the parish lies advantageously to the morning sun, so that the harvest is invariably a fortnight earlier than in most of the adjoining places.

In August 1773 the *Gloucester Journal* reported that 140 reapers were employed on one large Churcham farm. Maybe they slaked their thirst at Mr. Nind's cider house that was sold in 1811 with its mill, implements and household effects.

Birdwood is a hamlet lying on either side of the A40, within the parish of Churcham, where the **King's Head** cannot be missed. Fluttering flags and colourful signs invite the passer-by into its bars, pool room, skittle alley and guest accommodation situated in a long range of buildings, which have been extended and refurbished over the years since its days as a modest beer house. In 1923, when it was tenanted to Frank Ball, the Forest Brewery advertised the premises as a two-up, two-down beer house beside a 'Brick and Stone Built Cottage with three living rooms, Stabling, etc., with Stone

Sale of the King's Head at Churcham in 1937

The King's Head at Birdwood in 2004

and Timber erection of Coach-house, Urinal, Closet, etc' and let at £35 *per annum*. With Ball still the landlord, the **King's Head** passed to the Cheltenham Original Breweries in 1937, and later became a Whitbread pub. Almost opposite is the Springfield Hotel, a smallholding in 1927.

In 1863 George Hall kept the **Queen's Head** in Birdwood, which may have become the **King's Head** by 1891, and Thomas Akerman was running the **Bell** in 1876. The two royal inn signs might have represented loyalty to Queen Victoria and her son Edward VII, although a traditional picture of Charles II is shown on the existing **King's Head** sign. The sign of the **Bell** has always been popular due to its distinctive shape and sound, and that 'a bell speaks all languages'.

Before reaching Huntley an intriguing sign points the way to Soloman's Tump, where cottages are grouped around a junction of lanes and paths and two weathered and moss covered boulders. These lie about 30 yards apart and are recorded as mark stones indicating the parish boundary. The left-hand lane leads into Huntley with its one surviving inn, village stores, unusual church, golf course and equestrian centre. In the mid-19th century a tailor, saddler, grocer, draper, artist, carrier, blacksmith, wheelwright, farrier, shoemaker, castrator, butcher, painter, earthenware dealer, steam threshing machine proprietor and schoolmistress all lived in the village which then had a population of 533. The social needs of the inhabitants were provided by Joseph Stephens at his unnamed beer house and James Drinkwater at the **Red Lion Inn**.

CHOICE OLD WINES AND SPIRITS, HOME BREWED BEER, &c.

Well-aired Beds, Good Stabling, Lock-up Coach Houses, &c.

NEAT FLY AND POST HORSES TO LET.

An 1830 advertisement for the Red Lion

Deeds for the **Red Lion** date from 1732, and the building was well established as a coaching inn on the Gloucester to Hereford toll road by 1757 when it was described as 'formerly called The George but now called the Red Lion with stables, gardens and adjoining piece of garden formerly the site of a messuage called the Crown'. During the 19th century James Drinkwater was a long-term tenant offering 'old wines, spirits, home brewed beers, well-aired beds and good stabling' to travellers who could hire 'Neat Fly and Post Horses'.

Farmer James Dobbs, who was at the **Red Lion** in 1876, was followed by a succession of tenants who ran the inn around the turn of the century for Arnold, Perrett & Co. In 1903 an inventory was made of the pub and its contents when the tenancy changed from Julian Bannerman to Samuel Broom. It included the Bar with a '4 pull Beer Engine in Mahogany frame, Set of 5 two gallon Spirit Barrels, measures, decanters and Glass in bar cupboard'. In the Scullery and Brewery there were '2 iron furnaces, 7 iron saucepans, 3 enamelled saucepans' and a 'copper Beer warmer', and in the Cellar 'about 96 foot lead piping as fitted from beam to Beer Engine'. At that time there was a 'Front Hall, Club Room, Private Sitting Room, Smoke Room, Tap Room, Larder or Dairy, Kitchen, 7 Bedrooms and outside a Fowl House, Stable, Coal House, Orchard with fowl, Chaff House, Cider House with stone trough, Granary, Spirit Room', and a 'painted swinging sign "Red Lion" and Ironwork supports'. The Stock in Trade included 'one bottle of Medoc, one Pinot Noir, one bottle each of Brandy and Whisky, plus Cordials, Cherry Brandies, Martells, Ginger Wines, Angestura, Gin, Rum, Sherry, Ginger Beer, Guinness, Bass, a quart of Cloves, Lemons, 7 varieties of Cigars, 30 gallons of Beer and two gallons of old Beer'.

Sale of the Red Lion in 1937

In 1937 the **Red Lion** was one of over 200 licensed premises belonging to Arnold, Perrett which were passed to the Cheltenham Original Brewery, and was presumably taken over by Whitbread in the 1960s. A 1968 advertisement shows that the **Red Lion** was serving 'Hot and Cold Meals' in the bar, but does not offer any other information. The interior of the old part of the present building must date from the 17th century, with its beams and later panelled walls producing a cosy atmosphere. A notice on the wall claims that William Cobbett stayed at the **Red Lion** in 1826 because Cobbett wrote in his *Rural Rides:* 'I intended to sleep at Gloucester, as I had, when there, already come twenty-five miles, and, as the fourteen, which remained for me to go, in order to reach Bollitree, in Herefordshire, would make about nine more than either I or my horse had a taste for'. He continued 'I got to this village [Huntley], about eight miles from Gloucester, by five o'clock: it is now half-past-seven, and I am going to bed'.

Another early establishment at Huntley was the 'cidermill, cider house and press' owned by John Probyn, Lord of the Manor, who leased the property in 1771 for £55 to George Lodge. He was a 32-year-old rakemaker

The Red Lion at Huntley in 2004

who lived with his wife and three-year-old son at the cider mill. In the 20th century cider was made by the Knight family, farmers, fruit and cider merchants at Deep Filling Farm — an area within sight of May Hill, where traditionally the best cider is made.

At Huntley there was the elusive **White Hart**, kept by Thomas Harper in 1786, and the **Yew Tree**, occupied by John Phelps in 1903 when it belonged to a small brewery called Rogers & Co. This inn was taken over by Wintle's Forest Brewery, but was withdrawn from their sale of 1923 although the particulars survive: 'The Yew Tree Inn, Freehold Beer House, Huntley, Glos. Very Attractive Property, Brick and Stone-built with Slate and Tile Roof, just off the main road'. The small building contained three bedrooms, bar, smoke room, sitting room and a beer store. In the rear was a 'Timber erection of coach-house, Two-stall Stable, and Open Cart Shed' let to Mr. R. Bullock at £35 *per annum*. This is the last known reference to this pub.

At Huntley the A4136 branches south-west into the Forest of Dean, but this chapter deals only with the past and present pubs along the A40 to the Gloucestershire boundary at Lea Line. This important stretch of road was extensively realigned after being surveyed between 1823 and 1825 by Henry Welch for Thomas Telford. From Huntley the original road followed a route 'thro' a narrow rugged valley' past Woodend Farm to Dursley Cross. From the 1830s this was replaced by the present line together with the remainder of the route to Lea Line to provide an easier gradient over the hills for horse drawn vehicles.

At Dursley Cross, in Longhope parish, the original line of the Gloucester road can be identified as a footpath passing Dursley Cross House — a former inn of that name. In 1838 Thomas Beard occupied the **Cross Inn**, which continued to remain open despite the realignment of the main road. Throughout the 1860s and '70s James Browning was the landlord followed by Mrs. Jane Aston before Thomas Read's 'family had possession some 40 years, on Quarterly Tenancy, at the low Rent of Per £24 Ann.' During the 1920s the **Dursley Cross** was a fully licensed inn tied to the Forest Brewery. It was a substantial stone building with a 'Bar, large Club Room, Store Room, Kitchen, Pantry, Cellarage for Beers, Wine and Spirits, Three Bed Rooms, Lumber Room'. When it was acquired by Cheltenham

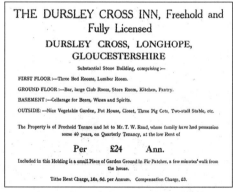

THE DURSLEY CROSS INN, Freehold and Fully Licensed

DURSLEY CROSS, LONGHOPE, GLOUCESTERSHIRE

Substantial Stone Building, comprising :—

FIRST FLOOR :—Three Bed Rooms, Lumber Room.

GROUND FLOOR :—Bar, large Club Room, Store Room, Kitchen, Pantry.

BASEMENT :—Cellarage for Beers, Wines and Spirits.

OUTSIDE :—Nice Vegetable Garden, Pot House, Closet, Three Pig Cots, Two-stall Stable, etc.

The Property is of Freehold Tenure and let to Mr. T. W. Read, whose family have had possession some 40 years, on Quarterly Tenancy, at the low Rent of

Per   £24   Ann.

Included in this Holding is a small Piece of Garden Ground in Fir-Patches, a few minutes' walk from the house.

Tithe Rent Charge, 16s. 6d. per Annum.   Compensation Charge, £3.

The 1923 sale particulars of the Dursley Cross

42

The former Dursley Cross on the old Gloucester road

Original Brewery in 1937, the **Dursley Cross Inn** was still tenanted by a member of the Read family. Despite its off-road position the inn survived into the late 1950s or early 1960s when it was converted into a private dwelling.

The ancient crossroads at Dursley was marked with a stone cross. The remains now consist of a 'base partly buried in the grass by a fence. It was moved here by the then publican of the Dursley Cross Inn from its position on a nearby grassy platt in order to enlarge the carpark'.

From the crossroads a country lane leads up to the **Glass House**, a lively and friendly little pub named after the 17th-century glassmaking that took place in Newent Woods. A manorial rental was paid by 'Widow Davis for the Glass house' in 1640, and three centuries later ploughing uncovered the site

The Glass House in 2004

of the kiln and fragments of glass. The **Glass House Inn** is shown on the 1888 Ordnance Survey map, and in 1891 John Haile occupied the beer house. A few years later the **Glass House** was tied to Lane Bros. & Bastow with Philip Smith serving behind the bar for some 40 years. From Glasshouse the road winds up to Clifford's Mesne where the **Yew Tree** still survives. Before the 20th-century county boundary changes this pub was in Herefordshire, so is featured in the companion volume *The Pubs of Ross and South Herefordshire*. Even so, a photograph has been included in the present work.

The Yew Tree at Clifford's Mesne in 2000

The Farmer's Boy at Boxbush in 2004

The Nag's Head at Boxbush in 2002

From Dursley Cross the present A40 meanders over the hills to Boxbush with its two pubs that are still open. In 1863 two beer retailers were recorded at Boxbush in premises that eventually became the **Nag's Head** and the **Farmer's Boy**. The **Nag's Head** was a Flowers beer house in 1903 when it was kept by John Hail, and in 1981 was described as 'snugly tucked into a bank on the A40' with a landlord who 'stood proud and friendly in front of his splendid casks of Smiles and Wadsworth'.

The **Farmer's Boy** from 1876 was owned and occupied by George Compton followed by Sydney Compton in 1927, and in 1981 was 'comfortable and cosy inside with ... a big roaring fire ... [and] signs of fairly recent renovation and restoration'. These are both popular names for country pubs, and the **Nag's Head** sign often signified that small riding horses or ponies were available for hire.

Between Upper Boxbush and Lea Line the Gloucester road 'has undergone extensive improvements and widening schemes. This makes it difficult to visualise it as a former toll road, but where realignment has taken place original sections have been left untouched'. In 1982 David Bick noted that:

> A tollhouse stood on the south side of the old road near the start of the new alignment which ran behind it at a higher level. Thus the building was sandwiched between the two, and by adding another storey and turning the back into the front, could be made to serve the new purpose. Or at least, that is what the physical evidence suggested.

Since then the ruined structure has 'vanished altogether'. Before 1842 the old road continued uphill to form a crossroads at Lea Line a few hundred yards further north of the modern crossing.

Part of Lea including Lea Line was in Gloucestershire before 19th century boundary changes. In 1596 there was a 'victualling house' at Lea Line, probably situated on the old crossroads to catch all passing trade. This may have been the later **George** of 1662, which was recorded in 1725 as a 'capital messuage formerly

This may have been the site of the George, later the Red Lion, then a school

called the George inn and later the Red Lion'. A deed of 1835 records an exchange of property between Lodge and Barrett of a 'schoolhouse formerly the Red Lion'. This suggests that Blenheim House 'a boarding establishment for young gentlemen', run by Mr. Irving FSA during the 19th century, stood on the site of this ancient hostelry.

Research shows the **George** at Huntley also underwent a name change to the **Red Lion** at around the same date. Originally the sign of the **George** referred to the patron saint of England, but when the Hanoverarian Georges came to the throne at the beginning of the 18th century, the name was identified with the ruling monarch. This was obviously not acceptable to these two innkeepers who changed their inn names to the **Red Lion** presumably showing their loyalty to the Stuarts who 'ordered that a heraldic red lion be displayed in public places'.

Within half-a-mile north of Lea Line stands a unique house called The Larches built with stone from the Wilderness quarry in the Edwardian style including towers and terraces that offer splendid views across South Herefordshire. This large mansion was built in 1907 for Francis Wintle of the Forest Steam Brewery at Mitcheldean. He introduced many modern features including central heating, plumbing and electricity, which were not generally installed at that time. The Larches was conveniently situated for Francis being only a three mile drive from his successful brewing, malting and milling business at Mitcheldean. After his retirement in 1923 he left The Larches and before 1934 had moved into Long Orchard at Lea. His company owned the nearby Railway Inn, which is covered in *The Pubs of Ross and South Herefordshire* together with the Crown also at Lea.

CHAPTER FOUR

Huntley to Mitcheldean

The existing A4136 developed as a major route linking the Gloucester road from Huntley through Longhope, Mitcheldean, the northern part of the Forest and Coleford to Monmouth and eventually to South Wales. Stretches date from the Roman period, but it is known that the original Roman road 'led south of Birdwood Coppice and by way of Little London to Mitcheldean. The section of the latter road in Churcham was in use in 1607 and described as a highway from Gloucester to Mitcheldean. By 1970 only a rough track or footpath survived, but in 2001 it served as part of the route of the Gloucestershire Way.

The road from Huntley to Mitcheldean was identified in the 1670s on Ogilby's itinerary, and since then the turnpike trustees and later county councils have improved, widened and realigned the route leaving abandoned sections to explore. This would have been the road taken by William Mountain's waggons in 1750, carrying

> Goods and Passengers as follows: by the Monmouth Waggon to all Parts of South Wales ... and all Places adjacent, these Waggons likewise carry for Cheltenham etc. and go through Huntley, Mitchel-Deane, and Coleford.

In 1813 George North was advertising his 'Old Established Waggons through Mitcheldean, Ross, Coleford, Monmouth ... and all Parts of South Wales, and the South of Ireland every Tues., Thurs. and Sat.', and in 1828 the route from the 'Huntley Turnpike' to 'Mitchel Dean' and 'Through the Forest of Dean' to 'Monmouth' was given as the main road instead of the one through Ross. In the 18th century the Mitcheldean inns advertised that there were 'neat Post-Chaises with able Horses and careful Drivers', or a 'new neat Post-Chaise, or Chariot' available for hire at 9d. a mile on the road leading to 'Gloster, Monmouth, London, Bath and Bristol'.

From Huntley to Mitcheldean the main road meanders its way through the parish of Longhope but avoids the village centre. In 1608 Longhope

47

possessed 'one Turner, two Sawyers, one Carver, and three Colliers or Charcoal-burners', there was also a reference to 'Three Saylors' who were either sail makers or sailors. In the past Longhope was known for the cultivation of plums, saw milling, tanning, nail making, manufacturing of agricultural implements and the growing of wheat, 'proof of this found in the fact that no less than five mills were built within a mile stretch of the Littlehope-Mitcheldean road'. Another important industry in the early 20th century was recorded in 1953 as:

> The blasting and burning of limestone ... A rambler along Hobbs' lane into a wooded area known as the Lime Kilns will pass the limestone quarry and will find the remains of some of the old kilns. The kiln is in the shape of an open-topped pit built above ground, with an entrance at one side at ground level. The coal and limestone were placed in alternate layers until the pit was full. The stone was then burned by slow combustion, raking the burned lime from the bottom and feeding from the top. The art of a limestone burner was never to let his fire out. Several old inhabitants can remember frying eggs and bacon on the lime-burner's shovel at the top of the pit. The lime was of excellent quality and was used by local farmers who hauled it away in three-horse wagons, those from the Forest of Dean bringing coal in their forward journey.

In 1863 many of the Longhope inhabitants worked in these occupations whilst others were employed as shop-keepers, a horse dealer, a boot and shoemaker and a carpenter. In the village there was also Henry Davis, a beer retailer, John Hobbs at the **Plough** and Thomas Milson at the **Yew Tree**. In 1953 the traditional industries 'no longer flourished', and since then the Hereford, Ross, Gloucester Railway has closed, together with the station at Longhope, the Longhope Manor Hotel and the Bradley Court Country Club, which

Mitcheldeane and Huntley District of Turnpike Roads, 1786.

NOTICE is hereby given, that the Tolls arising from the several turnpike gates herein after mentioned, will be Let to the best bidder, at the respective sums set opposite to their respective names, for the term of three years, to commence from the first day of January, 1787, at the house of Thomas Harper, innholder, called the White-Hart Inn, at Huntley, Glocestershire, on Tuesday the 17th day of October inst. between the hours of ten o'clock in the forenoon and five o'clock in the afternoon; and the person or persons who shall be declared the best bidder or bidders of the said tolls, any or either of them, must by himself, herself, or themselves, together with two sureties, give sufficient security for the payment of the rent or rents agreed for, in such manner as the trustees present shall think proper.

MITCHELDEANE DISTRICT.

	£.	s.	d.
Castle End Gate - - -	156	7	1
Lea Line Gate - - - -	83	12	11
Guns Mills Gate - - -	85	8	4
Gate at Mitcheldeane leading to Huntley	67	11	8
Gate at Huntley leading to Mitcheldeane -	80	0	0

HUNTLEY DISTRICT.

The gate at Huntley leading to Rofs -	120	0	0

By order of the trustees,
THOMAS RUDGE, Clerk.

*Sale of turnpike tolls in 1786
at the White Hart, Huntley*

was formerly an agricultural school housed in a large 'gothic style' mansion. Both are now nursing homes. Apart from written records it is only the names of the streets and houses that provide a reminder of Longhope's history.

In 1876 William Bradley was selling beer from his Longhope house, which was known as the **King's Head** in 1882, when he applied for extended opening hours. However, this beer house was unsuccessful and did not survive into the 20th century. Further along the main road is Royal Spring Farm which offers bed and breakfast accommodation in a spacious 16th-century farmhouse. Apparently the older part of this property was traditionally known as a 17th-century inn where Charles I called in search of refreshments in 1642, but finding that 'parties of soldiers marching ahead of the King had emptied the house of wine or ale, the sovereign quenched his thirst at the spring', hence the **Royal Spring**.

THE PLOUGH INN, Freehold and Fully Licensed
LONGHOPE, GLOUCESTERSHIRE

Stone-built Premises, well situate for business on the main Huntley-Mitcheldean Road, and comprise :

FIRST FLOOR :—Three Bed Rooms, Box Room, Club Room.

GROUND FLOOR :—Bar, Smoke Room, Tap Room, Kitchen, Beer Store, Coal House, Store Room and Back Kitchen.

IN REAR :—Small Garden, Two Closets, Urinal, and Timber erection of Store Shed. Nice Orchard, Three Pig Cots, and Large Building, etc.

The Property is of Freehold Tenure and let to Mr. A. J. Brain, a tenant of about 15 years' standing, on Quarterly Tenancy, at

Per   £50   Ann.

This Rent includes THREE COTTAGES adjoining which are Sub-let by the tenant producing Rents of £18 6s. per annum.

Land Tax, 4s. 3d. per Annum.   Compensation Charge, £4.

Sale particulars of the Plough at Longhope in 1923

About 1970, when the new course of the A4136 was built to avoid the village of Longhope, the **Plough Inn** was swept away, and the ancient crossroads, wayside cross and war memorial now remain unnoticed by motorists travelling along this fast by-pass. In the 1890s a Gloucestershire journalist wrote about curious inn signs in *Notes and Queries*, including one with an inscription swinging 'in front of a public-house at the foot of the hill at Longhope, and [which] bears representations of the cup and glass' similar to other signs reading:

Before you do this hill go up
Stop and drink a cheerful cup

And on the other side:

You're down the hill, all danger's past
Stop and have a cheerful glass

John Hobbs was the landlord of the **Plough** before the Godwin family who ran the pub during the latter part of the 19th century, when it was acquired by Wintle's Forest Brewery. In the 1920s Albert Brain was the

Sale of the Yew Tree at Longhope in 1937

publican of the fully licensed stone-built inn 'well situated for business on the
main Huntley-Mitcheldean Road'. It consisted of a bar, smoke room, tap
room and beer store below a club room, box room and three bedrooms.
Before Albert's death in 1966 he was helped by his daughter. His son-in-law
then took over as licensee, and when Gloucestershire County Council
announced their plans to demolish the **Plough** 'to improve visibility' along
the new by-pass a petition was signed by the customers. However, it failed to
save the pub with its 'many attractions such as a preserved wooden
mantelpiece which bears underneath it the trademark of the craftsman who
made it, and an unusual carved ceiling in an upstairs room where sing-songs
are regularly enjoyed'.

The **Yew Tree** in Longhope is the village's earliest known inn dating
from at least 1608 when it was kept by Thomas Dobbs. There is then a long
gap in its history until 1838 when the **Yew Tree** was occupied by Emanuel

The Yew Tree in 2002

Constance, who was probably related to the timber and wood turning family of that name. From around 1860 the Thomas family ran the inn, and were there when the Longhope Ancient Order of Foresters met to celebrate their 23rd Anniversary in 1882. The Thomas family still owned the 'Alehouse' in 1903, although John Woodward was listed as the publican. Sometime before 1937 Arnold, Perrett & Co. from Cheltenham acquired the inn with its 'yard, stables, coachhouse, gardens, lawns, and piece of orchard land and all other outbuildings' which was eventually taken over by Cheltenham Original Brewery and then Whitbread.

The **Yew Tree** remains open offering pub fare both to the locals and to passers by, including ramblers following the Gloucestershire Way. This long-distance route is described as 'a continuous walk of 100 miles through the distinctive areas of the Forest of Dean, Severn Vale and Cotswolds, conceived on the theme of Forest and Vale and High Blue Hill from the poem *A Song of Gloucestershire* by Will Harvey of Minsterworth'. Within a few hundred yards of the **Yew Tree** this waymarked route leads to the **Nag's Head** also in the parish of Longhope and described in chapter three. Unfortunately it is now impossible to follow — at least with drink in hand — the old saying recorded in 1953 'The Farmer's Boy went to the Cross to borrow the Nag to draw the Plough to the Yew Tree'.

From the Longhope crossroads on the A4136 the narrow Velthouse Lane leads through pleasant countryside to the **Red Hart** at Blaisdon. Along the way, the sight of Blaisdon Hall cannot be missed — a large ornate stone mansion built in the Jacobean style by the Crawshay family in the 1870s. Blaisdon Hall, with its gables, dormers and tower, was extended in 1907 and in the mid-20th century further buildings were added when it became school. A previous owner, Peter Stubs, was known for breeding champion Shire horses including one called 'Blaisdon Conqueror'.

The **Red Hart** was open in 1816 and enjoys being 'the only inn that has been found recorded in the parish'. In 1839 it was described as a 'house and garden', but it blossomed as an alehouse in the late 19th century under a succession of landlords named Hatfield, Woodman, Sims and Payne — all tenants

THE RED HART, Freehold and Fully Licensed

BLAISDON, GLOUCESTERSHIRE.

Built of Stone, with Rough Cast, occupying a good position, comprising :—

FIRST FLOOR :—Four Bed Rooms, Large Sitting Room, Box Room, Tank Room.

GROUND FLOOR :—Bar, Tap Room, Smoke Room, Beer Store, Large Store Room, Kitchen, Pantry, Wash-house, and W.C.

IN REAR :—Coach-house and Loft, Closet and Urinal, Small Garden, Brick-built Stabling for two, Loft over, and Two Pig Cots.

The Property is of Freehold Tenure, let to Mr. William Payne, a tenant of over 13 years' standing, on Quarterly Tenancy, at the low Rent of

Per   £24   Ann.

N.B.—The Rent of £2 per annum is paid by the Brewery for Orchard adjoining, which is let with the house. Compensation Charge, £4.

Sale particulars of the Red Hart in 1923

The
Red Hart
Inn
Free House

Blaisdon . Longhope . Gloucestershire . GL17 OAH

of Wintle's Forest Brewery at Mitcheldean. When the licence was transferred from Charles Hatfield to William Woodman an inventory and valuation was made of the 'Household Effects, Stock and Utensils in Trade'. Each room with its contents is listed — tap room, kitchen, scullery, passage, sitting room, three bedrooms and a landing with '3 meat dishes, 29 Dinner plates, Paraffin lamp and oilcloth'. Outside there were '2 oblong signs as fixed and writing thereon', whilst the drink stock amounted to '22 Galls XX, 54 Galls XX, 3 Quarts Gin'.

The 1923 sale particulars show that the **Red Hart** had been extended and then consisted of a 'Bar, Tap Room, Smoke Room, Beer Store, Large Store Room, Kitchen, Pantry, Wash-house, and W.C.' on the ground floor and 'Four Bed Rooms, Large Sitting Room, Box Room, Tank Room' on the first floor. Outside a coach-house, closet and stabling for two had been added. The **Red Hart** was not sold, but there was a change of tenant in 1924 when Gideon Price took over. He was still there there in 1937 when the **Red Hart Inn**, together with Wintle's other licensed properties passed to the Cheltenham Original Bewery. Gideon continued as landlord until 1952, and his photo is still hanging in the present cosy bar. Also featured on the walls is a framed valuation of 1903 and a Cheltenham Ales plaque serving as a reminder of its past link with the Cheltenham Brewery. In the mid-1990s, new owners took over and are recorded in an 'Ode to the Red Hart':

The Lamb at Abenhall in 2002

> To Guy and Louise
> With a splutter and a sneeze
> You got off to a shaky old start
> With a hell of a din
> You're finally in
> Ensconced, at the old Red Hart

From the late 16th century cider making was recorded at Blaisdon, and in the late 18th century the parish was said 'to contain many fruitful orchards'. In the 19th century John Dowding of Tanhouse Farm developed the famous Blaisdon Red Plum described in the W.I.'s history of 1975:

Blaisdon has a special fame that came about many years ago by a genetic freak in the horticultural world. In the orchard of Tan House, Blaisdon, a precarious sucker from a Victoria plum tree, perhaps trying to outshine its royal mother, grew from a sapling to a tree, producing an entirely new plum. Victoria may have been a royal fruit, but this plum had a majesty too, with its rich purple skin and golden flesh, delicious to eat and unrivalled for making jam, held up to the light its red texture like rubies. Loyal to its habitat, the 'Blaisdon' will not bear its fruit so flavoursome or prolifically outside the boundaries of Blaisdon.

From Longhope, the A4136 leads past the craft centre at Harts Barn before reaching a turning on the left to Abenhall, a separate parish until united with Mitcheldean in 1935. Abenhall, formerly Abinghall, lies on a

The Lamb sale particulars in 1923

supposed 'Roman road linking Lydney and the Severn crossing at Newnham with the settlement at *Ariconium* near Weston under Penyard'. The section through Abenhall now forms the bridleway, leading east of the church to Shapridge, which was abandoned when it was replaced by the present road in the 17th century. From 1769 the road was turnpiked, forming part of the route linking Mitcheldean with the Gloucester to Newnham road.

The **Lamb** stands at the junction of the A4136 and the Abenhall road, and was originally in Abenhall parish. It probably replaced a cider house kept by Jerermiah Goode in 1839, and was certainly established by the mid-19th century when the Abenhall Friendly Society met there, J. Haile being recorded at the **Lamb** beer house in 1863. By the turn of the century the **Lamb** was acquired by the Forest Brewery with Mary Stephens serving the pints. It was then known as a horse dealer's den with ponies and gigs tied up along the roadside and the dealers 'strutting about with long whips'. In 1923 Mr. Oliver Hail was running the fully licensed **Lamb** with its serving bar, parlour, sitting room and beer store below four bedrooms and two store rooms.

Like the rest of the Forest Brewery properties the **Lamb** was taken over by the Cheltenham Original Brewery in 1937 before passing to Whitbread. It later became a free house and, before renovation in the early 1990s, it offered 'A well stocked counter with piles of Pies and Sandwiches, Sausages and other fare' in the 'quite modest little pub' worth a 'stop when passing through the Forest if a light luncheon and a half of Flowers is what is required'. The refurbishment 'retained a two room, two bar layout' and the inn was due to have 'a restaurant with a distinctive and unusual wine list'.

In 1821 an innkeeper was recorded at Abenhall, probably at the **Rising Sun**, which was

St. Anthony's Well

54

owned by John Gwilliam in 1839. A fire at this isolated beerhouse in 1865 was described in the *Gloucester Journal:* 'A fire took place at the Rising Sun, a beerhouse between Mitcheldean and Littledean on Tuesday morning last, which completely gutted the premises (an old thatched building). The premises were insured'. Now two cottages called 1 and 2 Sun House stand on the site.

Also in 1865 a cider mill and cider houses occupied by John Joyner were offered for sale as part of the Church Farm and Shapridge estate. They were situated about half-a-mile west of the church.

Before leaving Abenhall it is a worth a detour for even the confirmed alcoholic to seek St. Anthony's Well for a slurp of the medicinal water. The stone-built well is picturesquely situated at the edge of the forest within half-a-mile of Gunns Mill. In the past its water was 'widely famed for curing cutaneous disorders, under circumstances some-what connected with the marvellous, its peculiar efficacy being combined with the rising of the sun, the month of May, and the visits to it being repeated nine times in succession'. Despite some exaggerations there remained ample proof that the water cured diseases of the skin. Maybe this curious ritual led to the nearby inn being called the **Rising Sun**.

Situated on a tributary of the Westbury brook, Gunns Mill enjoys a long history as an industrial site from at least the 15th century. Around 1743, the iron furnace was converted into a papermill by the Lloyd family. Joseph Lloyd insured his stock, utensils, dwelling house, paper mill, corn mill, granary and 'cyder house' all valued at £1,000. The papermill went out of production in 1879 and all its equipment was sold before 1890. The ruinous building stands in a sad state of neglect next to the house built by the Lloyds. From there the road leads south to Flaxley where no known licensed premises have existed except a possible victualler of 1670. Even so, the small picturesque village is worth a visit, as described in a 1970's guide, for there stands the remains of:

> Flaxley Abbey, a great moated house, founded in the mid-12th century as a Cistercian institution by Roger, Earl of Hereford, in memory of his father ... It is not open to the public, but a charming view of its battlemented façade is obtained from the road leading into the village.

Returning from Abenall, the A4136 is crossed on the way into Mitcheldean, a former market town which developed alongside the main highway from Newnham, Monmouth, Ross and Newent. In 1608 the town was flourishing with its industries of ironworking, cornmilling, weaving, tanning and innkeeping, but it fell into an economic decline during the late 18th century. In the 19th century an attempt was made to revitalise the town with the establishment of a brewery, cement works, gas works and quarrying, but it was during the 20th century that Mitcheldean underwent transformation, loosing its historic centre 'with the majority of the buildings in the High Street being demolished to widen the road and make way for more modern structures'. This was mainly due to the reuse of the brewery site in 1948 by the Rank Organisation, which became Rank Zerox in 1956. The site was expanded to accommodate a workforce of 4,700 producing photocopiers. This meant that housing estates were built, and roads widened to cope with the increase of traffic. Rank's have since reduced its staff and closed its main manufacturing operation, but the site is now used as a business park which includes the Mitcheldean Enterprise Workshops in the old brewery buildings.

A considerable number of inns once existed in Mitcheldean to cater for the passing traffic of wagons and coaches, the market traders and the townsfolk. As many of these inn sites are now not known or are uncertain, they have been approached in chronological order. The earliest known inns included the **Swan** or **Black Swan** and the **Bell** in 1581, and near the market place the **Garons** in 1616 and the **Talbot** in 1619. Some of these names reflect an earlier establishment — the **Swan** was in use as a tavern sign since the 14th century, and was popular during the reigns of Edward II and Henry VIII; the **Talbot** represents a type of hound used for hunting and derives its name from the Talbot family who featured the hound on their coat of arms. Although the Mitcheldean **Talbot** had closed by 1696, part of the building in the High Street became the **White Horse** by 1674.

By the latter half of the 18th century the **White Horse** had become an important meeting place as observed by the *Gloucester Journal* in 1761:

> At Mitcheldean in this county, on account of their Majesties Coronation, the Inhabitants expressed their Joy in a very distinguished manner. The principal Inhabitants met at the White Horse, and went in Procession from thence to the Church, preceded by a Band of Musick, where an excellent Sermon was preached, and two grand Anthems were performed. The Company afterwards returned to the White Horse to Dinner, where a fine buck was given by Maynard Colchester Esq., who regaled the Populace with a Hogshead of Liquor, and the Day was spent in giving every Proof of Loyalty and Joy which could become good Subjects upon so happy an Occasion.

With the turnpiking of the roads through Mitcheldean in the 18th century, William Price at the **White Horse** benefited from the coaching trade by hiring 'neat Post Chaises, with careful Drivers, and Saddle-Horses'. However, with increasing competition from the other inns at Micheldean the **White Horse** seems to have been the loser as a coaching inn, but it remained as a meeting place hosting the Mitcheldean Friendly Society meetings from 1809.

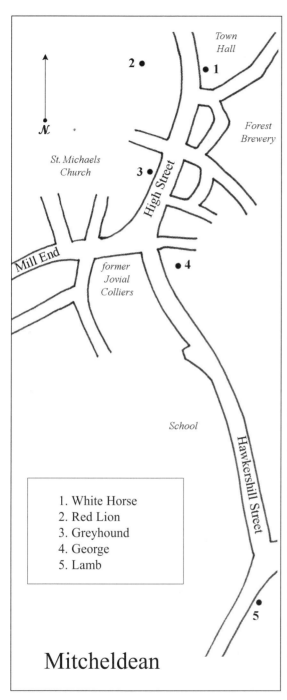

Town
Hall

2 ●

● 1

*Forest
Brewery*

*St. Michaels
Church*

3 ●

High Street

Mill End

*former
Jovial
Colliers*

● 4

N.

School

Hawkershill Street

1. White Horse
2. Red Lion
3. Greyhound
4. George
5. Lamb

●
5

Mitcheldean

*The pubs of Mitcheldean that were
open in the 1920s*

In 1830 William Pearce kept the **White Horse** but a few years later Giles Gardener occupied the 'White Horse Inn, Stables, Yard, Malthouse, and Garden'. Maria Parry was there in 1868, and in 1894 Cornelius Baynham was running the 'family and commercial hotel, the most replete in the neighbourhood; every accommodation at moderate charges'. This was about the time that Francis Wintle, from Mitcheldean's own brewery, acquired the premises.

During the 1920s and '30s, when Harry Preece and Isaac Herbert were running the **White Horse**, it was known that the 'public houses and inns were great meeting places, and probably fostered some of the street fighting', especially at election times when the 'public meetings were rowdy, with everyone sporting ribbons and favours'. At this time the **White Horse** remained a commercial hotel 'taking in visitors and doing wedding receptions'. At the beginning of the 21st century it is one of only two inns still open in Mitcheldean.

THE WHITE HORSE HOTEL, Freehold
and Fully Licensed
MITCHELDEAN, GLOS.

Occupying an important Position for Business within a few yards of the Brewery. The Premises
are built of Stone with Slate Roof, and comprise:—

SECOND FLOOR—Two Attic Bed Rooms.

ON HALF-LANDING—Two Bed Rooms.

FIRST FLOOR :—Four Bed Rooms, Sitting Room, W.C.

ON HALF-LANDING :—Two Bed Rooms.

GROUND FLOOR :—Hotel Entrance, Serving Bar, and Smoke Room, Commercial Room, Private
Sitting Room, Tap Room, with Entrance from Yard, Kitchen, Cellarage, etc.

IN REAR :—Approached by Gateway from Main Road, Stone-built Coach-house, or Garage, Small
Room adjoining, Stabling for two, Wash-house, Coal House, Bottle Store, etc. Range of
Stone-built Stabling with slate roof for 10 horses, Small Coach house, Lofts over and Granary
approached by Flight of Stone Steps. Pigs Cot, Public W.C. and Urinal, Large Kitchen
Garden, Timber and Corrugated-iron Roof construction of Skittle Alley.

The Property is of Freehold Tenure and let to Mr. Harry Preece, on Quarterly Tenancy, at the
low Rent of

Per   £40   Ann.

This Property is subject to a Chief Rent of 2s. per Annum, payable to the Lord of the Manor.
Compensation Charge, £6.

Proposed sale of the White Horse
in 1923

The other one is the prominent **George** situated in the centre of Mitcheldean opposite the church. It is now run by Pubmaster. The original **George** of 1620 stood on the west side of Hawker Hill until 1740. It was then reopened on its present site in a tall gabled house formerly called the Dunstone. In 1763 the *Gloucester Journal* advertised that the **George** was to be let. It had newly built stabling for 50 or 60 horses and 'meadow land with fruit trees capable

MITCHELDEAN.—WHITE HORSE HOTEL.

ALL THAT messuage or Inn known as the White Horse Hotel situate at Mitcheldean in the County of Gloucester and all outbuildings and appurtenances thereunto belonging comprising a stone built coach-house or garage small room adjoining stabling for two wash-house coal house bottle-store etc. range of stone built stabling with slate roof for ten horses small coach-house lofts over and granary approached by flight of stone steps pigs cot public W.C. and urinal large kitchen garden timber and corrugated iron roof construction of Skittle alley and all other outbuildings and appurtenances thereunto belonging TOGETHER with the site thereof and the land occupied therewith which said premises are now in the occupation of Isaac Herbert as tenant thereof.

Sale of the White Horse in 1937

The White Horse at Mitcheldean in 2002

of making 20 hogsheads of cider yearly, with a cider mill on the premises'. The following year the public were informed that:

> The George Inn in Mitchel-Dean, lately kept by John Roberts, is now taken and entered on by John Aldridge (late Service to Mrs. Pyrke) who has completely furnished the said Inn with everything convenient for the Reception of Gentlemen, Travellers, and others, and those who shall be so kind as to favour him with their Company may depend on good Entertainment of every Kind, with the most civil Usage, and a grateful Acknowledgement of their Favours by, Their most humble Servant, John Aldridge.

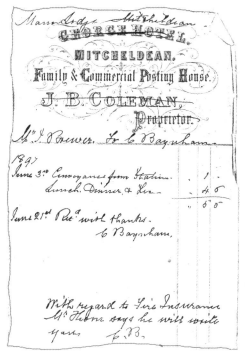

An 1897 billhead from the George

He also supplied post chaises, able horses, careful drivers and post-horses.

With improvements made to the roads by the various turnpike trusts there was competition between Ross and Mitcheldean as the coaching town on the route from Gloucester to South Wales. A notice in the *Gloucester Journal* in 1784 recorded that, according to Thomas Pinnel, a land surveyor, the distance from Monmouth to Gloucester via Ross was 26 miles and five furlongs, whilst the same journey via Mitcheldean was 25 miles and one furlong, a saving of one mile and four furlongs.

A few years later an advert was placed in the *Gloucester Journal* by James Graham at the **George Inn**, Mitcheldean where he announced that 'the new road through His Majesty's Forest of Dean, leading from Mitcheldean to Coleford and Monmouth, which is the high road from Gloucester to South Wales, is already greatly improved, and in a short time will be equal to any in this part of the country ... Graham has laid in a stock of admirable port and other wines, and every exertion will be made for public accommodation, Post chaises at 1s. per mile, and sober drivers'.

In 1803 it was reported that:

> The great travelling road to Monmouth from Gloucester now leads through Mitcheldean, which, with the good accommodation afforded to travellers,

will in process of time be probably the occasion of raising it to a considerable rank among towns of this description. Besides which, there are sufficient limitations in the double approach to the George Inn and large yard adjoining it, as well as the capacious stable-yards belonging to the other inns of the town.

During the 19th century coaches continued to run from the **George** to Coleford and Gloucester, but by 1842 passengers from Gloucester could 'proceed by Railway to Birmingham, and thence to London, Manchester, Liverpool, and most parts of England'. The rapid spread of the railway network saw a decline in coaching and its accompanying inns, but the Mitcheldean inns were not too badly hit until after the opening of the Hereford, Ross, Gloucester line in 1855, with Mitcheldean Road station a mile-and-a-half from the town.

A 1907 advertisement for the George

Landlords named Hale, Brain, Scudamore and Baynham ran the **George** until the 1890s when it was acquired by Wintle's Forest Brewery. The inventory and valuation of 1897 listed the bedrooms, dining room, commercial room, kitchen, beer house, skittle alley, bar, lobby and the cellars with a stock of gin, brandy, cherry brandy, ale, cider, port and champagne. In 1923 the third-floor attics were disused, so it is not surprising that the upper storey was deemed unsafe in 1947 and was removed and replaced by a flat roof. After the **George** passed to the Cheltenham Original Brewery, the inn signs were repainted and decorations and repairs were carried out, which in 1937 was included in the Wintle's sale. As a Whitbread pub under the Wyns it offered luncheons and dinners, and catered for weddings and parties in the 1960s.

Other 17th-century inns included the **Lion** or **Red Lion**, which was open in 1621, the **Cross Keys** of 1651

Proposed sale of the George in 1923

The George in 2002

and the **Shears** of 1695. The latter two were short lived, but the **Red Lion** survived into the 20th century before closing. Sharing the fate of the other Mitcheldean inns the **Red Lion** was taken over by Wintle's Forest Brewery at the end of the 19th century when George Newman was serving behind the bar. This fully licensed public house appears to have been withdrawn from the

THE RED LION, Freehold and Fully Licensed

MITCHELDEAN, GLOS.

Situate on the main road within a few yards of the Brewery. The Building, which is of Brick and Stone, comprises :—

FIRST FLOOR :—Five Living Rooms, Store Room, etc,

GROUND FLOOR :—Serving Bar, Small Bar, Tap Room, Two Beer Stores, Pot House, Private Sitting Room.

IN REAR :—Yard with entrance from main road, Coach-house, with Two rooms over, Harness Room, Stabling for five with Loft Over,' Open Cart Shed. Public Urinal, Two Brick-built W.C's. Small Vegetable Garden.

The Property is of Freehold Tenure and let to Mr. O٦ T. B. Haines, a tenant of about 10 years' standing, on Quarterly Tenancy at the low Rent of

Per   £24   Ann.

Apart from its Licence Value this Property occupies an Important Site with a Frontage of about 60ft. to the main road.

Compensation Charge, £3.

Particulars of the Red Lion sale in 1923

proposed sale of 1923, and was still trading in 1927. Ten years later the Youth Hostels Association announced that 'a hostel was established at Lion House, Mitcheldean, formerly an old coaching establishment'. In 1984 the former **Red Lion** was demolished to make way for a housing development, but the archway was retained forming an attractive feature.

In the early 18th century several more inns existed at Mitcheldean including the **Crown** of 1701, the **Swan** or **White Swan** of 1712, the **Bell** of 1740 in New Street, the **Seven Stars** of 1756 and the **King's Arms** of 1764, but only two survived the economic decline and stayed open into the mid-19th century. Stars Pitch is now the only reminder of the **Seven Stars** which stood on the west side of Hawker Hill in the mid-18th century. In 1830 John Watkins was the publican after which Thomas Lloyd took over. He appears to have been the last landlord before the inn closed around 1845.

The **Swan** stood on the site of Carisbrook House next to the former Market House, which was converted into a town hall in 1861 and in the 1920s was acquired by the Forest Brewery for use as a store room. In 1827 an inventory was made of the **Swan** posting house and its brewhouse. This was about the time that Thomas Pockett kept the inn which was often used for auction sales in the 1830s before its closure. The site was later occupied by the Carisbrook Temperance Hotel, which became a 'Boarding and Posting' establishment offering accommodation to tourists and cyclists at the beginning of the 20th century.

In 1764 Joseph Tibbs of the **King's Arms** 'finished another Stall Stable for twenty Horses ... bought four very good Chaise-Horses, and some Saddle Horses', and was offering 'the best Accommodation with civil Treatment' at his inn situated 'in the Pleasantest Part of the Town in the Road leading to Gloucester, Monmouth, London, Bath and Bristol'. Joseph was the brother of John Tibbs who had converted two small tenements and a former fives court into the Beaufort Hotel in Monmouth. The latter became a principal coaching inn, but Joseph at Mitcheldean did not appear to have been so successful. In 1773 William Querrell had another attempt at promoting the **King's Arms** by advertising that his inn was 'completely fitted up, the Rooms new floored, handsomely papered, and neatly furnished with new Beds etc., in such a manner as to render it as comfortable an Inn as any on the Road from South Wales'. He also hired horses and chaises at 'no more than 9d a mile'. With no further known references to this inn, it would appear that the **King's Arms** had closed before the end of the century possibly due to lack of trade, competition from the other coaching inns, and most likely that the preferred route to South Wales was still through Ross.

Throughout the 18th and 19th centuries covered waggons pulled by teams of four or five horses carried goods and passengers from Gloucester through Mitcheldean to South Wales. In 1750 William Mountain's wagons served 'Huntley, Mitchel-Deane, and Coleford from the Bell in Gloucester', and in 1814 'George North & Co's Old Established Wagons' lumbered through Mitcheldean to Ross and South Wales. In the mid-19th century John Evans, a baker, and John Bowery, a blacksmith, provided a carrier service from Mitcheldean to Gloucester. Even after the opening of the railway, Christopher Cottrell ran a horse-drawn wagonette twice a week to Gloucester from Platts Row. There is no indication of which inn was frequented by the carriers, but it was probably the **Red Lion**.

In 1839 the **George**, **Seven Stars**, **Red Lion** and **White Horse** were open together with the newly established **Rose and Crown**, which was short lived,

In this row of timber-framed building was once the Jovial Collier.

and the **Jovial Collier**, kept by James Merryman, a baker and beer retailer trading in a picturesque row of timber-framed houses which have fortunately survived into the 21st century. Towards the end of the 19th century, when James Phelps was running the pub, it was acquired by the Forest Brewery and became a 'typical pub of its time, with many little private rooms in which the customers were served and not expected to fetch their own beer from the counter. Before the Great War opening hours were long. At 6a.m. a row of pints would be drawn for the passing cement workers, and the house was still open at 11p.m. except on Sundays when hours were more restricted. Only men visited the pub, though women might send children to fetch their stout, and they never ventured inside themselves'. Shortly after 1906 the **Jovial Collier** closed, and in 1948 the building was used as a bakehouse.

In the High street the **Greyhound** was established as a public house in the 1860s with Thomas Trotter behind the bar. He was followed by Phineas Hatton, W. Cox and, whilst Merrick Phelps was there, the **Greyhound** was tied to the Forest Brewery. It occupied 'an important position for business', and its four storeys contained attics, bedrooms, a serving and private bar, a tap room, sitting room and kitchen with a cellar in the basement. In the yard there was a Pot House, outbuildings and an entrance to Platts Row. In 1937 the **Greyhound** was taken over by Cheltenham Original Brewery and some time between 1939 and 1958 it closed and was used as a post office.

Mitcheldean had its fair share of drunks causing disorder at the pubs and in the

THE GREYHOUND, Freehold and Fully Licensed

MITCHELDEAN, GLOS.

Occupying an Important Position for Business, the Building which is Stone-built with Slate Roof, comprises :—

SECOND FLOOR :—Attics.

FIRST FLOOR :—Three Bed Rooms, Two Store Rooms.

GROUND FLOOR :—Serving Bar, Private ditto, Tap Room, Sitting Room, Kitchen, etc. Unused cellar in Basement.

IN REAR : —Yard with entrance from Platts Row, Pot House, Coal and Lumber Store, Large Room over, Public Urinal and Two W.C's.

A Strip of Vegetable Garden opposite is held with this Property and in occupation of the Tenant.

The Property is of Freehold Tenure and let to Mr. G. E. Cox, a tenant of three years' standing, on Quarterly Tenancy at the low Rent of

Per   £30   Ann.

This Property is subject to a Chief Rent of 6s. 11d. per Annum, payable to the Lord of the Manor. Compensation Charge, £3.

Sale particulars of the Greyhound in 1923

streets. In 1891 Mary Ann Davis, described as a tramp from Cardiff, was charged by police officer Bowley 'for being drunk and disorderly at Mitcheldean'. She was found 'making a great noise and drunk in the street at 9 o'clock, with a bottle of whisky in her pocket', for which she was remanded for one week. By comparison in 1901, William Bennett, a drayman from Mitcheldean, was charged by P.C. Head with being drunk and refusing to quit an inn at Drybridge where he was employed. He was fined 5s. and 12s. 6d. costs by the court. In the early 20th century horse dealers gathered at certain times and 'some would be drunk and quarrel on the roadside'. This was when Fred Boughton, travelling back to Mitcheldean, often came upon drunks 'four or five trying to hold each other up and wobbling all over the road'.

In the past brewing and malting had been an important industry in Mitcheldean with records of a brewhouse in New Street in 1608 — a building in which John Hathway, a clothier, installed looms in 1617. By 1625 14 alehouses were brewing their own beer. In 1723 Mrs. Ann Hughes purchased 'All that Malthouse and Stable lately erected and built together with one piece of garden ground', and later that century Thomas Blunt, a surgeon, occupied 'two newly erected Messuages. Tenements or Dwelling house with the Brewhouse'. Towards the end of the 18th century Thomas Sergeant, a baker and maltster, owned a malthouse and brewhouse, whilst in 1839 there were at least eight maltsters with five inns all probably brewing their own beverages. Changes were rapid and by 1842 there was only one maltster listed with several tradesmen retailing beer.

Most pubs and beer retailers would have brewed their own beer until the start of commercial brewing during the first half of the 19th century, but it was not until 1868 that Thomas Wintle established the Forest Brewery at Mitcheldean. He found an 'exceptional favourable' site with the advantage of 'excellent water' obtained from the springs rising in the surrounding hills. The enterprise grew and by 1870 Thomas Wintle was described as a maltster, miller, brewer and corn miller at the Forest Steam Mills in Cinderford and at the brewery in Mitcheldean. For details of the history of this brewery see pages 22 to 25.

CHAPTER FIVE

Drybrook, Ruardean & Lydbrook

The villages of Drybrook, Ruardean and Lydbrook cover a scenic area in East Dean that was nearly all included in the parish of Ruardean in 1840, but Drybrook and Lydbrook became separate civil parishes during the first half of the 20th century. Now mainly rural, the landscape in the past was much affected by mining, quarrying and other industrial activities, which were served by an intricate network of tramways, railroads and navigation on the river Wye at a time when the Forest roads were mere tracks or non-existent. Today the motorist can easily explore the high and bye roads, cyclists can pedal along disused railway tracks, and walkers have a wide choice of riverside paths, footpaths and old tramways to discover.

The spread of industrial activity outside the villages led to the establishment of scattered settlements which characterise the Forest of Dean. At Ruardean Hill, Ruardean Woodside, Horse Ley, the Pludds and Plump Hill plenty of pubs served the local communities in the late 19th and early 20th centuries. Since the construction and improvement of roads it is hard to imagine that these drinking houses ever existed, and that the isolated **Mason's Arms** at Horse Ley above Lydbrook survived into the 21st century.

From Mitcheldean, two routes lead to Drybrook — one follows the winding lane from Mitcheldean church and crosses a wooded hill known as the Stenders, where a beer house known as the **Odd Fellows Arms** was open in 1841. The alternative follows the A4136, a typical twisting turnpike road built in the 1840s where, despite later improvements, a steep ascent has to be negotiated over Plump Hill below the Wilderness — a house originally built in the 17th century by the Colchester family. In 1824 they rebuilt the house which, after passing out of their ownership, was used as a sanatorium, an isolation hospital and an old people's home before becoming a residential field centre in 1968. It stands on an enviable site offering extensive views of the Forest of Dean, Vale of Gloucester and a stunning sight of May Hill.

Plump Hill, with its rocky outcrop and overgrown quarries, provides a pleasant landmark, and despite the interruption of traffic noise can be leisurely explored by following the waymarked Gloucestershire Way. Fred Boughton in his *Memoirs of Mitcheldean* recalls Plump Hill in the early 20th century when men were working in the limestone quarries, carthorses were hauling stone, and the milk was delivered by horse and float. He added:

> Just on down the road was the old Point public house, and down the rocky hillside in front of the Point was the Nag's Head. On a clear day there was a wonderful view from the Point. You could see the horseshoe bend in the Severn at Newnham and forty miles down the vale into Somerset. At Easter when the bore came up the Bristol Channel a crowd would stand by The Point and watch the Severn six miles away at Newnham.

From his description of the **Nag's Head** it is difficult to ascertain whether he was referring to the pub at the Point or one of the same name on Ruarden Hill, as no further information has been found since being recorded in 1903.

The **Point** on Plump Hill was the **Miners Arms** in the 1850s, but in 1863 Mr. G. Hobbs had changed its name to the **Point Inn**, and three years later hosted the annual dinner of the East Dean Benefit Society chaired by Thomas Wintle. The *Gloucester Journal* reported that 'about 120 persons were present and the dinner reflected great credit on Mr. and Mrs. Hobbs. The funds of the society are in a flourishing condition and many members have joined the club during the past year'. Peter and Mary Grimshaw were long standing tenants of the 'alehouse' at £32 a year when Wintle's Forest Brewery acquired it during the first half of the 20th century.

In 1923 the **Point** was described as standing 'on very high ground, and commanding Magnificent Views over the Severn Valley'; at that time the inn consisted of a 'Bar, Smoke Room, Sitting Room and Kitchen' on the ground floor, with 'Four Bed Rooms, Sitting Room, Store Room and Large Club Room' on the first floor. Outside were two beer stores, a coal store, a coach-house, a two-stall stable, pig cots and a yard with a well. In the 1930s the Wintle's licensed properties all

THE POINT INN, Freehold and Fully Licensed

PLUMP HILL, near MITCHELDEAN, GLOS.

Situate about one mile from the town on very high ground, and commanding Magnificent Views over the Severn Valley. The Premises are substantially built with Rough Cast Front and Slate Roof, and comprise :—

FIRST FLOOR :— Four Bed Rooms, Sitting Room, Store Room, Large Club Room.

GROUND FLOOR :— Bar, Smoke Room, Ditto, Sitting Room, Kitchen, Outside ditto, Two Beer Stores, Coal and other Stores, Coach-house, Small Yard with Well.

OUTSIDE :— Two-stall Stable, Pig Cots, Urinal, etc.

IN REAR :— Good Garden and Meadow, in all about Two Acres.

The Property is of Freehold Tenure and let to Mrs. Mary Grimshaw a tenant of about 27 years' standing, on quarterly Tenancy, at total Rents of

Per   £32   Ann.

Compensation Charge, £6.

Sale particulars of the Point Inn in 1923

passed to the Cheltenham Original Brewery. They carried out general repairs including outside painting and re-writing of the signs; this was when George Meek was the landlord. The pub survived the war years, but in the early 1960s it was demolished to make way for road improvements.

The main road leads to the southern end of Drybrook, where its church of 1817 serves as a useful landmark at Harry Hill. Known as the 'Forest Church', its guide book lists some unusual people who have been buried in the churchyard, including:

> the last man in the Forest of Dean to be hanged for stealing sheep. An unfortunate young man who died as a result of a stabbing incident in a local public house. The infant daughter of Henry Crawshay the only Iron King of the Forest, buried in 1842 ... Also, sadly, the seven month old baby son of the Reverend H.E. Nicholls, Vicar of this Parish in the middle years of the 19th Century.

The last named is now known for his interesting books relating to the history of the Forest of Dean. From the Holy Trinity church a road leads down to the centre of Drybrook, traditionally known as the Cross.

Drybrook was named after the brook that was crossed by an old route of Roman origin leading from Mitcheldean to Ruardean, now known as Morse Lane. The village grew and developed due to road improvements, mining and quarrying and the opening of the Mitcheldean Road and Forest of Dean Junction Railway in 1885. A halt was opened at Drybrook in 1907 providing a passenger service to Gloucester, which must have been a roundabout route because the link to Mitcheldean Road station was never completed. A few stories from Drybrook's past have survived. One dating from the Civil War and retold in *Nicholls's Forest of Dean* is of 'an act of cruelty perpetrated on a householder living in the little hamlet of Drybrook, who was struck down, and his eyes knocked out, for refusing to give up a flitch of bacon to a foraging party'. Another legend, relative to the same neighbourhood, preserves the memory of a skirmish called Edge Hill's Fight, named from the spot on which it occurred. 'It is true that some of the foresters suppose it to be the Great Fight [a traditional story] ... , an idea which perhaps have given rise to the story, were it not that a small stream which descends from the place in question bears the name of Gore Brook, from the human blood which on that occasion stained its waters'.

Another Drybrook story features a known highwayman, William Stallard, said to originate from Fownhope in Herefordshire, who lived above the Hawthorns in the 1790s. He was involved in the 'Bread Riots', when food was in short supply in the Forest, but was subsequently put in Gloucester gaol for horse stealing — a crime for which he was eventually hung.

In 1927, Drybrook's three pubs were well established in a village with plenty of shops, a doctor, a post office, a hairdresser, a beer retailer, a boot repairer and a watch maker. The school of 1862 had been enlarged to accommodate

Sale details of the Royal Oak in 1923 and 1937

286 children, and apart from Holy Trinity church there were Congregational, and United Methodist chapels.

At the Cross, the **Royal Oak** faced the **True Heart** on opposite sides of the Hawthorns Road. The **Royal Oak** was recorded as a beer house in 1852, and by 1863 the publican was Philip Jordan who served beer there for several decades. The premises were eventually acquired by the Forest Brewery with

Once the Royal Oak at Drybrook

William Heaven as tenant. A member of the Heaven family continued at the pub until the mid-1930s, but it eventually closed around 1960.

The same happened to the **True Heart** which appears to have been opened as a beer house in the late 19th century by Alfred Wintle from Bill

68

Mills at Weston-under-Penyard in Herefordshire. The pub passed to his brother, Francis, at the Forest Brewery, and was duly advertised in 1923 as 'occupying an important position at cross roads' with a club room, serving

Sale of the True Heart in 1923 and 1937

bar and tap room let to W.J. Morgan at '£20 Per Ann'. Also at the Cross was the premises of a beer retailer, which apparently stood next to the former **Cider Press**, an award winning licensed restaurant said to be housed in a former cider house.

The third and sole surviving pub in Drybrook is the **Hearts of Oak**, formerly called the **New Inn**, a beer house established in 1838. A decade later it became the meeting place of a miners Friendly Society, and in 1876 Joseph Meek was behind the bar when there was much competition for a good brew from many beer retailers in the area including James Marfell, a grocer, draper and wine retailer at The Morse, and James Griffiths, a stone merchant and proprietor of the Setting Sun Colliery. Before 1923 the **New Inn**,

The Cider Press Restaurant at Drybrook in 2002

with its club room, bar, tap room and pot house, was acquired by the Forest Brewery, and together with the other two Drybrook pubs was taken over by the Cheltenham Original Brewery in 1937.

It was during the 1970s that the **New Inn** was renamed 'to incorporate the three public houses which once served the village and re-christened the Hearts of Oak Inn' — a pub that has survived into the 21st century.

Drybrook, like other places in the Forest, has had its share of drunk and disorderly behaviour. In 1882 a collier named Abraham Matthews was charged with 'drunkenness and disorderly conduct' and fined 5s. plus costs.

> THE NEW INN, Freehold and Fully Licensed
> DRYBROOK, GLOS.
>
> Situate about 2 miles from the Brewery, built of Stone with Rough Cast, and Slate Roof, and comprises :—
> FIRST FLOOR :—Club Room, Five other Rooms.
> GROUND FLOOR :—Serving Bar, Tap Room, Sitting Room, Beer Store, Kitchen, Pot House, etc.
> IN REAR AND AT SIDE :—Stone erection of Coach-house with tile roof, Stabling for three, Loft over, Closet, Public Urinal, Stone erection of Stabling, and Brick Pig Cots, situate at other side of the house is a small Meadow and Garden.
>
> The Property is of Freehold Tenure, and let to Mr. A. T. Brain, a tenant of about 13 years' standing, on Quarterly Tenancy, at the Reduced Rent of
>
> Per   £25   Ann.
>
> Land Tax, 2s. per Annum.   Compensation Charge, £4.

When it was offered for sale in 1923, the Hearts of Oak was one of the many New Inns

> ALL THAT messuage or Inn known as the New Inn situate at Drybrook in the County of Gloucester and all outbuildings and appurtenances thereunto belonging comprising in the rear and at the side stone erection of coach house with tile roof stabling for three loft over closet public urinal stone erection of stabling and brick pig cots and a small meadow and garden situate at the other side of the house and all other outbuildings and appurtenances thereunto belonging TOGETHER with the site thereof and the land occupied therewith which said premises are now in the occupation of Walter Virgo as tenant.

The entry for the New Inn in the 1937 sale catalogue

The Hearts of Oak, formerly the New Inn, in 2002

The Hearts of Oak sign has a nautical flavour

At the **Royal Oak** in 1901 William Bennett, a drayman, was drunk and refused to quit the pub which was then kept by Arthur Reed. Although he was in the landlord's employ, he was charged by P.C. Head and fined 5s. and 12s. 6d. costs. Miners from Plump Hill, who were charged for being drunk at Littledean and Broadoak in 1891, were all charged 5s. plus costs.

From the Cross, the Hawthorns Road leads north from Drybrook to Lea Bailey passing the former **Crown Inn** in the Herefordshire parish of Hope Mansell, where the Miner's Friendly Society held their meetings. The history of this inn is described in *The Pubs of Ross and South Herefordshire*, but it is worth noting that Thomas Brain kept the pub in the 1850s. From there the road continues over the crossroads to Lea Bailey where a J. Brain kept a licensed premises in 1863. This was presumably the **Yew Tree**, which is depicted on the 1883 Ordnance Survey map and operated from a cottage now called the Old Cider Mill and bearing a date stone of *c.*1790.

From Drybrook, the ancient Morse Lane and the more recent Morse Road both lead to Ruardean. Along Morse Lane is the **Rose in Hand**, occupied by Richard Read, a shopkeeper, in 1876 when Thomas Baldwin was a beer retailer and butcher at The Morse. He took over the **Rose in Hand** at the beginning of the 20th century but had left by 1913. Despite being on a quiet

The Rose in Hand near Ruardean in 2002

The one time China Court in 2002

An old photograph of the Nelson Arms

road this inn has remained open into the 21st century. Along Morse Road there was also a beer house called **China Court**. This was kept by Robert Yemm at the turn of the 20th century, presumably in the existing cottage still called China Court.

Towards Ruardean the **Nelson Arms**, originally called the **Nelson**, had opened in the Morse Road in 1868, and in 1891 was run by W.W. Birt as an alehouse tied to A.J. Wintle. His Mitcheldean brewery did not own the property until the 1930s when a local smallholder, Albert Matthews, was licensee. It was included in the 1937 sale and as the **Nelson Arms**, this inn is still open.

The **Rose in Hand** contains the most popular flower used in pub names, but its full name is probably quite unique as is that of **China Court**. It seems unlikely that the **Nelson** was named

ALL THAT messuage or Inn known as the Nelson Arms situate at Morse Road Ruardean in the County of Gloucester and all outbuildings and appurtenances thereunto belonging comprising in the rear and at side two ranges of stabling beer store pot house club room brick closet pig cot public urinal etc. and all other out-buildings and appurtenances thereunto belonging TOGETHER with the site thereof and the land occupied therewith which said premises are now in the occupation of Albert Theophilus Matthews as tenant.

Sale of the Nelson Arms in the 1930s

The Nelson Arms still continues to serve customers

directly after the naval hero but, like these other pub names, may have been associated with local coal or iron mines called Nelson, Trafalgar, Rose in Hand and New China.

Morse Lane and Morse Road meet before reaching a crossways at Crooked End at the eastern end of Ruardean. The **Crooked End Inn** was recorded in 1775 when it was re-used as an independent church mission. At the time of writing a derelict chapel, originally founded by the Bible Christians, stands at Crooked End. It is understood that the place was named after the inn, but its sign may have referred to a bent staff carried by drovers or to a crooked billet — an oddly shaped stick or piece of wood used as a primitive inn sign.

In 2004 there were two pubs in the compact village of Ruardean, which commands far reaching views over the Wye Valley and the Forest of Dean. Charles Heath, the Monmouth antiquarian, described the village in 1828 as:

> a small parish, in the hundred of St. Briavels, in the Forest division. It is called Ruar-Dean (supposed to be a corruption of River-Dean), because it is situate on the river Wye, and to distinguish it from the neighbouring places of Mitchel Dean and Little Dean: which abound with pit coal and iron ore ...

The View at Ruar-Dean Church unfolds itself, which is a scene of great grandeur. Here both sides of the river are steep, and both woody; but in one the woods are intermixed with rocks. The deep umbrage of the Forest of Dean occupies the front; and the spire of the church rises among the trees.

Ruardean village developed along an ancient road leading from Mitcheldean to Monmouth. Its church dates from the 12th century and the 180ft. high tower and spire present a prominent landmark. From the churchyard a footpath leads north-west to the scanty remains of a manor house that was allowed to be crenellated in the 14th century. It then continues to the Lodgegrove Brook and the Herefordshire boundary. The contents of the parish chest revealed that during the 17th century the churchwardens accounted for 'Bread and Wine on Whitsunday 4s. 8d.' in 1677 and in 1682 2s. 0d. 'For to make the compayne drinke going on prosscessioning and for a peall to ring them home' and 8s. 0d. 'to Philip Hatton for ale for to make the company drink when we bargend with the founders and workmen that assisted them' with the bells and the erection of a clock.

The population of Ruardean rose from 845 in 1801 to 1,293 in 1881, during a period when the inhabitants were mainly employed in husbandry combined with either mining or a trade. Towards the end of the 19th century an annual sheep and cattle fair was held at Ruardean. This may have attracted four Frenchmen with their two performing Russian bears to the neighbourhood in 1889, which led to an unfortunate and tragic incident reported in the *Gloucester Journal*:

Somewhere in the neighbourhood of Nailbridge the report was started that a child had been killed at Cinderford, and a woman very much hurt, by the bears. The report, it seems, was a pure fabrication, but the poor Frenchmen and their quadrupeds who had been objects of interest at once received the attention of a hostile mob. Without enquiring as to the truth of the story, scores of young fellows and boys who had collected intimated their intention to dispatch the brutes. To this end stakes were torn up, garden clothes props, stones, brickbats, and other weapons were used to attack the bears. Their keepers, unable to speak a word of English, went down on their knees and in great distress implored, by gestures, to be left alone. Their entreaties were in vain, and several times the men were struck with either sticks or stones, and one received a serious blow in the neck with a half brick. In this way a couple of miles were traversed, and at 6 o'clock it was estimated that a mob of 200 persons had collected. The bears became very excited, and in the middle of the road within sight of Ruardean the smaller of the two beasts was killed outright by a heavy pole.

Two of the Frenchmen escaped into a wood, and made off the best way they could to Cardiff. The other two, worn out with fatigue and fright, sank to the ground, letting the second animal go free. The beast jogged on as fast as it could, but was again captured and was shot dead. Some persons who took pity on the strangers invited them into their house and gave them shelter. The neighbourhood continued in a most excited state for some time.

Over a hundred years later John Belcher in *The Forester* of 18 April 2002 added to the story:

The perpetators were from Cinderford and Steam Mills, many straight out of the public houses still wearing their pit dirt and clothes and looking for trouble. The main upshot of all this was that it became a Forest-wide joke to taunt 'Who killed the bears'? to anybody from Ruardean just to provoke them. Even today it can rankle; memories of injustice have a long life, especially in the Dean.

Daphne Booth, in her *A Look Back at Ruardean 2000*, recalled:

During my early days Ruardean was a compact friendly village where the inhabitants knew each other. The dwellings were the older type of cottages which are visible today, but no council homes or newer private houses existed ... There was a Brewery in the centre of the village, which employed more men. Later these premises became a Bacon Factory — which closed sometime in the very late 1920s.

Today the sleepy village of Ruardean still shows signs of a busier past when, in the 18th century, four inns were trading. Two have survived to the present day — the **Angel** near the church and the **Malt Shovel** a short walk away. In 1760 a Friendly Society held their meetings at the **Angel**, and in 1829 James Burgess, the publican, was paying 7s. 6d. Poor Rate to the overseers. He was followed by John Court in 1835, and during the 1860s and '70s George Smith, a cattle dealer ran the pub. At the end of the 19th century Alfred Wintle from Bill Mills in Herefordshire owned the **Angel**, which was then tenanted to L.J. Phelps. After Alfred's death in 1895 his properties were left in the hands of trustees, and at a later date the **Angel** passed to his nephew Francis Wintle at the Forest Brewery. In 1937, when the brewery and over a hundred licensed premises where taken over by the Cheltenham Original Brewery, the **Angel** was in the hands of Thomas Morgan as tenant.

ALL THAT messuage or Inn known as the Angel House situate at Ruardean in the County of Gloucester and all outbuildings and appurtenances thereunto belonging comprising in the rear a small garden two closets and two pig cots and all other outbuildings and appurtenances thereunto belonging TOGETHER with the site thereof and the land occupied therewith which said premises are now in the occupation of Thomas Morgan as tenant.

The description of the Angel from the 1937 catalogue

The Angel at Ruardean in 2002

The **Malt Shovel** has a sign that claims a founding date of 1742, but the early 21st-century landlord assumes that 'The Malt Shovel was an ancient drinking house with its own brewery established in the year 1110 making it the oldest pub in England!' The **Malt Shovel** was certainly open in 1774 when a Ruardean Friendly Society was using the facilities. During the 1830s it was kept by Thomas Thompson, whose family continued to own the premises into the early 20th century when Isaac Hale was innkeeper. As with other local licensed houses the **Malt Shovel** was eventually acquired by Wintle and in 1937 was taken over by the Cheltenham Original Brewery.

R.W. Phelps was the 'proprietor' of the **Malt Shovel** in 1968, and in the early 1990s this Whitbread pub was considered to be 'A typical Forest local, friendly, basic but with all the essentials, a good coal fire, a welcoming smile, a decent pint and digestible snacks. The decor is clean and unlikely to get in the way of conversation'. Since then many alterations have taken place including the addition of the 'Downing Street Dining Room' which features

> ALL THAT messuage or Inn known as the Malt Shovel Inn situate at Ruardean in the County of Gloucester and all outbuildings and appurtenances thereunto belonging comprising in the rear a stone erection of stabling coach house two pig cots closet and small strip of garden and all other outbuildings and appurtenances thereunto belonging TOGETHER with the site thereof and the land occupied therewith which said premises are now in the occupation of Harold Bowkett as tenant.

The Malt Shovel was included in the 1937 take-over

windows from Number 10 Downing Street. In 2002 the *Citizen* newspaper reported that 'The owner of one of the Forest of Dean's most famous landmarks — the Malt Shovel pub — has said he is being forced to shut down because of controversial housing plans set to go-ahead next door'. At the middle of 2004 the houses have yet to be built and the **Malt Shovel** remains open.

The Malt Shovel at Ruardean in 2002

In Daphne Booth's recollections she wrote 'At the West End opposite the Malt Shovel and a few yards westerly stands the house where the Horlicks of Malted Milk fame originated' — certainly a different 'brew' to the one at the inn! It was in an old granary, where malt was produced for the brewing industry, that the brothers James and William Horlick 'conducted experiments to produce the distinctive Horlick recipe'. The brothers then left Ruardean to seek their fortune in London, and eventually moved to America, where they were successful with the malted milk drink that bears their name. James Horlick, who was given a baronetcy in 1914, died in 1921. In 1997 *The Forester* reported that plans were being made to preserve the old granary, but in 2004 it still stands in a derelict state near the **Malt Shovel**.

In the mid-18th century there was also the **Crown** in Caudle Lane, near where a row of almshouses was thatched in 1781. Opposite the church was the **Bell**, an inn of some importance which appears to have been closed during or shortly after the Second World War. In 1776 a Friendly Society met

RUARDEAN.—THE BELL INN.

ALL THAT messuage or Inn known as The Bell Inn situate in the Town of Ruardean in the County of Gloucester opposite the Church there with the stable garden and all other outbuildings and appurtenances thereunto belonging TOGETHER with the site thereof and the land occupied therewith.

The description of the Bell in the Arnold, Perrett catalogue

there, and in 1840 James Evans was the owner and occupier of the **Bell Inn**, 'Stable Yard, Malthouse, Yard and Garden', which became the principal place in Ruardean. It stayed in the same ownership into the last quarter of the 19th century, but by 1891 it had been acquired by Arnold, Perrett & Co., and in 1906 the tenancy was transferred from Elizabeth King to Eric Ellis. In an inventory of that date the **Bell** contained attic rooms, four bedrooms, a box room, laundry, club room, sitting room, tap room, wine cellar, and a bar with drinking tables, a brass gong, pewter spirit measures, wooden spirit kegs and corkscrews. Outside, a long sign read 'Bell Commercial Hotel', and a smaller sign informed visitors that the premises were licensed. The 'stock in trade' included bottles of whisky, sherry, brandy, port and cordials with over 70 gallons of beer in the cellar. In 1937 Arnold, Perrett & Co. were taken over by the Cheltenham Original Brewery, but the **Bell** obviously did not last long in their management and was eventually demolished, although the adjoining malthouse still survives, having been converted to a dwelling.

From Ruardean, minor roads lead south to settlements at Ruardean Hill, Ruardean Woodside and the Pludds, all of which lie on beds of sandstone and shale and form the Forest of Dean coalfields, where colliers worked the Coleford High Delf, a deep and productive coal seam. In this area in 1788 two pits called True Blue and Windrills were in production, and in 1835 workings near Ruardean Woodside belonged to Newham Bottom Colliery. This was when coal mining was the chief occupation in Ruardean and boys aged between 10 and 15 years were employed to work a 72 hour week, either working ventilation doors for 3s. 6d. a week or dragging hods of heavy coal on hands and knees for 8s. or 9s. a week

THE JOVIAL COLLIERS, Freehold Beer House
RUARDEAN WOODSIDE, GLOS.

Stone-built and Rough Cast, comprising :—

FIRST FLOOR :—Four Bed Rooms, Club Room, Box Room.

GROUND FLOOR :—Bar, Tap Room, Sitting Room, Beer Store, Kitchen, Larder.

BASEMENT :—Cellarage.

OUTBUILDINGS :—Consist of Two Sets of Stabling, Granary, Loft, Pig Cots, Urinal and Closet.

IN REAR :—Nice Garden, and Two Meadows, in all about Five Acres.

The Property is of Freehold Tenure, and let to Mr. John Gibbs, on Quarterly Tenancy, at the Reduced Rental of

Per   £50   Ann.

Proposed sale of the Jovial Colliers in 1923

ALL THAT messuage or Inn known as the Jovial Colliers situate at Ruardean Woodside in the County of Gloucester and all outbuildings and appurtenances thereunto belonging comprising two sets of stabling granary loft pig cots urinal and closet and in the rear a garden and two meadows containing about five acres and all other outbuildings and appurtenances thereunto belonging TOGETHER with the site thereof and the land occupied therewith which said premises are now in the occupation of John Gibbs as tenant.

The Jovial Colliers changed hands in 1937

The one-time Nag's Head on Ruardean Hill

— an inhumane method that lasted until the end of the 19th century. Mining gradually declined and after the Second World War the True Blue mine closed, although opencast mining continued. The miner's social life centred around the numerous beer houses that were established in these outlying settlements.

At Ruardean Hill — standing at 950 feet this is the highest point in the Forest of Dean — there was the **Nag's Head**, owned and occupied by A.W. Baldwin in 1891, before becoming an Alton Court Brewery pub in 1903 and then tenanted by Richard Edwards. After the Ross based brewery closed the **Nag's Head** was taken over by the Cheltenham Original Brewery in 1962. It continued for a while as a social centre for the local community but closed sometime before 1980.

The sign of the Roebuck at Ruardean

By 1841 a beer house had already been established at Ruardean Woodside, which became the **Jovial Colliers**. It was kept by George Wilks in 1891 after it had been acquired by Alfred Wintle's brewery. John Gibbs was the tenant in 1923 paying a rent of £50 a year. Gibbs was still there in 1937 when the pub was taken over by the Cheltenham Original Brewery, but had left by 1939. It survived the Second World War, but around 1960 was closed and converted into a dwelling — fortunately the name has been kept.

The lanes lead around Ruardean Woodside to a modern housing estate called Roebuck Close. This was named after the **Roebuck** that once stood there. Apparently the original

79

Roebuck of 1862 moved to new premises, and from the late 19th century until 1933 was run by the Bradley family. It was then sold to the Alton Court Brewery. In 1968 Graham and Joan Roberts at the **Roebuck** were welcoming visitors to the Forest of Dean 'to savour the congenial atmosphere and colour their local knowledge', but the site was more valuable as a housing estate.

Eddy's Lane winds up to the isolated cottages at the Pludds, renowned for its extensive views. By the 1980s this settlement had lost its shops, choral society, cricket club and beer house, but the village hall seems to have been given a new lease of life. The beer house of the late 19th century was called the **Royal Oak** and was kept by George Meek as a tenant to Arnold, Perrett & Co. When the company was taken over by the Cheltenham Original Brewery, the Pludd's beerhouse (then with a shortened name — the **Oak**) was conveyed including a communal arrangement for the use of the pump.

ALL THAT messuage or tenement used as a Beerhouse and known as the Oak Inn with the garden ground courtyard and pump and all outbuildings and appurtenances thereunto belonging situate at or near the Pludds in the Township of East Dean in the County of Gloucester All which said premises are part of the piece or parcel of land distinguished as Number 114 on the plan of Ruardean Walk referred to in the Second Report of the Dean Forest Commissioners TOGETHER with the site thereof and the land occupied therewith RESERVING unto the owner or owners for the time being of the messuages or cottages adjoining the said premises on the east a right at all reasonable times in the daytime to enter the said premises and use the said pump forming part thereof such other owner or owners as aforesaid from time to time paying one moiety of the expenses of renewing the said pump and the suction pipe attached thereto and of keeping the same respectively in repair.

The 1937 catalogue entry included details of the water pump at the Oak

The one time Oak or Royal Oak at the Pludds

From Ruardean the main route leads south-west to the steep-sided village of Lydbrook which still retains many features of its complex industrial past. Upper, Central and Lower Lydbrook developed along a narrow valley formed by the Lyd brook, a stream that worked mills and forges from at least the 16th century. From about 1800 there was an expansion in the iron working and a tinplate works was established. By 1863 there were also a stone merchant, coal masters, and chemical works. The wharves along the Wye at Lower Lydbrook provided an ideal outlet for the products, together with the tramway completed in 1812. The railway system was eventually established, including the dramatic viaduct of 1874 which spanned the Lydbrook valley. With all this industrial activity it is not surprising that Lydbrook had numerous inns and beer houses scattered throughout the village at various periods. Out of at least 24 past and present ones, only six remained open in 2004.

IN THE HEART OF THE ROYAL FOREST OF DEAN **visit the unspoilt old**

ROYAL SPRING INN

LOWER LYDBROOK (6 miles from Ross on Ross-Coleford Road, B4228. Turn left at Lower Lydbrook sign). 9 miles from Monmouth.

4½ acres of own Woodland — ideal for Children to explore.

Free House — Bar Snacks — Car Park

A 1970s advertisement for the Royal Spring

The Royal Springs in 2002

Before reaching Lydbrook proper, Vention Lane descends steeply past the **Royal Spring Inn** to join the B4229 beside the river Wye. The **Royal Spring** was an early 19th-century beer house that had been established by the Harrison family below the Vention Lime-Kilns which were in full production in 1824. In the second half of the century the Wheatstones acquired the premises, but it was not until the late 19th century that John Wheatstone named the pub the **Royal Springs** after the nearby springs in the Royal Forest of Dean. The pub's own history states that the Wheatstones remained at the **Royal Spring** until 1971, after which a succession of landlords kept the pub. In 1991 Jon Hurley wrote in his *Guide to the Forest of Dean Pubs*:

> The steep climb is worth the effort just to sip a pint and admire the view of the Wye valley below. The two bar Royal has an energetic couple turning it round and their recent activities include a beer garden with stream and two old lime kilns which they promise to restore.

Below the **Royal Spring** on the left of Vention Lane is a steep wooded slope. Here was the **New Inn**, but there are no longer any visible signs of this

The 1806 sale of the New Inn as advertised in the Gloucester Journal

unlikely site for an inn. It was the home of George Westone in 1773 when a 'Cock Match' was held between the gentlemen of Monmouth and the gentlemen of Gloucester. The *Gloucester Journal* did not report who won this cruel sport, but in 1806 it advertised the forthcoming sale of the inn.

In 1829 Mrs. Pearce was paying Poor Rate for the **New Inn**, the land and the Coal Wharfs described as being at Waters Cross. She was followed by John Thompson paying for the same premises in 1835, and Richard Harrison in 1840.

The house and gardens of the **New Inn** were situated below the tramway leading from Lydbrook to Bishops-wood and above the present B4234. The tramway was completed in 1812, and up to 1951 the section from Vention Lane to Lower Lydbrook 'was used under toll for supplying Incline Cottages with coal by horse-drawn road carts'. This route is now preserved as a public footpath and provides a splendid way to the top of the former incline and viaduct at Lower Lydbrook. After the mid-19th century the **New Inn** either re-opened or was replaced by the **Queen's Head** beer house kept by John Bennett and then James Bailey until it closed around 1890. It is remembered by the locals as the **Parrot**.

The B4234 follows the Wye to the **Courtfield Arms** at Lower Lydbrook, a fairly large establishment which has grown from its earlier origins as another **New Inn**. In 1837 it was owned by Colonel Francis Vaughan from Courtfield and John Ward was the tenant paying Poor Rate. At a later date it was taken over briefly by Leonard Jones who changed its name to reflect its connection with the Vaughan estate on the other side of the Wye. An event occurred at the **Courtfield Arms** in 1901 as reported in the *Dean Forest Guardian*:

82

SMOKER. — A smoking concert was held at the Courtfield Arms Hotel on Saturday evening last, to assist the amalgamated Friendly Societies of Lydbrook in raising funds towards holding their annual fete and gala in mid-summer. The concert was largely attended, and a very friendly evening was passed. Mr. J. Masters occupied the chair, and performed this duty in a style that is 'all his own,' and well-known in the neighbourhood, his efforts to make the company enjoy themselves, needless to say, meeting with a decided success. ... Messrs. Diamond and Baines (banjo comedians), of Ross rendered several songs.

In 1903, when the tenancy passed to Oliver Knight, it was described as an alehouse tied to the Alton Court Brewery. It appears that the Knights extended the original building to form a hotel, which the Courtfield estate put up for sale in 1920 as:

a Pleasantly-Situated Wayside and Residential Fully-Licensed Hotel' containing a large club room, six bedrooms, a bathroom, a bar, bar parlour, tap room, sitting room, kitchen, breakfast room and two cellars with a coach house and a two-stall stable.

In the late 1920s C.F. Plint took over the hotel, and was still there in 1939 when the **Courtfield Arms** was advertised as an 'old fashioned hotel' offering accommodation to 'tourists and motorists' and serving Ind

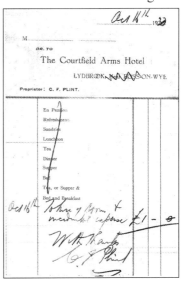

A 1936 receipt from the Courtfield Arms

Sale of the Courtfield Arms in 1920

The Courtfield Arms in 2002; it is now called the Waterside Inn

Coope & Allsopp Ales and Stouts. During the second half of the 20th century the hotel grew sufficiently to provide an 'ideal setting for conferences and dinners'. In 2002 torrential rain caused high floods at Lower Lydbrook, but despite placing sandbags the cellars of the hotel were flooded. It was also in 2002 that the hotel had a complete refurbishment and name change. It is now the **Waterside Inn**, with a restaurant specialising in Bangladeshi and Indian food.

Where the B4234 turns south and heads up the Lydbrook valley, a steep and long flight of steps leads to the top of the former viaduct that carried the Severn and Wye Valley Railway. It dominated the Lydbrook landscape until is was dismantled in 1965. At the top the railway workers could slake their thirst at the **Rising Sun**, whilst at the bottom of the steps the workers at the former iron works, forges and tinworks could choose whether to drown a pint at the **Saracen's Head,** the **Sawyer's Arms,** the **Tinman's Arms,** the **Recruiting Sergeant** or the **Forge Hammer**. The exact site and dates of the **Rising Sun** and the **Saracen's Head** are unknown, but the remainder were all established around the mid-19th century, except the **Forge Hammer** which existed in 1837 when James Price kept the inn. At the beginning of the 20th century it was owned by the Wickwar Brewery, and in 1906 the tenancy passed from Joseph Hall to H.A. Walker in an agreement stating that:

The Forge Hammer in 2002

the house has averaged 196 barrels per year and we think under good management would do considerably more, as the present tenant is not out for the business, the accommodation has just been much improved. There is also a fair trade done in wine and minerals. If the tenant understood butchery, with a good wife to assist in the house, we think he could do some trade, as there is no butcher at Lydbrook.

The premises consisted of a club room, bedrooms, tap room, large tap room, cellars and a kitchen. Outside was a 'Large Hanging Trade Sign with Iron Supports' and stables, and the stock in trade was valued at £8 2s. 9d. for beer, bitter and stout.

In 1991 the **Forge Hammer** was a free house described as:

A two barred, whitewashed inn near the Wye with red rexine seating, horsey prints, brasses and the heads of three former denizens of the Forest ... There is also an attractively tiled fireplace surround in which dusty electric logs glowed.

The **Recruiting Sergeant** was short lived as a pub, the **Sawyer's Arms** was sold as a dwelling house in 1930, and the **Tinman's Arms** became a general store and off licence and struggled on until 1980 when it finally closed.

In a bundle of deeds dating from 1698 it is recorded that the **Anchor** was purchased by Thomas Wilce in 1808, and remained in the Wilce family until

The one-time Sawyer's Arms in 2002

Sale of the old Sawyer's Arms in 1930

1856 when William Russell, an iron master from Bishopswood, acquired the property. His family operated forges and mills in Lydbrook, and his father had established wireworks next to the inn. On the north side were the 'Lidbrook Iron and Tin Works', and apparently the horses working in the tinplate works were stabled at the **Anchor**. As occurred with many other pubs, the **Anchor** was sold to Arnold, Perrett & Co., in this case for £2,000 together with its 'stables, coach-house and other outbuildings ... also all that known as the Market Hall situated near the said Anchor and all that piece of meadow land between the Anchor Inn and the Railway there', and in 1937 it was taken over by the Cheltenham Original Brewery. The market hall had been built by William Russell in 1873 and became the principal meeting place in the village. After the First World War it was used as a cinema, but was demolished in the early 1970s.

Lydbrook's ironworks and tinplate works ceased to operate after 1930, and although new factories were built on the disused sites the lack of business

Sale of the Anchor at Lydbrook in 1937

The Anchor Inn in the 1990s

A late 19th century beer token from the Anchor Inn

forced many pubs to close well before the middle of the 20th century. This included the **Anchor** which was closed and de-licensed in 1954. In 1967 the premises were sold to Edwards Transport, and the former inn fell into disrepair. In 1980 there was a movement in the village to re-open the **Anchor**, where in the past silent films had been shown, children had played on the swings and round-abouts and the Rugby Club had used it as changing rooms. Following a petition signed by 101 names, the planners allowed the **Anchor** to re-open later that year after complete renovation.

During the course of his work the new landlord uncovered:

> a number of artifacts, which he has used to give character to the furnishings; in the Lydbrook bar, the history of the village is depicted in documentary and photographic form, and in the other, known as the chart room, a nautical flavour has been introduced. This is also apparent at the front of the premises, where the herb garden is decked with anchors salvaged from sunken wrecks dating from the 16th century (one having been recovered from the river Wye). In the restaurant ... [is] a huge 10-foot fireplace ... incorporating a beam from Ruardean Church belltower which

has lain in a field for some years ... the walls bear two large paintings of the Forest of Dean Stone Quarries.

Among the intriguing items that he has recovered ... [was] an advertisement for a cook and kitchen maid (preferably mother and daughter) whose combined wages were to be the princely sum of 15 guineas a year.

In the early 1990s a 'new broom was sweeping furiously, carpets were being tacked and the paint was flying', and an experienced chef was offering 'excellent fare'. The beers included a 'creamy Free Miners Ale'. Still under the same management in 2001, the landlord was offering a friendly welcome with an interest in the history of the old hostelry, serving a good glass of wine in interesting surroundings.

The one-time Bell at Lydbrook

At Upper Lydbrook on the west side of the B4234 is a cottage, hardly recognisable as a former inn, but which has nevertheless retained its name, the **Bell Inn**. It was recorded in 1792, and in 1808 a Friendly Society held their meetings at the inn. It was frequented by 'workers from the local wire works who would draw a nine gallon barrel of cider or ale for their shift's work. Making wire was very thirsty work'. During the second half of the 19th century the **Bell** was owned and occupied by John Ward, and remained as a free house until it was acquired by Wintle's Forest Brewery. In 1937 it was taken over by the Cheltenham Original Brewery as:

All that messuage or inn known as the Bell Inn ... comprising a small yard two closets and public urinal in the rear a small garden in the front and a vegetable garden in the rear and at the side and also stone built stabling with loft over and all other outbuildings. In occupation of Mrs. Mary Beard as tenant.

She was still at the **Bell** in 1939; it is not known when this pub closed.

On the opposite side of the road was the former **Prince of Wales**, a handsome house which still displays its name. This pub was owned and occupied by William Jones in 1876, and stayed in the same family ownership until at least 1935.

Opposite the Bell was the Prince of Wales

Also at Upper Lydbrook is the **Jovial Colliers**, reputed to date from 1854, and kept by the splendidly named River Jordan before Alfred Jones took over in the late 19th century. This was when 'beers and cider were drawn from the wood' for the men from 'Lydbrook Deep Navigation Pit, probably railway workers and certainly men of the Lydbrook Chemical Works'. After the Chemical Works closed in 1919 Alfred sold the 'Jovial Collier and the cottage and outbuildings erected thereon' to the Alton Court Brewery in 1923. In turn it passed to West Country Breweries in 1962, and was later acquired by Whitbread. It has undergone considerable alterations and expansions, but is now the only pub open in Upper Lydbrook.

The Jovial Colliers at Upper Lydbrook in 2002

Georges' Bristol Beers were on sale at the Crown and Sceptre when this undated, but early, photograph was taken

Opposite the **Jovial Colliers**, Church Road climbs steeply past a row of cottages. The one displaying a date stone was the **Crown and Sceptre**, kept by John Jones in 1863 and Edward Stephens in 1879. Also known as the **Flag**, it was taken over by Scobie and Stephens Brewery at the beginning of the 20th century and remained open until the First World War.

Church Road continues uphill and zig-zags around Lydbrook church, which was consecrated in 1851. As stunning views emerge from the edge of the Forest, a clever navigator will find the remote **Mason's Arms** at Horse Ley, where only liquid refreshments are served and can be enjoyed in its

---

HAWSLEY.—MASON'S ARMS.

ALL THAT messuage or Inn known as the Mason's Arms situate at Hawsley near Lydbrook in the County of Gloucester and all outbuildings and appurtenances thereunto belonging comprising pot house closet three pig cots stone erection of stabling with loft over meadow and garden containing in all three-quarters of an acre or thereabouts and all other outbuildings and appurtenances thereunto belonging which said premises are now in the occupation of Alfred Powell as tenant AND ALSO ALL THAT cottage adjoining now in the occupation of Mrs. Burns as sub-tenant of the said Alfred Powell and all outbuildings and appurtenances thereunto belonging TOGETHER with the site thereof and the land occupied therewith.

The catalogue entry for the Mason's Arms in 1937

tranquil garden. The main building dates from before 1787 and became a beer house around 1870 with its name given at a later date. It was probably extended after being purchased by Francis Wintle's Forest Brewery at the turn of the 20th century, and was kept in turn by James Brain, William Baldwin and Alfred Powell until it was taken over by the Cheltenham Original Brewery in 1937. During Powell's tenancy the beer house was called the **Bush**, a name by which it is still commonly known. This earlier name was not forgotten in 1990 when an iron made bush was erected in the grounds.

Returning to Upper Lydbrook, the main road leads up and past the site of the **Queen's Head**, a building 'erected in 1856 on all that plot or piece of meadow land ... commonly called the Brook patch', which was 'bordered on the east by the turnpike road from Mirey Stock through Lydbrook towards Ross', and was occupied by Thomas Watkins before James Phelps purchased the property in 1873 with a mortgage from Alfred Wintle at Bill Mills. In 1889 the 'Inn or Public House known by the sign of the Queen's Head' which then consisted of 'three bedrooms, three rooms on first floor, Cellar, Woodhouse (with passage through for use at any time) Bakehouse or Back kitchen (with use at any time for Baking purposes) Pigscot and garden', was let to Alfred Phelps, a collier. In 1891 the public house was conveyed to Messrs. Garton & Co. and taken over by the Anglo Bavarian Brewery who appear to have closed it. The precise site is now uncertain.

The 1891 sale of the Queen's Head

Amongst one of the last properties at Upper Lydbrook on the east side of the road is the **Yew Tree**, a former beer house established in the mid-19th

Sale at the Yew Tree in 1901

century probably by Joseph Moore. By the end of that century George Knight was serving beer there, when an auction sale of 'Cottage Properties and Accommodation Land' advertised in the *Dean Forest Guardian* was held in the inn. From around 1903 the Smart family ran the establishment until at least 1939. it closed sometime afterwards.

Upper and Lower Lydbrook, with its busy industrial sites, riverside trade and network of railways and tramroads, attracted many thirsty drinkers throughout the centuries. Apart from the inns and beer houses that have already been mentioned there were a number of short lived pubs, but their sites have not, as yet, been identified. These include an alehouse at Hangerberry in the 1740s, the **Puddlers Arms** of 1850, and the **Royal Forester**, **Swan** and **Cross Keys** of 1868. At Lydbrook House there had been a 'capacious Malt-House' and a 'Brew-House and Cellar' both occupied by Mrs. Ann Pearce in 1856. In the past cider was produced by Mr. Constable at Lower Lydbrook. He was 'the local cider maker for many years and himself took a flagon of cider to work each day. It did him no harm as he lived into his nineties'. In the mid-19th century Lydbrook nearly had its own brewery, when it was suggested in a sale poster that the 'celebrated Tin-Plate Works of Messrs. Allaway & Partridge' offered 'unusual advantages for the opening there of various Businesses and callings, particularly that of a Brewer'.

CHAPTER SIX

Nailbridge to Staunton

A number of assorted buildings are clustered around the busy crossroads at Nailbridge, where the present A4136 leads from Mitcheldean through Brierley and Berry Hill to Staunton on the western edge of the Forest of Dean. This is an ancient route where traces of Roman paving have been discovered; it is now an important route leading from Gloucester to Monmouth and South Wales, which was turnpiked in the late 18th century. The other roads that lead to the Nailbridge junction are the A4151, which passes through Cinderford and Steam Mills and was built as a turnpike road during the mid-19th century to link Littledean and Nailbridge, and a quieter road leading to Drybrook and Ruardean — the area covered in chapter five.

An early photograph of the Old Engine Inn

Nailbridge is named after a bridge carrying the Gloucester to Monmouth road over the Dry brook, and its industrial past is easy to trace from early Ordnance Survey maps. Remains of the tramway, the Mitcheldean Road and Forest of Dean Railway are easily identified. These served the former collieries, engine works, quarries, chemical works, Brain's brickworks and a flour

Sale of the Old Engine Inn in 1870

Sale of the Old Engine in 1923

mill at Steam Mills that was originally owned by Timothy Bennett and acquired by Thomas Wintle, the brewer from Mitcheldean, during the 1870s. He equipped the mill with 'the new Elite system, a recent invention, which was installed by Messrs. William Gardner and Sons, milling engineers, Gloucester'. In 1927 Nailbridge had a working blacksmith, two haulage contractors, a timber merchant, a cycle agent, at least two shops and no less than five licensed premises, of which four were owned by Wintle's Forest Brewery.

Due to road improve-ments, closure of industrial sites and rebuilding it is difficult to locate all these former drinking dens at Nailbridge. The **Old Engine** at Steam Mills appears to have been the earliest and longest running pub, which was first recorded in 1856. William Matthews was the publican in 1863 and he remained there until his death in 1870. The **Old Engine** was then offered for sale together with 'the Stables, Coach-house, Waggon house, Loft, Wash room, Cellar, Machine house (but not the machine), [and] underground reservoir, capable of holding 38 Hogsheads'. From the beginning of the 20th century Thomas James served a long tenancy at the fully licensed **Old Engine**, 'Well placed to command a steady trade within about 2½ miles from the Brewery'. In 1923 the inn consisted of a serving bar, public bar, smoke room, a pot house and a coachhouse, stabling for four horses and cellars for beers, wines and spirits. It must have survived well into

94

the 20th century as its small modest sign still hangs on the outside wall of this former pub.

The **Mitre** was a beer house also situated at Steam Mills in the 1890s, and run by W.G. Payne during the 1920s. It was 'Well placed to command Local and Passing Trade', and offered a serving and public bar, a smoke room, club room and a pot house. When Charles Dowding was tenant in 1937 the **Mitre** was taken over from the Forest Brewery by the Cheltenham and Original Brewery Company Ltd.

Situated on the western side of the Nailbridge road junction was the **Railway**, a fully licensed inn that opened in the 1870s when Aaron Meek anticipated the opening of the Mitcheldean Road and Forest of Dean Railway. Towards the end of the 19th century the Dunkley family ran the **Railway** for a number of years. In 1913 Richard Read was the tenant of this stone-

The Old Engine in 2002

THE MITRE INN, Freehold Beer House
STEAM MILLS, CINDERFORD, GLOS.

Well placed to command Local and Passing Trade, substantial Stone Building, comprising :—
FIRST FLOOR :—Six Rooms, Lumber Ditto.
GROUND FLOOR :—Serving Bar, Public Ditto, Smoke Room, Kitchen, Smaller Ditto, Club Room. Pot House, W.C.
IN REAR :—Public Urinal and Closet, Cellarage in Basement.
The Property is of Freehold Tenure and let to Mr. W. G. Payne, on Quarterly Tenancy at the Reduced Rent of

Per   £35   Ann.

Compensation Charge, £6.

Sale of the Mitre in 1923

THE RAILWAY INN, Freehold and Fully Licensed
NAILBRIDGE, GLOS.

Situate about 2 miles from the Brewery and occupying a commanding position at the junction of four cross roads.   The Premises are built of Stone and Rough Cast with Slate Roof and comprise :—
FIRST FLOOR :—Four Bed Rooms.
GROUND FLOOR :—Bar, Tap Room, Smoke Room, Sitting Room, Kitchen, Beer Store.
OUTSIDE :—Yard, Pot House, Coach-house, Two-stall Stable, Pig Cot, Coal Shed, Two W.C's., and Strip of Flower Garden.
The Property is of Freehold Tenure, and let to Mr. Richard Read, a tenant of over 10 years' standing, on Quarterly Tenancy at the Rental of

Per   £40   Ann.

This Rent includes Two Cottages adjoining, which are Sub-let by the tenant at total inclusive Rents of £18 4s. per annum.
Compensation Charge, £6.

Sale of the Railway in 1923

built pub with its bar, tap room and smoke room, plus a pot house and coachhouse in the yard. This Wintle pub, like the others, was taken over by the Cheltenham and Original Brewery in 1937, but both the **Mitre** and the **Railway** have since closed.

Proposed sale of the Bridge Inn in 1923

Sale of the Bridge House Inn in 1937

Standing opposite the former Nailbridge Halt Station was a beer house and bakery called the **Bridge** tenanted to Joseph Brown in 1923. This was probably the **New Bridge** owned and occupied by James Barnett in 1891 before being acquired by Francis Wintle at the turn of the century. Known as **Bridge House Inn** in the late 1930s, when it was tenanted to Thomas Cannock, it was taken over by the Cheltenham based brewery and later became Bridge House.

The main Monmouth road leads through the Forest to a small settlement called Brierley, the childhood home of Winifred Foley, author of *A Child in the Forest*, first published in 1974 as a 'vivid and personal story of life and hardships faced by a Forest of Dean miner's family in the 1920s'. This popular book and its sequels were published by the Forest of Dean Book Shop in Coleford and have had several reprints. When a child in the 1920s, Winifred remembered the remoteness that was part of the Forest life:

... the Forest of Dean was remote and self-contained. We were cut off from the world — from the rest of Gloucestershire by the Severn estuary, from Monmouthshire by the River Wye; and where our northernmost hills stopped, we stopped. A *Royal* Forest, it had been. Ten by twenty miles of secluded, hilly country; ancient woods of oak and fern; and among them small coal mines, small market towns, villages and farms. We were content to be a race apart, made up mostly of families who had lived in the Forest for generations, sharing the same handful of surnames, and speaking a dialect quite distinct from any other.

In the early 19th century Brierley Hill was a tiny place nestling between the wooded Astonbridge Inclosure and numerous coal workings named 'Strip at it', 'New Mine' and 'Young's Colliery'. The earliest cottages were built near a quarry where there was a beer house that became known as the **Quarrymans Arm** — the meeting place of a Friendly Society in 1853. It appears to have been replaced by the **Swan** — a former 'cottage by the road' which opened as a licensed premises a few years later. In 1860, while Mr. W. Karn was there, it was known as the **White Swan**. By 1879 it had lost its pureness and regained its former name under the Brown family, tenants of the Smarts, who later ran the pub themselves until at least 1927. In 1990 the **Swan**, by then a Whitbread pub, was described as 'Externally, a pleasant looking little white-washed boozer with useful parking', but its bar was 'awkwardly laid out with a long bench', and the lounge was 'equivalent to the parlours in miners' terraces'. Even so, the **Swan** has survived into the 21st century offering the usual range of food and drink.

From Brierley, the A4136 passes a pleasant picnic site at Edge End and continues along a section of road that was constructed in the mid-19th century by the turnpike trustees. This leads to a crossroads at Five Acre, which lies south of a well populated area where six pubs still survive to serve the communities at Five Acres, Berry Hill, Joyford, Shortstanding and Christchurch.

The Swan at Brierley Hill in 2003

The Gamekeeper's Inn was, until recently, the Rising Sun

The existing **Gamekeeper's Inn** was until recent times known as the **Rising Sun**, a beer house established in the mid-19th century. Early long-term landlords include James Young and James Cooper, but by 1927 Mrs. Emily Byatt was in charge. During the 1980s the old pub was 'totally renewed' featuring 'bare stone, beams and blazing logs'. Keeping up to date with modern trends, in 2002 it was offering an 'Extensive Game Menu from Kangaroo to Wild Boar'.

From the crossroads at Five Acres, the B4432 leads north to the **Globe** at Berry Hill. It was a modest beer house that was kept by Albert Hughes in the late 19th century. He was followed by Thomas Gwilliam who was there in

The Globe at Berry Hill

1901 when the Brothers Friendly Society celebrated their anniversary. For the occasion dinner was served in the Club Room at 6p.m. and, after a long toast list, the rest of the evening was 'devoted to conviviality and harmony, and songs were sung. A hearty vote of thanks was given to the Host and Hostess for the excellent arrangements and very good dinner'. The Trafalgar Brass Band played and 'gave the greatest satisfaction'. Arnold Martin was the **Globe's** landlord during the 1920s and '30s, and may have met the young Dennis Potter who was born in 1935. Potter became the 'Forest's greatest literary son', a talented but controversial playwright who was born at Berry Hill and frequented the pub at a later date.

In Potter's *Changing Forest*, published in 1962, he wrote:

> At the Globe, my favourite pub, the fireplace was piled high with huge, blazing lumps of local coal, and the early arrivals were smacking their hands over it, talking in low, cold voices. Some of them had come through the lanes or across 'the meand', or even through the wood, now a huge soft cathedral of cold. The Forest is beautiful at this time in a different, more aloof fashion than when green with summer, and the feel of the place becomes more immediately apparent. I suppose one feels a return to the sense of isolation and severely separated villages, that, too, there is something unbearably evocative about the stamping of feet outside the blazing windows and the bustle of coats, hats, greetings which follows.

Acclaimed for his many television dramas including *Pennies from Heaven*, *Blue Remembered Hills* and *The Singing Detective*, Dennis Potter is commemorated in the library at Ross on Wye, the town where he lived from 1959 until his death in 1994. Before Potter's death the **Globe** was transformed with 'everything opened up, bright white, upholstered and carpeted with gas logs, and playing Everly Brothers' tapes'.

From the **Globe**, a minor road leads through Joyford to the thriving and popular **Dog and Muffler** found tucked away at the end of the lane. Known as the **New Inn** in 1838, it was owned by James Hall, a Redbrook maltster and brewer, and leased to John Hill an innkeeper and gardener as 'All that messuage tenement and dwelling house situated at Joyford ... commonly called or known by the name of the New Inn with the yard garden and outbuildings'. In 1857, when John Hill was paying a half yearly rent of £12 10s., there was a dispute over his fixtures and fittings 'purchased by him at the time of entry'. In the latter part of the century, about the time that Edward Fox owned the property, the inn was renamed the **Britannia**. This name survived until the mid-20th century when a new landlord decided to rename the pub the **Dog and Muffler**. According to a local imbiber, this unique and amusing name depicted a dog wearing a

The Dog and Muffler in 2003

miner's muffler or scarf. The dog belonged to the then landlord who around that time had purchased a mine.

The **Dog and Muffler** has grown out of all proportions since its modest beginnings as a beer house, and has doubled in size since the description in Jon Hurley's critical pub guide of 1991:

This attractive little pub is way off the well trodden track but worth finding just the same. ... Tidy and cosy, it has genuine old world charm and dedicated hosts to keep it that way. There are old oak beams, nooks and crannies, soft and comfortable old chintzy chairs in the tiny lounge, plus a well-stocked bar ... gleaming copper and brass items hang from the ceilings.

In the late 19th century there was another beer house at Joyford at a junction of several unclassified roads. It was owned and occupied by Charlotte Harrison from 1879 to the end of the century, and was known as the **Albert**, which suggests an earlier establishment of at least 1861 when the prince died. Thomas Howells was running the **Albert** in 1903 for the representatives of the Harrison family, and an Emily Howells was recorded there in 1935 before it eventually closed.

The road going south-west from the **Globe** leads to the **King of Spain**, a modern and more exotic name for the former **King's Head**, possibly the oldest inn in this part of the Forest. At the Gloucester Record Office a bundle of deeds includes an Abstract of Title dating from 1772 recording 'All that Cottage tenement or dwelling house wherein the said John Phipps did inhabit and dwell together with his garden and pigscot'. In 1786 the property was left to his son, who died in 1827 and left the 'house then resided in together with the Barn Stable Garden and all outbuildings' to his wife Mary. The barn and stable had been extended and converted into a 'messuage or dwelling house', which became the inn around 1830. In 1858 the whole property was split into three lots and the 'dwelling house commonly called or known as the King's Head inn with the stable piggery and garden' was conveyed to Edwin Morgan Godwin for £160. The **King's Head** remained in the ownership of the Godwin family until the early 1900s when Ernest Beach took over the beer house and stayed there until at least 1939. The 'friendly

The King of Spain was at one time the King's Head

free house' of 1984 was still offering 'a good selection of brews' in 1991 before being renamed the **King of Spain**.

Just south of the **King of Spain** is another pub called the **Pike House**, which stands at the corner of a major crossroads. It is a rather modern looking flat-roofed building, obviously rebuilt on or near the site of the original **Cross Keys** that was recorded here in 1856. This became the **New Inn** under the Jones family, who managed the pub until the 1930s when it had been acquired by Arnold, Perrett and Co. In 1937 the Cheltenham Original Brewery took over. At a later date the pub was renamed the **Pike House** commemorating a former tollhouse that stood at the crossroads

The Pike House at Berry Hill

101

The Sale of the New Inn (Pike House) in 1937

between 1840 and 1888. The pub continues to enjoy a good trade, serving a
variety of food as well as drinks.

From the Lower Berry Hill crossroads a road leads north past the two
previously mentioned inns and through Christchurch, with its Gothic style
church built in 1812, to the **New Inn** at a place called Shortstanding. The
New Inn and the **Royal Oak** were both marked on the 1877 Ordnance
Survey, but the latter was refused a licence in 1903 because of 'misconduct'
and became a private house called the Oaks. The **New Inn** was owned by the
Tomlins from the 1870s to the 1900s, and Allen Lodge was behind the bar in
1927. In 1984 it was operating as a 'Basic one bar pub' and in the 21st
century still has a welcoming atmosphere.

From Shortstanding a narrowing but well used road leads to Symonds Yat
where the famous 500 foot craggy rock forms a natural platform for a superb
view of the river Wye's horse-shoe bend. This divides Symonds into East and
West of the river; the name Yat meaning an 'opening or gate' possibly through
the five lines of fortification that covered the cliffs. These date from the Iron
Age, and Symonds probably 'takes its name from Robert Symonds, a High
Sheriff of Herefordshire in the 17th century'. Due to parish and county boundary
changes, most of the past and present Yat inns now lie in Herefordshire and have
been described in *The Pubs of Ross and South Herefordshire*.

Following her Gloucestershire research the author would like to add that
the existing **Royal Hotel** originated from a range of 19th-century buildings
used as an alehouse known as **Rocklea** before a hotel licence was granted in
1903. This was the same year that George Davis of the **Folly** inn was refused
a renewal of his licence at this unknown site.

Almost midway between Shortstanding and Symonds Yat is a place
called Hillersland and the **Halfway House Inn.** This is a modern name for an
inn that originated from at least the early 18th century. It stands on an old
route which was turnpiked by the Dean Forest Trust from 1827 to 1888. In
1747 this property was described as 'All that messuage or cottage or
tenement where the said Susannah Jones then Dwelt commonly called or
known by the Name or Sign of the Cock together with the Stable at
Hillersland'. Susannah left the property to her only child, Mary, who was
eventually married to Samuel James, a pawnbroker.

Sale of the Rock in 1937

The **Cock** was an early inn sign often indicating that cockfighting took place on the premises. This may have been the reason that in the mid-19th century its name was changed to the **Rock** after the nearby outcrop at Symonds Yat. In 1879 James Gwilliam was a grocer and alehouse keeper at the **Rock.** In 1891 the inn was owned by Garton & Co. and was later acquired by the Anglo Bavarian Brewery then Arnold, Perrett & Co. before being taken over by the Cheltenham Original Brewery in 1937.

In the 1960s and '70s Mr. S. Harding was the proprietor, but by 2002 the **Halfway House** had become a tea room and bed and breakfast establishment

The Halfway House in 2003

— not a traditional inn, although it did retain a dining licence. Nearby is the Symonds Yat Rock Motel which had a 'Licensed Restaurant and Qualified Chef' in 1975.

English Bicknor is a quiet parish almost cut off between the meandering Wye and the present main roads, and is accessible by car only from Christchurch or Lydbrook. Its history is long and complicated, running from the construction of Offa's Dyke in the 8th century to the building of 20th-century village houses. The majority of the inhabitants were previously employed in industries associated with iron, charcoal, coal, timber, lime and agriculture, but

A 1970s advertisement for the Rock Motel

103

apart from a few handsome houses the village now has a suburban appearance in a scenic setting.

A path signposted 'Coldwell Walks' leads to Symonds Yat along a scenic route landscaped in the late 18th century along the top of towering limestone crags named Raven, Ship, Needle and Quarry Rocks. Far below are glimpses of the Wye between the trees, and before reaching Symonds Yat Rock the attractive moss covered spring-fed Coldwell is passed. The return is down a steep path to the riverside and along a delightful stretch to Common Grove at English Bicknor.

It was near here in 1808 that John Whitehead Warre was drowned. This young man, born in Oporto and related to the famous port shippers, was with his family enjoying an excursion down the Wye in a pleasure boat from Ross to Monmouth. When they arrived below Coldwell Rocks the family and boatman pulled up on the shore for a picnic. After eating their 'cold collation' John decided to bathe, but was apparently seized with cramp and sunk to the bottom.

Around the time of this unfortunate accident two former pubs were probably still open in English Bicknor — the **Bear** and the **White Hart** — and at a cider mill by the Wye at Coldwell Rocks cider was made from 'excellent orchards of cider apples'. The **Bear** once stood at the entrance to the churchyard where the former almshouses of 1858 still stand. It was the meeting place of a Friendly Society in 1787 and 1788, and the manor court met there once a year during the early 19th century. In 1838 John Price was the owner and it was tenanted to William Badham, but some time before 1858 the inn was demolished and replaced by the almshouses which have since been converted to a private dwelling.

South of English Bicknor church on the west side of the road was a malt house owned by Joseph Ambery in 1838. Still called the Malt House, the property can still be identified although rather hemmed in by modern houses. Further south, on the opposite side of the road, was the **White Hart** dating from at least the 17th century when it was owned by William Rudge, junior, and his wife. In 1767 'All that Messuage or Tenement called or known by the Name of the White Hart situate and being in the said Parish of English Bicknor' was in the possession of John Evans, who lived at the smithy on the other side of the road. In 1790 the inn was conveyed to William and Mary Ambery who later closed the inn and 'pulled down the building'. It was replaced by a private house known as Bicknor Cottage when conveyed to the Rev. James Davis and Miss Alice Davis in 1857. The last recorded beer retailer at English Bicknor was Mary Jones in 1879.

From Berry Hill, the A4136 bypasses Coleford to reach the north-west fringe of the Forest, where Staunton lies high above the Wye Valley. The

The White Horse in Staunton

original road through the village was diverted by the Turnpike Trustees in the early 1830s leaving an attractive traffic-free centre. The post office of 1989 was housed in a 17th-century building, which at one time was the **Royal Oak**, a cider house with memories still stretching to 'cider drinkers sitting around an old oak tree' as J.A. Cockburn wrote. It is understood that this inn was known by the sign of the **Ostrich** in 1799, but apparently its name was changed to the **Royal Oak** around 1832. James Carver was a busy man in 1845, he was the publican, pigman, cider maker and blacksmith. He left the running of the **Royal Oak** to Mrs. Carver in 1863 because he had taken over the tenancy of the **White Horse**. Although the **Royal Oak** closed around 1890 a cider retailer was recorded at Staunton in 1894.

The existing **White Horse** inn faces the A4136, but the original building of 1813 was rebuilt in the 19th century so as to accommodate the turnpike road. In 1845 William Morgan owned the inn, and by 1863 James Carver from the **Royal Oak** was serving behind the bar and shoeing horses in the adjoining smithy. He appears to have been followed by John Hicks, a plumber, who ran the **White Horse** for at least a couple of decades around the turn of the century during which period the Alton Court Brewery from Ross acquired the premises.

When the Alton Court Brewery ceased to function, its pubs were taken over by the Cheltenham Original Brewery in 1962. The list included the 'inn in the Parish of Staunton known as the White Horse with the blacksmith's shop outbuildings garden and land thereto adjoining'. In recent years the **White Horse** was serving a 'mixed clientele of locals and a regular trickle of ramblers in this rather off the beaten track village'. In 2002 the enthusiastic owners were advertising 'Under New Ownership — Lunchtime Bar Food — Evening Restaurant Menu' and the inn continues to thrive.

In 1901 the local press reported several cases of drunkenness at Hillersland and Staunton. At the **Rock Inn** a collier named Amis White 'refused to quit after a row and a fight' and was fined 10s. and 7s. costs. Another collier, John Tye was summoned for assault at the **White Horse** and for 'being drunk and disorderly and refusing to quit the place'. In November a case of drunkenness was reported as follows:

> Robert Witts, a collier of Crossways, near Coleford was summoned by P.C. Wiltshire for the above offence at Staunton on the 11th November — the officer said he found defendant at 11.30pm lying down in the village fast asleep. He woke him up and found defendant was drunk — Fined 5s and 8s costs.

Those interested in myths and legends are attracted to Staunton with its ancient stones, wells and crosses. From the **White Horse** a winding forest path leads to the massive Buck Stone which is surrounded by legends dating from Celtic times. Standing in this magnificent vantage point overlooking the Wye Valley the Buck Stone rocked on its own axis until 1885 when it was vandalised by a group of touring actors accompanied by an innkeeper from Monmouth. They managed to tip the huge stone from its plinth, which caused it to shatter into several pieces. Luckily the public demanded the stone to be repaired and replaced, where it remains today. According to Roy Palmer's *Folklore of Gloucestershire* the Buck Stone acquired its name in the 13th century:

> When King John was hunting nearby — at Staunton — a member of his retinue displeased him so much that the man's death was decreed. Courtiers pleaded, the king relented and pardoned the man provided a buck were killed during the day's sport. A suitable animal appeared, and was shot close to a great rock from then on called the Buckstone.

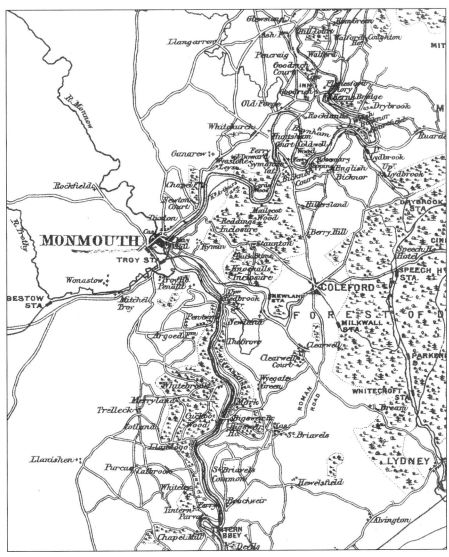

A 1914 map showing many of the places in the western part of the Forest of Dean mentioned in the text

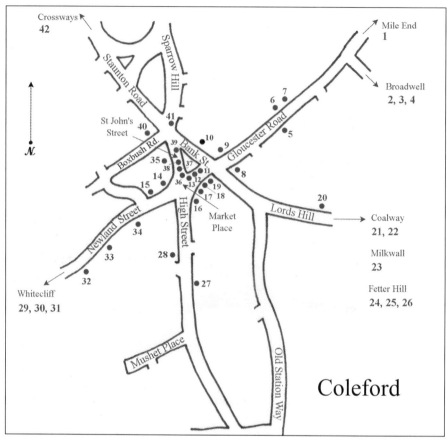

1. **Royal Forest**
2. Roving Jockey (?)
3. Rising Sun
4. **Bird in Hand**
5. Lamb / Pig & Whistle
6. Jovial Colliers
7. Rose in Hand (?)
8. Bear / Royal Oak
9. **King's Head**
10. Queen's Head / Jenny Lind
11. Buck / White Hart
12. **Angel**
13. Market Tavern
14. **Old White Hart**
15. Coach & Horses
16. Unicorn
17. Fleece

18. Feathers /
    Plume of Feathers
19. Butcher's Arms
20. Plough
21. **Britannia**
22. **Crown**
23. **Tufthorne**
24. George
25. Royal Oak (?)
26. Vine Tree
27. Red Lion
28. **Forest House**
29. Bear (?)
30. Folly
31. Nag's Head /
    Travellers Rest
32. Bell

33. Mason's Arms
34. **Market Tavern /**
    White Horse /
    Shinnanigen's
35. White Swan
36. Railway
37. Dennises
38. Victoria
39. George
40. Help me through the World /
    Mason's Arms
41. Prince of Wales
42. Crossways
    Three Parrots (?)
    Harp (?)

Coleford, showing the positions of pubs.
Those open in 2004 are shown in bold.
Those whose precise positions are uncertain are shown with (?)

CHAPTER SEVEN

Coleford

The traditional route from Gloucester to Coleford closely followed the existing A40 to Huntley, then along the road which now forms the A4136 to Edge End, where the original Mitcheldean to Coleford road (now the B4028) leads through Mile End. In the centre of the town is the Market Place, where an isolated church tower stands on the Tump in the middle of a busy crossroads. The prominent tower features an 'embattled parapet with pinnacles as the continuation of stepped diagonal buttresses, with clock faces on the south, west and north sides'. This was the site of an earlier chapel dating from at least the 1480s, which was enlarged in the 1740s and replaced by a larger octagonal chapel in 1821. It was demolished in 1882, apart from the tower, and in 1968 the Market Hall of 1691 was also demolished to improve traffic flow.

In 1900 Coleford was described in a guide book as:

> A market town of much imporrtance ... in the midst of some of the finest forest scenery. The Great Western and Severn and Wye Joint Railways have stations here. In the centre of the town is a Town Hall and Market House, and a market is held here every Friday — stock markets on the 3rd Tuesday of the month, and Coleford fair on June 20th.
>
> Coleford is largely supported by the Forest of Dean collieries and iron mines in the locality today, and its fortunes are largely bound up with the success or non-success of the mines.

From the late 18th century, Coleford and the Forest of Dean benefited from the turnpiking of the roads leading to Gloucester, Monmouth and Chepstow. In 1796 the *Gloucester Journal* announced that 'the new road thro' his Majesty's Forest of Dean, leading from Mitcheldean to Coleford and Monmouth, which is the high road from Gloucester to South Wales, is greatly improved, and in a short time will be equal to any in this part of the county'. Road improvements led to an increase in travel, trade and transport, and thus in the various businesses associated with coaching and carrier services. In

1830 nine 'Inns and Public Houses', two maltsters, one brewer and three blacksmiths were recorded at Coleford. A few years later they were joined by a saddler and a wheelwright, and about 16 beer retailers — the latter due to a change in the legislation. In a *Glance Back at Coleford* published in 2000, Keith and June Webb wrote:

> During Victorian and Edwardian times, Coleford was a hive of small shops, offices, business premises and countless public houses. Some of the town's better buildings were originally hotels or hostelries, as the distance which could be travelled in a day in times past, usually meant an overnight stopover was required when doing business or visiting in the area.

Coleford milepost

Throughout its long history Coleford has never been short of a drinking place offering good quality beer. In 1483 an Aleconner was appointed to 'examine locally brewed ale and ensure it was good and wholesome, and appropriately priced'. There is some evidence to suggest that the **Angel** and **King's Head** stand on sites occupied by inns in 1608, and in 1653 William Worgan was dwelling in a 'messuage and garden ... being the Inn in Colford'. Twenty years later a deed relating to the present **Feathers** survives as the earliest known reference to a named inn in the town. During the 18th century these three established inns were competing with nine others in Coleford. Since then, over 40 names of past and present inns, taverns and beerhouses have been recorded in the town and its neighbourhood with nine open.

Approaching Coleford along the B4028, a built-up area at Mile End is where the **Royal Forest** stands near the crossroads. In the late 19th century John Brown owned and occupied this alehouse, where the local colliers came to slake their thirst. In 1901 the new landlord, Richard Edwards, had problems with some of his customers according to the *Dean Forest Guardian*:

> Amos Jones and George Hale, colliers, of Broadwell Lane End, were summoned by Mr. Richard Edwards, landlord of the Royal Forest, Mile End ... Prosecutor said [that] on Saturday, 12th May, the defendants came to his house and asked for beer which he refused to draw, as the defendants were both the worse for liquor. He asked them to leave several times, but they would not do so, and commenced to use bad language. He eventually ejected Jones and when he was returning to the house he met

The Royal Forest at the beginning of the 21st century

Hale coming out. Both defendants continued to act disorderly when outside the house,—The Chairman said both defendants had been there before, and Amos Jones,who had a very bad record, would be fined £2 and 8s. costs, and Hale would have to pay £1 and 8s.

In 1937 the **Royal Forest** passed from Arnold, Perrett & Co. to the Cheltenham Original Brewery. The inn eventually became a Whitbread pub and in 1968 was serving an 'In-the-Basket-Menu at Weekends'. By the late 1970s Ron and Irene Mitton were offering 'a very extensive menu including Severn Salmon, Trout, Steaks etc.'. Sadly this 'much renovated bright and breezy pub' of the 1980s became neglected, but fortunately has been given a new lease of life.

. ALL THAT messuage or Inn known as The Royal Forest Inn situate at or near Mitcheldean Lane End in the Township of West Dean in the County of Gloucester bounded by the turnpike road leading from Coleford to Lydbrook by waste land of the Forest of Dean and land formerly of the late John Perry on all or the most parts and sides thereof and containing an area of three-quarters of an acre more or less TOGETHER with the cottage with the outbuildings and appurtenances thereunto belonging erected on the land or on some part thereof.

Sale of the Royal Forest in 1937

111

From Mile End a slight detour leads south to Broadwell, where three beer houses were recorded in 1841. One of these may have been the unlikely named **Roving Jockey** occupied by Henry Morgan in 1852 when it was advertised for sale in the *Gloucester Journal* as 'All that Messuage or Dwelling House now used as a Beer House, and called the Roving Jockey, with the Outbuildings, Gardens and Land'. The other two probably became the **Rising Sun** and the **Bird in Hand**.

The former stood at the road junction and eventually became a large pub dispensing beers and ciders from hand pumps to the Real Ale brigade in the 1980s, but a lack of business since then saw its closure a few years later.

Fortunately the **Bird in Hand** has survived into the 21st century, transforming itself from a modest beer house run by Mary Marlin in the 1890s to a premises that 'underwent radical alteration'. A century later various beers were on offer together with home-made dishes.

From Mile End the B4028 becomes the Gloucester Road before it reaches Coleford town centre. In the past, a few beer houses and inns lined this street including the longest survivor — the **Lamb** — which was on the east side of the road. In the early years of the 20th century it was tied to the Blakeney Brewery and was run by the Jones family. In 1901 the following incident was reported in the local press:

The Bird in Hand in 2002

112

Frederick Lambert and James Dixon, youths, of Coleford, were summoned by P.C. Hewitt for causing an affray at Coleford on Sunday, the 5th May.—The officer said on the night named he saw the two defendants outside the Lamb Inn, Gloucester Road. They were making use of bad language towards each other, and commenced to fight. Witness went towards the defendants, and Dixon ran away, but was stopped by a gentleman. Lambert had his coat off and Dixon had his hat off.—The Chairman said the defendants should not make such fools of themselves, and they would be bound over in the sum of £10 each to keep the peace for six months, and pay 6s. 6d. each costs.

At one time the **Lamb** was also known as the **Pig and Whistle**, inevitably depicting a sign of a pig playing a whistle. It was eventually acquired by the Stroud Brewery and in 1962 was taken over by the Cheltenham Original Brewery who appear to have closed the premises.

On the opposite side of the Gloucester Road was an earlier pub called the **Jovial Colliers** which dated from at least 1766 when it was the meeting place of a Friendly Society. Between 1830 and 1870 the innkeepers included Thomas Godwin, George Porter, David Smith, Thomas Powell, Thomas Hale and William Pullin who possibly served the last pint before it closed around 1885. Next door was a beer house recorded in 1861 as the **Rose in Hand**.

This collection of pub names are worthy of some explanation, the **Roving Jockey** seems unique, and may have been named after its landlord. The **Rising Sun** was a popular pub sign in the Forest of Dean, and the **Bird in Hand** probably copied the proverb 'a bird in the hand is worth two in the bush', in this instance the bush meaning a rival house. The **Pig and Whistle** is a nickname possibly derived from 'peg o'wassail' an ancient saying wishing 'a measure of good health'. The **Jovial Colliers** — a favoured name in the Forest — was obviously named after those working in the local industry, who were not likely to be jolly after their long shifts until they had visited the pub.

On each corner of the Gloucester Road facing the Market Place were two inns conveniently placed to catch the newly arriving coaches and carriers during the 18th century. The **Bear** stood on the east side with the present **King's Head** opposite. The **Bear** of 1798 changed its sign several years prior to the banning of bear-baiting in 1835, and it is understood that it later became the more traditionally named **Royal Oak**. William Court was the innkeeper in 1839 and by 1842 was also a 'spirit dealer, auctioneer, upholsterer, and inspector of weights and measures'. He was followed by a succession of landlords until Arthur White, recorded there in the 1890s, served as the last known publican before it was closed in 1910. The site was

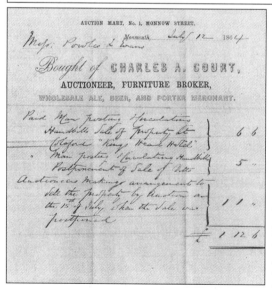

To be SOLD by AUCTION, by Messrs.

COURT & SON

AT THE

ANGEL HOTEL, COLEFORD,

On FRIDAY, the 15th of JULY, 1864,

At Three o'clock in the Afternoon, subject to conditions of Sale, the

FREEHOLD INN

CALLED

THE KING'S HEAD,

With the Garden, Coach-houses, and other Outbuildings thereto belonging.

The King's Head sale in 1864

re-used as an auction room and a second-hand store for some time before being completely redeveloped.

The **King's Head** in Bank Street faces the Market Place, and in 2002 was covered in scaffolding while undergoing a 'facelift with the help of a heritage grant aid ... aimed at helping and encouraging those responsible for the repair of historic buildings in the conservation area to preserve and enhance them and, where appropriate, reinstate any lost architectural

The Kings Head in 2004

features'. The **King's Head** is a prominent building standing on a site where an inn has existed for many centuries. A traditional story dates from the Civil War when Coleford supported the Parliamentarians. In 1643 the Royalists marched through the town, barricaded a mansion and burnt down the market house. In retaliation their commander, General Lawdy, 'was shot with a silver bullet from the window of a house' where the **King's Head** now stands.

The **King's Head** became one of Coleford's coaching inns and in the 1830s and 1840s, when Thomas Porter kept the hostelry, the *Forester* coach travelling from Gloucester to Monmouth called at the inn every morning at eight. Porter ran the **King's Head** from 1829 for at least 25 years and was followed by James Griffiths and a long line of successive landlords. In 1864 'The Freehold Inn called the King's Head, With the Garden, Coach-houses, and other Outbuildings' were to be sold by auction. The sale was postponed but the auctioneers made a charge of £1 12s. 6d. for 'making arrangements' and 'Circulating Handbills'. Other sales were held at the inn including the auction of 'Four highly-valuable Coal Gales [mines], comprising (and known as) The Speedwell Colliery'.

After Arnold, Perrett & Co. acquired the **King's Head** in the early years of the 20th century, the local police 'couldn't cope with malefactors eluding them when they came in the front door', so the 'police successfully asked the magistrates to order the bricking up of one of the two back doors' — a story related by Ray Allen to the *Forest Review* in 1998. Arnold, Perrett

& Co. were eventually taken over by the Cheltenham Original Brewery in 1937.

Alongside the **King's Head** is the narrow Spout Lane which once led to a brewery and an alehouse which was called the **Queen's Head** in 1856, but is also recorded as the **Jenny Lind**. Apart from these names little is known of the premises which closed shortly after 1881. On the left hand side of the lane is a stone building — the sole remains of Coleford's own brewery dating from 1833 when John Trotter from Coleford became involved with 'All that messuage,

Tenement or cottage with a building sometime used as a skinhouse but then lately converted into a Brewery ... at a place called the Spout', better known as 'All that Brewhouse or Public Brewery with the Counting house, storehouse, furnaces, yard and appurtenances' where John Trotter established his brewery. It was then leased to

The remains of the Coleford Brewery in 2002

H. Courteen, S.G. Gregg and Charles Wadley until 1858. After this the brewer Henry Salmon took over the premises and he was followed by Harry Clark who appears to have served as the last brewer before it closed towards the end of the 19th century.

At different periods there were a number of inns overlooking the Market Place, but only the **Angel**, the **Old White Hart** and the **Feathers** survived into the 1990s. It appears that the original **White Hart** was renamed the **Buck** by Richard Porter who kept the inn in the 1830s. This new sign remained until it closed around 1860. The **Buck** stood to the right of the existing **Angel**, which has been successfully transformed into a 21st-century establishment. Its luxurious accommodation, Real Ale Bar, Malt and Hops Tea Room and live music in the Kavern Bar caters for all tastes, but it somehow manages to retain the feeling of its historic past which dates back to the 17th century. Also known as the **Great Inn**, it became the town's principal coaching inn and the place for public meetings and assemblies. The Excise Officer was based here, but in 1741 he was moved to another alehouse before returning to the **Angel** in 1792.

It was during the early 19th century, when William Roberts kept the **Angel**, that auctions of property were held at the inn, including the sale of Cinderhill farm at St. Briavel's in 1806. Roberts was followed by Thomas Holden, a long-serving landlord from 1810 until the 1830s when William

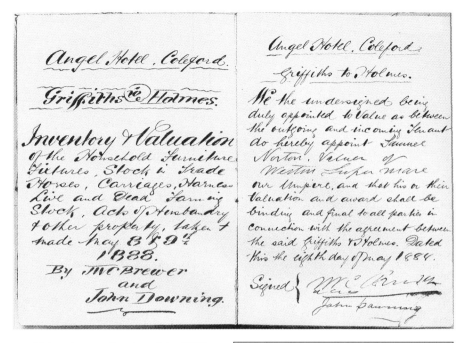

Valuation at the Angel in 1888

Batten took over. An 1831 incident is commemorated on a plaque and reads: 'Through this archway Warren James the leader of the Foresters in the Dean Riots was brought on 15th June 1831 after his capture'. The rioters had thrown open the Forest inclosures made by the Crown to protect the trees, because they excluded the animals that had always grazed the Forest. After his trial at Gloucester, James was found guilty and transported to Tasmania. During the middle years of the 19th century James Dennis was an active innkeeper who erected a long wooden sign reading 'Angel Hotel James Dennis' which stretched from the inn to the market house. By 1863 James Dennis had handed over the running of the **Angel** 'commercial and

Sale of the Angel in 1898

117

posting house' to William King, while he traded as a 'wine & spirit agent, & agent for the Phoenix Fire Assurance Co.', situated at the back of the **Angel**.

From thereon various landlords kept the 'Angel, family and commercial hotel and posting house'. When the tenancy changed in 1888 from James Griffiths to George Holmes an inventory was made of the 'goods and effects' in the 'Dining Room, Commercial Room, Coffee Room, Bar, Tap Room, Private Sitting Room, Kitchens, Pantry, Mangle Room, Club Room, Bedrooms, Store Room and Cellars', all valued at £932 13s. 9d. Ten years later another tenant was required, but there was concern because 'the client has not yet definitely decided on taking the Angel Hotel' due to complications over valuation and commission. Eventually the owner, Mrs. E.R. Payne, took on Edward Highley, an experienced innkeeper from the town's **Old White Hart**.

THE ANGEL HOTEL
COLEFORD :: **FREE HOUSE**

First-class Residential Hotel in the centre town of the Dean Forest with every modern sevice. Ideal headquarters for every class of tourist. Famed for its excellent cellars and good food.

BASS & WORTHINGTON ON DRAUGHT

CARS FOR HIRE — COMMODIOUS YARD AND GARAGES

Phone & Telegrams : Coleford 13. *Proprietor P. W. Paddock.*

A 1939 advertisement for the Angel

The Angel in the 21st century

118

Throughout the 20th century the **Angel** continued as an hotel and from the 1980s gained a reputation for its Real Ales. Then 'new owners experienced in upmarketing' undertook a 'massive refurbishment programme'.

On the left of this old coaching inn was at one time a more modest establishment known as the **Market Tavern**. This catered for the market traders in the early 19th century until it closed around 1850, although it may have remained open as one of the

The one-time Market Tavern

many unnamed beer houses that existed at that time. On market days the Market Place presented a busy scene with colourful stalls, penned animals, tethered horses and parked wagons with farmers and traders discussing business at one of the inns or taverns.

The **Old White Hart** (not to be confused with the previously mentioned **White Hart**) is wrapped around the corner of St. John's Street and the

The Old White Harp in 2002

119

Market Place. Its long range of buildings date from at least 1731 when William Morgan owned the **White Hart Inn** 'together with the Stable, Garden, Brewhouse and appurtenances'. Later Morgans were recorded

A 1939 Advertisement for the White Hart

there including Thomas, who was connected with the Market House and from 1838 to 1845 collected the 'tolls, pens, fair tolls etc.' which averaged about £75 a year. After the Morgans left in 1861 Henry Kear kept the **Old White Hart** and was followed by Edward Highley until 1898 when he took over the tenancy of the **Angel**. In 1906 the inn was romantically called **Ye Old White Hart** by the proprietor, George Probyn, and this name continued under Orlando Coole throughout the 1920s and 1930s. In the 1980s the **Old White Hart** was a 'comfortable pub with modern lounges, small log fire, boxed beams, and the inevitable horse brasses'.

The only other known inn on the north side of the Market Place was the **Coach and Horses**, an early inn recorded in 1719 and sold to William Peters in 1752. The confirmation of the sale in 1761 survives as the last reference to this inn. On the opposite side of the Market Place is a white building — the

Sale of the Unicorn in 1921

former **Unicorn Inn** — now called Unicorn House. In 2002 the owners received a heritage grant for external repairs. The *Forester* newspaper reported: 'This is seen as particularly important since the property fronts on to one side of Mushet Walk, the pedestrian route linking the old and the new parts of the town centre, which now also boasts the Mushet pavement plaques'.

The **Unicorn** dates from the mid-19th

The one-time Unicorn in 2004

century, and was kept by Edward Smith in 1879. It was later acquired by J.W. Watts, who owned numerous properties in Coleford. From the beginning of the 19th century Sara Reeves kept the **Unicorn** for over 30 years, and remained there after J.W. Watts died in 1821. His properties were offered for sale including the 'Unicorn Hotel' consisting of 'Two Front Bars, Smoke Room, Large Sitting Room, Kitchen, Pantry and Scullery' on the ground floor, and a 'Sitting Room, Five Bedrooms and Boxroom' on the first floor, and 'Large Underground Dry Cellarage'. After the sale, Sara remained at the **Unicorn** for a few more years until Charles Radford took over around 1935. The inn has since been closed.

Between Unicorn House and the present **Feathers** was an inn called the **Fleece** only recorded in 1849 by S.G. Gregg, a surveyor in the town. The sign of the **Fleece** suggests an earlier establishment, as the name refers to the importance of the wool trade.

A few doors away from the **Fleece** is an almost hidden entrance leading to the **Feathers**, another of Coleford's old inns. The doorway is set well back from the Market Place, and belies the extent of this building, which is best seen from the car park. In 1672 the inn came into the possession of Richard Sladen and his wife Mary, the daughter of the former proprietor named Stirley Kedwin. In a deed of 1737 it was 'commonly called or known by the Name of the Plume of Feathers or Old Inn' and was divided into two — the inn kept by the Sladen family until passing into the hands of George Wintle then Richard Smart who ran the inn for its owner, Henry Jenkins, in the 1820s; the other part became a separate house.

Henry Jenkins, described as an innkeeper and stonemason, was forced to sell the **Feathers** in 1827 in order to pay his creditors. He had previously been declared bankrupt in 1819 and served time in a debtor's prison. In 1827 the following notice appeared in the *London Gazette*:

> A meeting of the Creditors of Henry Jenkins, late of Coleford ... Innkeeper and Stone-cutter, an Insolvent Debtor, who was discharged from the King's Bench-Prison, in or about the month of February 1820, will be held on Saturday the 10th day of February next, at the Office of Messrs. Powles and Tyler, in the Town of Monmouth at Twelve o'Clock at Noon precisely, to approve and direct in what manner, and at what place or places the real estate of the said Insolvent shall be sold by public auction.

After this meeting 'All that commodious Inn and Public House called the **Feathers Inn** ... together with two large Yards, four large Stables & other attached Buildings' was auctioned with his other properties. John Edwards was recorded at the **Plume of Feathers** in 1830 when North's Wagons and Thomas Plaisted's carriers ran a service from the inn's yard to Gloucester. From the mid-19th century a long line of successive landlords kept the **Feathers**. It everntually became a Courage pub, described as 'unpretentious and friendly' and 'snugly hidden away', but in 2004 its doors were closed and its windows barred. The remaining pub in the Market Place once stood on the corner with Lords Hill. The **Butcher's Arms** was a beer house and shop which was run by James Cullis in the 1860s and 1870s. It may have continued as a beer retailers until the end of the century.

From the centre of Coleford roads lead out in all directions like the spokes of a wheel, and each one leads past sites of former pubs and inns including three that were

The Feathers in 2002

122

Coleford, Glocestershire.

TO BE SOLD BY

AUCTION,

BY

WHITE & SON,

AT THE

King's Head Inn, in the Town of Coleford,

ON FRIDAY, THE 23rd. DAY OF MARCH 1827,

Between the Hours of THREE and FIVE in the Afternoon,

SUBJECT TO SUCH CONDITIONS AS SHALL THEN BE PRODUCED,

The Undermentioned

FREEHOLD

PROPERTY,

Being the real Estate of HENRY JENKINS, late of Coleford aforesaid, Innkeeper and Stone Cutter, an Insolvent Debtor, who was discharged from the King's Bench Prison, in or about the Month of February, 1820.—VIZ :

All that commodious INN and PUBLIC HOUSE, called the *Feathers Inn*, situate in the centre of the said Town of Coleford, together with two large Yards, four large Stables, & other attached Buildings, with the Appurtenances thereto adjoining, late in the occupation of Mr. GEORGE WINTLE, and now of Mr. RICHARD SMART, as Tenant thereof.

A compact built DWELLING HOUSE and GARDEN, pleasantly situated in the said Town of Coleford, adapted for the Residence of a small genteel Family, with attached and detached Offices, late in the occupation of Mr. ROBERT JACKMAN, and now of Mr. WELLER, as Tenant thereof, built only a few years ago, and conveniently fitted up at a considerable Expense, together with a two stalled Stable to the said Premises adjoining, late in the occupation of Mr. LOWE, Surgeon, and now of Mrs. ANN BAKER.

A desirable newly-erected MESSUAGE and SHOP, late in the occupation of Mr. LOWE, Surgeon, and now of Mr. JAMES POWELL, as Tenant thereof, situate in the Market-Place of the said Town of Coleford.

A small DWELLING HOUSE, with the Appurtenances, late in the occupation of Mr. RICHARDS, Exciseman, and now of Mr. WATKINS.

Seven QUARRIES of excellent STONE, situate at Birch Hill, Howlers Slade, and Barn Hill, in His Majesty's Forest of Dean.

For a view of the Premises, apply to the respective Tenants, or to Mrs. ANN BAKER, in Coleford; and for further Particulars to Messrs. POWLES & TYLER, Solicitors, Monmouth, or the Auctioneers, Coleford.

AWBREY, PRINTER, MONMOUTH.

Sale notice of the Feathers in 1827

open in 2004. Firstly, Lords Hill follows an ancient route to Coalway, and passes the former **Plough** with a date stone over the arch initialled '1828 H. W.' The pub would have overlooked open fields before Bell's Hotel and Forest of Dean Golf Club was created. It had opened by 1851 as a beer house, and Edward Wilcox was recorded there in 1863. After his death 30 years later

The Britannia on the corner of Coalway Cross in 1930

John Arnold & Sons acquired the pub and appointed Mary Fox as tenant. George Tillings was the landlord in 1935, but the **Plough** has now been closed for a number of years.

At Coalway, the hamlet has expanded since four cottages were built there in the 18th century. The locals at the beginning of the 21st century had a choice of two pubs — the **Britannia**, which had been run by Henry Hawkins for John Arnold & Sons at the beginning of the 20th century and in 1981 was 'a fairly basic hostelry ... before becoming a 'Pubmaster', and the **Crown** dating from the 1870s. This pub was taken over by

The Britannia at Coalway in 2002

The Crown at Coalway

Arnold, Perrett & Co., and passed to the Cheltenham Original Brewery in 1937. Some time before the beginning of the 21st century the **Crown** became a Free House and is still open.

From Coalway a road skirts Colcford to Milkwall where the **Tufthorn** serves the local community. Although still open its documentation

The Tufthorn at Milkwall in 2002

125

is elusive, but back in 1962 it was acquired by the Cheltenham Original Brewery from the Stroud Brewery as that 'messuage or Inn in Tufthorne Lane, Perry Grove Milkwall near Coleford known as the Tufthorne Inn with the outbuildings and land ...'

From Milkwall the cycleway to Fetter Hill follows the course of the Coleford Railway which opened in 1883, was taken over by the Great Western Railway the following year and was closed in 1917. At Fetter Hill, former industrial sites including quarries, stone works and brick making have been reinstated as forest, but the men working there were able to down a pint at either the **George** or the **Royal Oak** beer houses. Both were open in 1903 with the **George** tied to Lloyd & Yorath, but owned and occupied by John Porter. It appears to have closed after World War Two but the building can still be identified, unlike the **Royal Oak** which was run by L. Banks in the

The George at Fetter Hill with the railway directly behind

early 20th century but was later demolished. Amongst the quarries at Dark Hill was a cottage called the **Vine Tree** in 1837 which was probably the same **Vine Tree** kept by James Polly as a beer house in 1859.

From Coleford's market place the High Street leads south to join the B4228. On the left there is ample free parking for the shoppers, tourists and those visiting the Great Western Railway Museum, housed in the original goods station of 1883 — the only remaining part of this railway site. A modern doctor's surgery stands on the site of the **Red Lion**, a Whitbread pub that succumbed 'meekly to the demolition power of the bulldozer'. In 1732 'All that Messuage Tenement or Dwelling House called or known by the

Sale of the Red Lion in 1921

name of the Red Lyon situated and being in the town of Coleford aforesaid with a Brewhouse, Two stables and backside and Garden' was sold by William Morgan to Richard Browne and Richard Symonds for the sum of £80. From thereon it passed through the Browne and Mabbett families until 1775, when it came into the ownership of John White. During the 1830s and 1840s Thomas Grindell kept the inn, and Edmund Jones did so in 1858. John W. Watts purchased the premises towards the end of the 19th century, and supplied the Whittingtons at the **Red Lion** from his own wine and spirit business in St. John's Street.

In 1921 John Watts died and his properties including the **Red Lion** were offered for sale. At that date the property consisted of 'Front Bar, Private Bar, Living Room and Back Kitchen, good Underground Cellars, Club-room and Four Bedrooms'. Attached to the building was a 'useful Yard with Premises recently used as a Carpenter's Shop; Malt Houses, Stabling for Four Horses and Piggeries', let to Mr. Albert Edmunds at £25 a year. The **Red Lion** was later acquired by the Stroud Brewery, taken over by the Cheltenham Original Brewery in 1962 and so passed to Whitbread, but 'failed to stay in business despite a fight from regulars who managed a stay of execution by appealing to English Heritage to help them retain this centuries-old pub'. It was demolished in 1992.

On the opposite side of the High Street are the council offices housed in a former temperance hotel, and the present licensed **Forest House Hotel** dating from 1797. From the early 1800s it had been the home of the famous Mushet family, pioneers in the development of the iron and steel industries at Whitecliff and Darkhill. A splendid way to Whitecliff is by foot along Rock Lane, an ancient hollow way that steeply descends to the Whitecliff valley and ends exactly opposite the blast furnace associated with David Mushet. The massive furnace bears a date stone of 1800, and in recent years has been extensively repaired.

At least three pubs are known to have existed in Whitecliff, 'a long struggling hamlet on the Newland road'. It was named after the rock face where a quarry is still worked. The **Bear** was a coaching inn at an unknown date and site, but the **Folly**, which is now a heap of stones

127

The one-time Nag's Head at Whitecliff

alongside Rock Lane, was a beer house recorded as early as 1757. John Taylor appears to have been the last beer retailer and shopkeeper before it finally closed some time after 1879. The **Nag's Head**, on the east side of the road, although now closed, still retains its name. It was known as the **Travellers Rest** in 1830 when Jeremy Trigg was the landlord, but in 1842 it had reverted to its original 18th-century name the **Nag's Head**. Arnold, Perrett & Co. purchased the inn at the turn of the 19th century and built an Edwardian extension in 1907. The Cheltenham Original Brewery took over the **Nag's Head** in 1937 and within a short time it was closed.

Returning to Coleford's Market Place along Newland Street, three former pub sites are passed on the south side of the road. They were

---

NEWLAND.—THE NAG'S HEAD,

ALL THAT messuage or dwellinghouse used as a Public House and known as The Nag's Head with the outbuildings garden and cottage and all other outbuildings and appurtenances thereunto belonging and the piece or parcel of pasture land or orcharding adjoining the same containing altogether four acres and twenty-three perches (more or less) situate at Whitecliffe in the Tything of Coleford in the Parish of Newland in the County of Gloucester.

Sale of the Nag's Head in 1937

COLEFORD.—MASON'S ARMS.

ALL THAT messuage or Inn known as the Mason's Arms situate at Coleford in the County of Gloucester and all outbuildings and appurtenances thereunto belonging comprising in the rear a yard W.C. urinal and timber and brick built outbuildings and all other outbuildings and appurtenances thereunto belonging TOGETHER with the site thereof and the land occupied therewith which said premises are now in the occupation of Frederick Hinton as tenant.

Sale of the Mason's Arms in 1937

128

*The Mason's Arms is now
a motorcycle shop*

recorded by the the surveyor, S.G. Gregg, in 1849 as the **Bell**, opposite the Baptist Chapel, the **Mason's Arms**, now a motorcycle shop, and the **White Horse**, which became a modern theme pub called **Shinnanigen's**, but is now more prosaically called the **Market Tavern**. Despite extensive research no further references have been traced, except that either the **Bell** or **Mason's Arms** was occupied by Sarah and Elmes Bozeley, beer sellers in Newland Street during the mid-19th century.

St. John's Street leads north from the Market Place, and was originally called Birmingham Street before the new church was built and dedicated to St. John in 1880. Near its corner the old stone wine vaults are now offices but 'a hundred years ago John W. Watts bottled Bass's Pale Ale and Guinness's stout in his own cellars, and supplied families with ale in casks from nine gallons upwards', before the premises were sold after 1921 to S.J. Highley.

Further along on the same west side is a building with a balcony. This was once the **White Swan**, kept by Alfred Webb for J.W. Watts at the turn of the 20th century. After Watts's death in 1921 the **White Swan** was sold as a three-storied licensed house consisting of 'Front Bar, Private Bar, Tap Room, Living Room, Cellarage and Coal Shed' on the ground floor with four bedrooms and a sitting room on the upper floors. It was acquired by Wintle's Forest Brewery and taken over by the Cheltenham Original Brewery in 1937 as 'All that messuage dwelling-house or beerhouse

The White Horse became Shinnanigen's and is now the Market Tavern

Lot 2. The Stone-built and Slated **Single Licensed House**, with a Double Frontage of about 29 feet to St. John Street, and with Entrance at rear from Old Tramway Lane, known as

The "White Swan," Coleford.

The Accommodation includes :—

On Ground Floor —Front Bar, Private Bar, Tap Room, Living Room, Cellarage and Coal Shed.

On First Floor —Two Bedrooms and Sitting Room.

On Second Floor —Two Bedrooms.

There is a good Pump on the Premises, and Gas is laid on

It is now let to Miss Mary Fox on a Quarterly Tenancy, at the low Rental of £16 per annum.

The White Swan sale in 1921

known by the name or sign of the White Swan'. It probably closed around 1950.

On the east side of St. John's Street four pubs or beer houses existed at different periods during the 19th century. Starting from the Market Place end there was the **Railway**, kept by

COLEFORD.—THE WHITE SWAN.

ALL THAT messuage dwellinghouse or beerhouse known by the name or sign of The White Swan with the appurtenances thereto belonging and usually occupied therewith situate in St. John Street Coleford in the County of Gloucester formerly in the occupation of William Mason but now in the occupation of Samuel Peters and bounded by messuages and premises of Messrs. Pont & Adams a messuage or premises now or formerly belonging to or in the occupation of Tom Hill the old Monmouth & Forest of Dean Tram road and by St. John Street aforesaid on all or the most parts or sides thereof.

The 1937 sale of the White Swan mentioned the 'old Monmouth and Forest of Dean Tram road', which bordered the pub grounds

The Victoria is now a book shop

The one-time George in St. John's Street

Edwin Stephens in 1867; **Dennises**, in 1891 run by the Cheltenham Brewery for the executors of James Dennis and continued by Lydia Cullimore in 1903; the **Victoria**, kept by A. Jenkins in 1860, which became a coffee tavern and now houses the excellent Forest of Dean Bookshop; and next door the **George**, open in 1839 and now a shop. The **Railway** was probably named after the tramroad which operated between 1812 and 1872, and not the Severn and Wye Railway which did not open until 1875 or the Coleford Railway which opened in 1883. The **Victoria** and **George** were probably both named after the two monarchs.

At its northern end, St. John's Street meets the junction of Boxbush and Staunton roads and Sparrow Hill. Standing on the corner of Boxbush Road is the former **Help Me Through the World**, which closed in the 1990s, but still displays its sign. It was open in 1867 and re-named the **Mason's Arms** in 1877, a name that was kept for

131

The former Help Me Through the World in 2002

over a century. In 1901 George Jones was the owner and occupier of this beer house, which was later acquired by Wintle's Forest Brewery. While Frederick Hinton was the tenant in 1937 it was taken over by the Cheltenham Original Brewery and passed to Whitbread. The 'plain pub on outskirts of town' closed shortly after 1984 before re-opening as **Help Me Through the World** in the 1990s, but did not survive into the 21st century. The original and unusual sign relates to the drunkard's cloak — a barrel with holes for the head and hands which was fitted on a drunkard as a punishment during the Commonwealth.

Until demolished in 1939 the **Prince of Wales** had stood at the bottom of Sparrow Hill. It had been kept by Robert Morgan in 1891 before it was acquired by the Redbrook Brewery. After World War One, Ind Coope had taken over the premises which was run by the Harris family until its closure. Apart from a pub recorded in 1861 as **Crossways** on the Staunton Road; the **Three Parrots** of 1755 and the **Harp**, both at unknown sites, this completes the list of past and present pubs in Coleford and its neighbourhood.

A number of Friendly Societies and Beneficial Clubs were active in Coleford during the late 18th and early 19th centuries. By means of a weekly subscription they provided a form of insurance for the less wealthy against sickness, disability and old age, and were usually associated with public houses. From 1766 a Beneficial Club met at the **Jovial Colliers**, and from 1777 a Friendly Society met at the **White Hart** together with a New Widows Club in 1812. Other meeting places were at the **Feathers** from 1784, the **King' Head** in 1785, the **Angel** in 1788, the **Nag's Head** in 1790 and the **Bear** in 1798, where the Female Friendly Society met in 1813, and the **Red Lion**, the meeting place of a Friendly Society in 1802 and a Benefit Society in 1827.

Towards the end of the 19th century there was a rise in the Temperance Movement to encourage less incidents of drunkenness which were numerous at this period. The *Dean Forest Mercury* of 1882 reported the 'Painful Death near Coleford' of William Brown, a 66-year-old hawker, who after making his rounds in the Forest 'had partaken of too much drink'. He took a lift in a wagon which unfortunately overturned. William received fatal injuries and died later that night. Several cases of 'drunk and disorderly behaviour' were reported in 1885, including one involving Fred Joynes, a collier, who was fined 10s. with 7s. costs. Mary Muir and George Jones were each fined 7s. for using obscene language in Newland Street, and a publican was fined for permitting drunkenness on his premises.

In 1901 the Temperance Movement was holding meetings at the British School in Coleford, and at the Methodist chapels at Clearwell and Bream. During that year mainly colliers and tramps were charged for 'being drunk and disorderly', but there was also the case of Ben Dobbs who 'had a very bad record'. He was a Coleford fishmonger who was fined £1 with 8s. costs for being drunk in charge of a pony and trap. He managed to reach his house, but as he was helplessly drunk his wife 'got him into the house and put the pony in the stable'. Then there was Edward Harris, a quarry labourer, who was 'very drunk and staggered across the road and fell down near the Town Hall'. Maybe he was making for the water trough, erected in 1897 to commemorate Queen Victoria's Diamond Jubilee, which in the past was used 'to dowse unruly drunkards who had been thrown out of the many public houses in town'. The authorities made attempts at closing some pubs by not renewing their licenses 'to cut down on working class drinking', but it was slow to take effect until restricted licensing hours were introduced.

*Effigy of a Forest of Dean miner from a 15th-century brass
in Newland Church*

CHAPTER EIGHT

Newland, Redbrook, Clearwell & Bream

Newland is probably the most attractive village in the Forest of Dean, providing a picture little changed since 1939 when R.P. Beckinsale wrote the following in his *Companion into Gloucestershire*:

> The pretty, clean-looking village of Newland has grown up in the shape of
> an irregular square around its spacious churchyard. The clearing, which
> originated probably during the reign of King John, lies in the winding
> valley of a tributary of the Wye, from which it is hidden by the high ridge
> crosscd by the lane to Redbrook. The houses on the east side of the square
> are unusually large and substantial for a forest village and several of them
> are clad prettily in evergreen shrubs and creeping plants. Spout farm would
> do credit to a Cotswold town, and adjoining it, some way back from the
> road, is the Dower House, built in the late eighteenth century by Squire
> Probyn, whose crest, an ostrich's head with a key in its mouth, explains the
> name of the very hospitable inn near by.

Before boundary changes Coleford, Newland, Clearwell, Bream and Redbrook were all hamlets within the large parish of Newland, and joined by a network of old roads. In medieval times many of the crossroads were marked with wayside crosses, examples of which still exist at Newland and Clearwell. Some of the old roads are now only footpaths and bridleways. A typical example is the Burial Path leading from Coleford to Newland which took its name from its earlier use when coffins had to be carried from Coleford to be buried at Newland church. It now forms a pleasant and attractive walk along green lanes and field paths which gradually dip down to Newland village.

More accessible routes to Newland from Coleford either follow Scowls Road from Crossways or Newland Road through Whitecliff, Millend and Scatterford. Whichever route is followed, the remains of the Coleford Railway, which opened in 1883 along the former tramroad of 1812 and conveyed Forest coal to

Monmouth, are visible. The railway was taken over by Great Western Railway, and a small station to serve Newland was built near Cherry Orchard Farm. The railway ceased to operate in 1917 and the station has since been converted into a private house.

The beautifully proportioned church of All Saints is known as the Cathedral of the Forest and dates from the 13th century. Its history is well documented; the Miner's Brass is unique and its rich collection of early monuments is rare in such a small place. The village has certainly benefited from the generosity of its inhabitants who funded almshouses, established a grammar school and provided a meeting room. Most of these buildings, including the present **Ostrich Inn**, are situated in a long range of buildings overlooking the churchyard.

The **Ostrich** is well worth a visit — the low ceilinged and beamed interior dates from 1694 when the house was rebuilt by the Probyn family who leased it from Bell's Charity, a charity for the poor dating from the 16th century. The present landlady claims that some of the internal features have been dated to an earlier period. Sometime before 1816 the house became an inn and its sign represents the Probyn crest. In 1849 'All that Messuage or dwelling house and Inn called the Ostrich Inn with the Stable Coachhouse outbuildings garden and appurtenances' was leased to Philip Ducavel, another local landowner, until his death in 1855. He was buried in the church opposite and his memorial reads:

> Philip John Ducavel Esq.
> d. Dec. 16 1855 Aged 77
> His mortal remains rest in a vault
> on the north side of this churchyard

The Ostrich in 2002

After Philip's death the **Ostrich** was leased to his sister Jane Bevan then Henry Salmon. At that time water to the inn was 'the usual supply of Spring Water running by Pipes through the ground'. By 1863 H. Freeman was in charge of the **Ostrich**. At the beginning of the 20th century, when Robert Pring was the innkeeper, the Trustees of Bell's Charity still owned the property. By the late 1970s the pub was well-run and the beer was 'not just served properly but actually seen to be so as all the trappings of draught beer selling were clearly visible behind the counter, the pipes, nozzles and barrels etc.'

Newland was not always such a quiet place as it is now. In 1882, the *Dean Forest Mercury* reported 'A Row at Newland' when Henry Smith and Frank Rooms were charged with assaulting Thomas Morgan, a wheelwright. He was waiting at the **Ostrich Inn** for his son who was 'ringing at the church', when the two offenders came in and started arguing with him and 'words ensued'. Morgan went into another room, but was followed by Smith who knocked him over, then 'both fell upon him, and he was kicked and rendered almost insensible'. The case was heard by the bench at Coleford Police Court. Nearly ten years later the same paper reported that the landlady, Anna Parry, was summoned 'for selling drink to a drunken person and for permitting drunkenness'.

It is understood that an earlier inn existed in Newland called the **Ram**, which was used for vestry meetings during the mid-18th century. The sign of the Ram has been in use for many centuries, and usually signifies a place associated with clothworkers or sheep rearing. It appears in the arms of the Worshipful Company of Clothworkers and other livery companies connected with the wool trade and is a popular name found in other parts of Gloucestershire.

From Newland a minor road leads north then west to Upper and Lower Redbrook and the river Wye. Redbrook is also approached by a shorter footpath through Forge Wood, which partly follows the line of an abandoned road. In 1828 the Monmouth antiquarian, Charles Heath wrote the following:

> This hamlet is divided and distinguished by the names of Upper and Lower Redbrook, from standing one above the other on the banks of the Wye, part of which is situated in Monmouth and part in Gloucestershire, a small brook adjoining the turnpike road ... dividing the two counties. Lower Redbrook works were formerly the property of the English Copper Company in London, who carried on a considerable trade in that line here, till they sold them to the late Mr. David Tanner of Monmouth. They were held, for some time, under his assignees, by Mr. Thomas James,— who, at the expiration of his lease, removed to a like manufactory at Lidney,—so that they are now in ruins.

Over the centuries Redbrook became an industrial place where the waters of the Valley and Red brooks powered blast furnaces, copper smelting and tin

Sale of the Redbrook Brewery in 1855

The Redbrook Brewery around 1905

The Old Brewery House in 2003

plate works, several corn mills, a 17th-century paper mill and two breweries. Not all of these were working at the same time, and most had ceased by the end of the 19th century. Iron ore and charcoal were readily available from the Forest of Dean, transportation was supplied by barges on the river Wye, and industrial growth was aided by the construction of the Monmouth Tramway from Coleford in 1812, the completion of the Monmouth to Chepstow turnpike road in 1824, and the opening of the Wye Valley Railway in 1876. With a decline in these operations, Redbrook has gradually been transformed into a rather delightful place.

The Redbrook Brewery was established in 1825 by Richard Sims, and was later acquired by James Hall and run as the Redbrook Upper Brewery until his death in 1844. The brewery was then advertised 'To be Let or Sold' in 1855 with its 'Genteel Residence' and 'large commodious Malthouse, capable of making 1,200 quarters of Malt per season, with a good trade; also a small compact three-quarter Brewery attached, with a constant supply of excellent water'. The brewery was offered for auction two years later to enable the purchaser 'to carry on the extensive Malting and Brewery business long connected with the property'. It was

Ind Coope provided the beers at many of the inns in the Forest in 1939

In a previous life this building in Upper Redbrook was the Old Inn and probably the Queen's Head

acquired by Thomas Burgham whose family ran and expanded the business which supplied at least 22 licensed properties either owned or tied to the Redbrook Brewery. Little is known of the other 19th-century brewery, which was operated by the Ansleys who lived opposite their Flour Mill at Upper Redbrook.

At its industrial height Redbrook was known to have 'consisted largely of inns' which is an exaggerated figure for the five ale houses established by the mid-19th century at Redbrook. The property called the **Old Inn** at the top of Upper Redbrook was probably the **Queen's Head** kept by the Hawkins family from at least 1906 until 1939. Opposite was the **Founder's Arms** kept by William Page in 1835, Amos Hodges in 1859, C. Mason in 1863 and Mrs. E. Morgan in 1906, before it closed its doors to the public. Overlooking the Wye at the bottom of the hill was the **Bush**, which

Once the Founder's Arms at Redbrook

139

The one-time Bush Inn

despite a series of different landlords survived as a pub into the mid-1990s. It was much used by the hungry rambler following the Offa's Dyke Path or the Wye Valley Walk, both long distance walking routes which, meeting at Redbrook create some excellent circular routes.

The Wye Valley Walk continues southwards towards Chepstow, crossing the Wye by an iron footbridge which was originally constructed to carry the Wye Valley Railway from Monmouth to Chepstow. The line opened in 1876 and was amalgamated with the Great Western Railway in 1905 before closing in 1956. On the opposite bank, at Penallt in Monmouthshire, in the shadow of the old bridge, is the **Boat Inn**, which continues to be a popular refreshment stop for Wye Valley walkers. Although in Wales, this inn must be included in this book because its carpark is in Redbook on the east bank of the Wye, the approach being by the old railway bridge. In Heather and Jon Hurley's *Paths and Pubs of the Wye Valley* published in 1986 this unique inn was described as:

The Wye in flood near the Boat Inn at Penallt in December 1997

140

an interesting old inn with plenty of beams, a quarry tiled floor and a comfortable range of furniture. ... In summer the many visitors who find this quaint spot may sun themselves in the hilly garden whilst listening to the chinking of water, as it runs merrily in little waterfalls off the bank and into the river below.

In 1848 there were two pubs at Lower Redbrook, both situated below the former tin-plate works which finally ceased production in 1961. The **King's Head** was run by B. Lambert in 1859, and from at least 1879 to 1906 the Taylors kept the inn. It was later taken over by Arnold, Perrett & Co. and passed to the Cheltenham Original Brewery in 1937 after which it was closed.

The Fish and Game as bed and breakfast only

The **Bell Inn** was temorarily closed in 1992 and was re-opened as the **Fish and Game**, before becoming a bed and breakfast establishment. At the beginning of the 21st century it was reopened with a flourish by a new landlord — an experienced publican from the Harewood End Inn in Herefordshire.

There was a radical change by 2003

From the southern end of Newland, a minor road leads past Scatterford to Clearwell, another attractive Forest village. Its name is romantically derived from the 'Spring Amongst the Clovers', but in 2002 the 19th-century stone wellhouse was in a neglected state. The clear water certainly played a role in the development of the village and its past industries of nailmaking and tanning. Other employment was provided in the iron mining, quarrying and stoneworking industries or rural crafts. In recent times Clearwell has been promoted as a tourist attraction with Clearwell Castle, originally Clearwell Court, which was gutted by fire in 1929 and left empty until it was restored and converted into an hotel, now described on its sign as a 'Neo-Gothic Mansion *c.*1730'. Clearwell Caves, where iron ore has been mined for thousands of years, opened its caverns to the public, and the unique Puzzle Wood, originally open iron mines dating from Roman times, offers a picturesque walk arranged in the form of a puzzle. At the peak of tourism in the 1980s Clearwell was able to offer accommodation at Clearwell Castle, the Lambsquay Hotel, Tudor Farm and at the **Wyndham Arms** with the **Lamb** and **Butcher's Arms** both offering 'Good Food and Good Ale'.

All these pubs were still open for business at the beginning of the 21st century, but two much earlier inns have long since closed — an unnamed inn or lodging house that was granted a lease in 1518, and the **Carpenter's Arms**, which was the meeting place of the Clearwell Friendly Society in 1787. This establishment probably stood within the group of houses that are now called Carpenter's Cottages. In the early 1800s a 'Malthouse Cydermill

The Butcher's Arms in 2002

142

and Orchard together with the buildings thereto adjoining and belonging' were situated in Clearwell in the possession of Thomas Jones.

It appears that a beer house called the **Nailer's Arms** was situated somewhere in Clearwell during the latter part of the 19th century, when it was run for a longish period by members of the Smith family.

In 1802 the friendly society had moved to the **Butcher's Arms**, which still exists in the East Street. From the mid-19th century W.M. Constant was the keeper of this alehouse, which was later acquired by Lloyd & Yorath when Charles Creed was the landlord. Around 1908 Mike Morgan took over the **Butcher's Arms** where his family remained for many years.

In 1980, a Forest newspaper in its 'Pub Profile' reported:

> The moment you step through the door into the bar at the Butcher's Arms at Clearwell in the Forest of Dean, you enter an age which has all but passed. The locals know this pub as Mike's, after the landlord's father-in-law, Mike Morgan, who first took over the pub 72 years ago. And it hasn't changed since. The main bar is fairly small, low ceilinged, with ancient beams supporting the floor above. There is an open fire over which is a slate mantlepiece, and in one corner of the room there stands a battered old Joanna. Drinks are served through a small window, almost a hatch, which opens onto a tiny bar behind. It would be unfair to call this pub quaint, but it certainly has a sense of history, unsurpassed by any other public house in the Forest of Dean. Landlord Milson Dovey and his wife Ivy are proud of the pub's original character. The Butcher's Arms has been run by the family for generations, and not one of them has altered it.

The article also reveals that the Forest of Dean Caving Club met there once a month in the Club Room upstairs — a huge room where the Harvest Festival Dinners were held.

The **Butcher's Arms** eventually changed hands in 1985 when the 'brewery decided to sell the premises'. It was acquired by the Cotterills who had experience in the licensing trade. They decided to rename the pub **Dovey's** to retain the former family connection, but by the 1990s it had reverted to its original name. By this time it had been transformed — Jon Hurley wrote in his guide that 'Beams have suddenly sprung from behind plaster, a log fire complete with tasteful stone surround has also appeared, and it burns well, filling the low roofed bar with the poignant pong of another fading autumn'.

The central junction of roads at Clearwell is marked with a 14th-century wayside cross, which was much restored and redesigned by John Middleton in 1866 when he rebuilt the church. Opposite the cross is the **Wyndham Arms**, a 17th-century building with an overhanging timber-framed gable. There is a local tradition 'that the oldest parts of the house date from 1340, and though

The Wyndham Arms in 2003

this may seem extravagant there may be a good deal of truth in the claim' as R.J. Masefield wrote in an unpublished and undated journal.

The inn was named the **Wyndham Arms** after the family who purchased the premises as part of the Clearwell estate in 1698. Thomas Wyndham rebuilt the mansion in 1728 from a design by Roger Morris, whose castellated Gothick style led to it becoming known as Clearwell Castle instead of court. No doubt the **Wyndham Arms** was well established before its first known reference in 1821. During the last quarter of the 19th century William Cole kept the inn; he was followed by Maynard Keyes, a long term landlord from at least 1903 to 1935 when it was tied and later acquired by Arnold, Perrett & Co. Similar to other Arnold, Perrett houses the **Wyndham Arms** was taken over by the Cheltenham Original Brewery in 1937 as:

> All that messuage or Inn known as the Wyndham Arms situate in the village of Clearwell in the Parish of Newland in the County of Gloucester with the coach-house stables yard gardens and pasture land thereto adjoining and belonging and all other outbuildings.

The recent history of the **Wyndham Arms** follows from 1973, when John and Rosemary Stanford purchased the property for £19,000 and then transformed it into a prestigious hotel and restaurant renowned for its excellent food. In the 1980s it was described as 'a completely modernised period pub with a comfortable and relaxing ambience'. In 2002 the *Forester*

The Lamb in 2003

reported that the Stanfords had sold the business to a new owner, who planned to 'expand the hotel enormously'. The new owner went on to state that 'At present there are 17 bedrooms and one luxury suite. By this time next year I expect there to be about 30 bedrooms', but in the 2004 *Royal Forest of Dean Visitors' Guide* only 16 rooms are listed.

In 1879 there were two beer retailers at Clearwell one of which was probably represented by the **Lamb**, still open in West Street. George Edwards kept the beer house in 1891, when it was one of 22 licensed premises that were tied to the Redbrook Brewery. The inn was acquired by Ind Coope, and served Burton Ales well before World War Two. More recently, the **Lamb** took on a new lease of life offering 'Quality Bar Meals', wine 'by the bottle and by the glass' and beer from Ansells.

The *Dean Forest Mercury* of 1891 reported several incidents at Clearwell that were associated with drinking and pubs. James Wyatt, a bill poster from the Scowles, was charged for being drunk and disorderly, and, at the **Lamb**, Thomas Morgan, a collier, was charged for assault. James Fox, landlord of the **Butcher's Arms**, and William Cole who kept the **Wyndham Arms** were both summoned for supplying beer and rum to boys of 13 and 15 years of age. At Clements End, a collier named Charles Brooks from Clearwell was charged for being drunk on a Sunday and causing a disturbance. He was fined 5s. plus costs.

ALL THAT messuage or Inn known as the Travellers Rest situate at Stowe in the Parish of Clearwell in the County of Gloucester and all outbuildings and appurtenances thereunto belonging comprising stone outbuildings comprising stabling and coach house pig cots barn etc. also a stone and timber erection of coach house urinal and closet and a garden in rear and front AND ALSO a piece of land containing about five acres with a road stone quarry worked by the tenant and all other outbuildings and appurtenances thereunto belonging TOGETHER with the site thereof and the land occupied therewith which said premises are now in the occupation of Harold George Miles as tenant.

The 1937 sale of the Travellers Rest

From the west end of Clearwell, Margery Lane leads to a small settlement called Stowe, where the former **Travellers Rest** has seen better days. It opened as a beer house around 1850 to cater for the limeburners, quarrymen and farm labourers working in the neighbourhood. In 1879 Charles Knight was the beer retailer, some time before Arnold, Perrett acquired the premises at the turn of the century when James Berrow was pulling the pints. He was followed by Harold Miles in the 1930s when the Cheltenham Original Brewery took it over.

In the 1980s the **Travellers Rest** was described by Jon Hurley in his *Forest of Dean Pub Guide* as 'a trifle antiseptic with its modern furniture, space invaders and fruit machines. There is however, a smaller bar with intimate lighting'. Regretfully this popular pub was damaged by fire in March 2002. The *Forester* reported 'Licensee Andrew Richards and his wife

The Orepool at Sling in the 1930s

146

Maureen were saved from almost certain death in their blazing pub near St. Briavels when three Dalmatian family pets raised the alarm'. Once they had escaped from the building the fire fighters were called, but 'it took more than two hours to bring the blaze under control and at the height of the incident more than 30 firefighters were at the scene'. In December 2002 its windows were boarded up and it was surrounded by scaffolding — apart from its sign it appeared to be well closed. It is still closed in 2004, apparently awaiting a new life.

Travelling east from Stowe past Clearwell Quarry and across a staggered crossroads, the **Orepool Inn and Motel** cannot be missed. It now caters for all types and ages in its various bars, function room and beer garden. Traditionally known to have existed as an inn for many centuries, the present **Orepool** certainly dates from the mid-19th century when the Old Sling Ore mines were at their peak production. Charles Case was the publican in 1879,

The Orepool Inn and Motel

whilst during the 1890s and 1900s members of the Keyes family kept the inn.

Standing at the Sling road junction is the **Miner's Arms** — a beer house that had been established in the late 19th century. Since 1984 this former 'One bar free house' has undergone a complete transformation. It is now open all day and on Thursdays and Saturdays the 'Best Live Music in the Forest' can be heard and enjoyed.

The Miner's Arms at Sling in 2003

Within a mile of Sling is the **Montague,** formerly the **Miner's Inn** at Clement's End. In 1891 it was a beer house run by Richard Nash for Wintle's Forest Brewery, and it may be that its name was changed at

Sale of the Miner's Inn in 1937. It is now the Montague

that time to avoid confusion with the neighbouring pub. Was this unique
name — the **Montague** — chosen solely to commemorate William
Montague of the Forest of Dean Iron Co., who died in 1847 or is there a more
deep-seated reason?

In 1990 the **Montague** was 'definitely worth stumbling upon if you were
respectable, middle-aged and you regard the comforts of life important'. The
same still applied in 2002 when David and Jenny Chapman were running the
pub which was then known for 'Good food, good company in a congenial

The Montague at Clement's End

Sale of the Oakwood Inn in 1937

The Oakwood Inn in its glorious setting

atmosphere with a welcome to all the family and ample parking in a pleasant part of the Forest of Dean'.

From Clement's End, the forest road leads south-west through Oakwood where the former **Oakwood Inn** closed its door around 1960 to be converted into the existing dwelling. The premises were recorded as a corn mill from 1520, and was last used as a mill shortly before World War One. It had become licensed in 1900, but was probably an earlier cider house which became 'a very popular place for the local declining sheep badgers [Forest term for sheep keeper] to meet on Sunday mornings after a stroll around their free running Forest sheep'. Charles Trueman kept the **Oakwood** during the 1930s as an Arnold, Perrett house, from which it passed to the Cheltenham Original Brewery in 1937.

Before reaching Bream, a detour along

The one time Oakwood Inn in 2002

Sale of the Miner's Arms at Bream Tufts in 1937

the waymarked Gloucestershire Way by foot leads south across Bream's Meend near the site of the **Miner's Rest**, a former Arnold, Perrett beer house kept by Alfred Phillips in 1903. However, it was short-lived and closed a couple of years later. Along this route, remains of old workings are clearly visible before reaching the B4231 leading from Coleford to Bream. On the roadside a former pub was renovated during 2002 at a place called Bream Tufts. In 1891, this was yet another establishment that was known as the **Miner's Arms**, a beer house owned and occupied by Thomas Billy. After his death William Camm ran the **Miner's Arms** and as an Arnold, Perrett pub it was taken over by the Cheltenham Original Brewery in 1937 together with two parcels of land.

The **Miner's Arms** was also known as the **West End**, and as a Whitbread pub in the 1970s enjoyed a reputation for 'a good sing on a

Now closed, this was the Olde Winding Wheel Inn and previously the West End and the Miner's Arms

Saturday night'. It was after the brewery sold the 'compact pub', that the new owners changed its name to the **Olde Winding Wheel**. As with many pubs that suffered a rather unnecessary change of name, there was a brief period of success before the **Winding Wheel** closed for good in the early 1990s.

150

The names of these last mentioned pubs, inns and beer houses reflect the main occupations in the past of the inhabitants of Bream, who worked in the iron ore mines at Devil's Chapel, Bream's Grove and Noxon, the coal mines at the Flour Mill and Princess Royal collieries, and at the many small drift mines scattered throughout the Bream area. The life of these miners was recalled by William Camm in 1978 in his interesting booklet *Bream Through the Ages*:

> In days gone by a boy working down a mine would often become a miner for life, in fact there was not much employment otherwise. ... The accidents and coal dust on their lungs all had to be taken in their stride. ... Today a miner in our village streets, in his mining gear with carbide lamp, tea tin and heavy hobnailed boots ringing on the road as he walked, would be a very uncommon sight, yet only a decade or so ago it would be unusual not to see them.

Bream is the largest village in the Forest of Dean, consisting of Bream itself, Bream's Eaves, Bream Woodside, Bream Tufts and Mill Hill. In 1608 Bream was a small place with its houses clustered around the junction of the main Newland to Lydney road with the minor route to Parkend. This area became known as the Maypole, where a 40 foot high pole once stood. It was the centre of the village until the development of the High Street took over with its pubs, shops, school, library and community centre. From 1795 the Forest of Dean Trust gradually turnpiked the road from Newland via Bream to Lydney, and in the 19th century a new turnpike road was built from Bream to Parkend. The population of Bream grew to 2,700 in 1927, and 'the inhabitants were mostly employed by the Princess Royal Colliery Co. Ltd.' Trains ran from Whitecroft station on the Great

---

BREAM—THE CROSS KEYS INN.

FIRST ALL THAT piece of land at Bream in the Parish of Newland containing about 36 perches and delineated and coloured pink on the plans drawn on a Conveyance dated 18th May 1908 and made between The King's Most Excellent Majesty (1) Edward Stafford Howard (2) and Arthur Leonard Smith (3) and on a Conveyance dated 19th January 1914 and made between The King's Most Excellent Majesty (1) the Right Honourable Walter Runciman (2) and Nellie Smith (3) TOGETHER with the messuage or Inn known as The Cross Keys Inn and the outbuildings erected thereon

Part of the 1962 conveyance of the Cross Keys

151

The first Cross Keys after closure

Western Railway, and alcoholic beverages were available at eight licensed premises.

At the Maypole, the original village centre, four inns existed in earlier times. Two of them were traditionally known as the **Live and Let Live** and the **Dolphin**, and although no known records have survived, it is understood that the **Live and Let Live** stood facing the High Street on the Newland to

The Hedgehog, now the Keys, was previously the Cross Keys

Lydney road, and the **Dolphin** was on site of the existing Dolphin Cottage on the west side of the High Street.

Almost adjoining was the **Cross Keys**, a large stone building which had opened as an inn before 1792 when a Friendly Society met there. During the latter part of the 19th century George Wintour was licensee for a number of years before the Stroud Brewery acquired the premises. Under a succession of publicans, including Hannah Brice, William Camm and Richard Yarmouth, the **Cross Keys** continued to trade until 1962 when it was taken over by West Country Breweries Ltd. Part of the site was redeveloped, and the old inn was closed, but the license and the name were transferred to another property a little further north on the High Street. The newly opened **Cross Keys** became a Whitbread house and in the late 1970s was found to be a 'busy, informal and without frills, a man's pub'. Since then it was, for no apparent reason, renamed the **Hedgehog** — but is now a free house simply called the **Keys**.

Opposite the old **Cross Keys** was once the **New Inn** housed in one of Bream's oldest buildings dating from at least 1637 when George Gough owned the property. It became an inn some time before 1814 and is clearly marked on Bryant's map of 1824. At that time it must have served as a coaching inn for travellers on the Newland to Lydney road, for the road leading from the High Street to Parkend was then only a mere track. From

The New Inn at Bream in the 1930s

153

the mid-19th century the Hewlett family kept the **New Inn**, which at the turn of the century was owned by Barnard Bros., before it was taken over by the Ross based Alton Court Brewery. In the 1930s it was kept by Len Crosse and his wife and was mainly a weekend pub, although the Crosses were very popular with the locals. They retired at the beginning of the Second World War and a London couple, Ray and Peggy Whitehead, took over and stayed until the early '50s. In 1962 the 'messuage or Inn known

The former New Inn at Bream in 2003

as the New Inn and the cottage and outbuildings erected thereon' were acquired by West Country Breweries, and some time after H. Skidmore served behind the bar, the old inn was closed.

The **New Inn** appears to have been the most important inn at Bream, where the 'Odd Fellow's Lodge the Duke of Wellington, the Old Wake committee, the R.A.O.B. and the Vernon Lodge' held their meetings. Until 1924 the Bream Fair was an annual event held in a field near the **New Inn** and the Maypole. In 1979 William Camm, a nephew of the earlier innkeeper at the **Cross Keys**, wrote the following about the Wake:

> Whit Monday was the day this was held in the same field as the Fair, very much consisting in the main of English games, many of which are vanishing, or have done so. The prizes were all, by and large, children's clothes, which were hung on a line stretching across the road from the New Inn to the Cross Keys opposite, a quaint event. Its origin is lost; it went defunct, then was revived in the early 1920s ... the New Inn being its headquarters. It was held for a few years but ... it faded out, and I doubt whether we shall ever see its like again.

154

The former **New Inn** was purchased by the Dean Heritage Museum, who were planning to restore the building, but it has since been sold and its intended future is unknown to the author.

Further up the High Street on the east side there was at one time the **Two Swans** also known by the locals as the **Double Ducks**. It was originally a beer house that traded from at least 1869 until the late 1930s when Jim Price served as the last landlord.

Opposite the War Memorial, at the top of the High Street, is the existing **Rising Sun**, which despite its position on the outskirts of the earlier village centre was recorded as an inn in 1787. The oldest part of the building dates from 1729, but since then this prominent and popular pub has been extended. For a brief period in the 1990s it was renamed the **Village Inn** after it had been 'completely gutted and extended'. From the late 18th century the **Rising Sun** was the meeting place of a local Friendly Society, a venue for political meetings, the headquarters of a Rugby Club and a place to roller skate! Several members of the Morse family kept the inn which eventually became an Arnold, Perrett pub and in 1937 was taken over by the Cheltenham Original Brewery. In 2002 the **Rising Sun** was named the 'Forest of Dean Pub of the Year' by the Forest branch of CAMRA, an honour that was recorded in the *Forester*:

> The Rising Sun impressed the judges because of the range and quality of its beers and the publican was quoted 'We pride ourselves on our choice of beers from small breweries and we always have guest beers.

The Two Swans at Bream in the 1930s

155

A 1937 photo of the Rising Sun

We have between four and six beers on at any one time and, since we
moved here three and a half years ago, we've had about 400 different
beers.

The **Mason's Arms** and the **King's Head** both plied their trade in
Bream's Eaves area, and either one of them fit the description of 1858 of
'All that Messuage or Dwelling now used as a beerhouse in the occupation
of George Cole' that had been newly built in 1825. The site of the **Mason's
Arms** is shown on an early Ordnance Survey map just to the north of
'Bream Eaves Inclosure No 2'. It was here that Susan Skipp retailed beer
for over 50 years until the late 1930s. The **King's Head** is shown on the

ALL THAT messuage or Inn known as The Rising Sun with the stables
buildings yards and appurtenances thereunto belonging and a butcher's shop
TOGETHER with the site thereof AND ALSO ALL THAT piece or parcel of land
thereto adjoining and belonging containing by admeasurement one acre and
thirty-six perches more or less which said premises are situate as to the main part
thereof in the Tything of Bream in the Parish of Newland in the County of
Gloucester at a place known by the name of St. Anne's Cross and as to a small
portion of the said messuage and buildings are situate in the Township of West
Dean in the said County of Gloucester.

The Rising Sun sale details in 1937

The Rising Sun in 2003

more detailed Ordnance Survey map of 1883 so can be identified. It was acquired by Wintle's Forest Brewery in the late 19th century, and a member of the Wintle family was the publican in 1901 when 'an extension of one hour was granted to Mr. Henry Wintle, landlord of the King's Head Inn, Bream, on the occasion of a concert on the 24th November'.

Sign of the Rising Sun

During the 1920s and '30s John James kept the **King's Head**, followed by Edith James in 1937 when the Cheltenham Original Brewery took over the establishment. The **King's Head** continued for a few more years with Mr. D. Price serving as the last landlord before it closed and was converted into a private house.

With a dozen drinking dens open in and around Bream in the 1900s, it is not surprising to learn that drunkenness was a problem. It was mainly beer and cider that was consumed in large quantities by the parched farm labourers and the thirsty miners 'anxious to wash away mouthfulls of coal dust'. The Temperance Movement was very active at this time in

ALL THAT messuage or Inn known as The Kings Head situate at Bream in the County of Gloucester and all outbuildings and appurtenances thereunto belonging comprising a garden in rear and at side with stone outbuildings namely stabling pig cots two closets public urinal etc. and all other outbuildings and appurtenances thereunto belonging TOGETHER with the site thereof and the land occupied therewith which said premises are now in the occupation of Mrs. Edith James as tenant.

Sale details of the King's Head at Bream in 1937

trying to persuade people away from the 'demon drink'. Thus in 1902, 'Temperance Sunday was duly observed at the Primitive Methodist Chapel in Bream, it being the fourth anniversary of the Band of Hope's connection with the chapel'. The local paper continued: 'In the afternoon and evening Mr. Dutton delivered two very powerful sermons, dealing with drink as a curse and total abstinence as the cure ... He also dwelt most particularly on the increase amongst drunkenness in women, a fact that was to be deeply deplored'. In 1911 a temperance society known as the Rechabites demonstrated in full force at a Gloucester District meeting held at Bream. Banners were displayed representing this society together with the World Wide Temperance Fraternity, the Abstinence Brotherhood and another advising 'prevention Better than Cure'.

CHAPTER NINE

St. Briavels, Hewelsfield & Brockweir

From Coleford the B4228 leads south through Sling to the attractive villages of St. Briavels and Hewelsfield, both lying on a high plateau above the river Wye. Minor roads from all directions meet at St. Briavels, as do some ancient routes which now serve as footpaths and bridleways. These include a steep track that leads down past Lindors Farm to a former ford across the Wye that was replaced by Bigsweir Bridge in 1827, and one called the Portway which led eastwards into the heart of the Forest of Dean. Hewelsfield Lane was another which led south to Hewelsfield and was replaced by a turnpike road which now forms the present B4228.

The historian, Arthur Clarke, writing in 1953 describes St. Briavels as:

> Boldly silhouetted against the sky, The Church and Castle ... challenge all who travel the lower reaches of the River Wye. Situated on an eminence 800 feet above sea-level the Castle watches over a gap in the wooded flank of the Forest of Dean. Twice daily the tide sweeps up the river to its feet and where it ceases is Bigsweir.

Whereas in 1974 a travel writer wrote the following in *Gloucestershire Life*:

> As a village, St. Briavels is particularly attractive for apart from the neat grouping of inn, post office, paper shop and butcher's shop around a quarter sector of the castle moat, it straggles in hapazard fashion uphill and round corners in delightful back lanes such as Pistol Lane and Barrelwell Lane.

The line of Offa's Dyke, constructed in the 8th century, can be followed through the parish of St. Briavels. It forms a section of the 168 mile long Offa's Dyke Path, which opened as an official walking route in 1971, and is now well established as a National Trail. Accommodation is available in the many bed and breakfast establishments, and at the **George Inn** and the Youth Hostel at St. Briavels. Since 1948 the Youth Hostel has been housed in the castle, a splendid building dating from Norman times with many features

*The entrance to St. Briavels Castle
in the 19th century*

including its magnificent gatehouse still remaining. The castle was visited by King John, Henry III and Edward II, when it was the headquarters of the Constable who served as the Warden of the Forest. In the early 19th century a court was held in the former chapel, a debtor's prison was housed in the gatehouse and according to Charles Heath 'The Castle is now a public house'. He continued in his 1828 *Excursion Down the Wye*:

> The traveller may pass a little time very pleasantly, in surveying these ruins, with the attendant scenery here noticed; and, being half-way between Chepstow and Monmouth, in the village will meet with a clean room, and his horses taken care of, at either of the two public houses, which adjoin the side of the road.

A century later Ivor Davis, in his *Village in the Forest,* recalled that 'outside the moat and facing the valley were two cottages called the Malt Houses. Whether they were ever used for brewing beer for the castle I do not know', but it is known that the gaoler of the debtor's prison kept an alehouse in the castle, which probably served as the **Castle Inn**.

In 1987 medieval revels were relived at St. Briavels Castle by the Far Isles Medieval Society who laid on a 15-course feast and period music for their members who were all dressed in suitable costumes. The *Citizen* reported:

> Only now and again do they break with tradition. A modern cooker was used for the preparation of the feast which included venison, trout, salmon and beef washed down with mead, beer, cider and fruit juice.

A much earlier tradition, known as the Bread and Cheese Dole, has survived to the present day at St. Briavels. After the evening service on Whit Sunday, small pieces of bread and cheese are thrown from the Pound Wall to the waiting crowd. The event is said to date from the 12th century and was recorded in 1779 when the morsels of food were thrown to the congregation from the gallery inside the church. This caused such an uproar that:

About 1857, or perhaps a year or so later, the unseemly custom was transferred from the church to the churchyard, the bread and cheese being thrown down from the church tower. Later on it was transferred to the road outside the church gates. It now lasts but a few minutes. A few years ago all the roughs of the Forest used to come over, and there was much drinking and fighting; but now it is very different. The custon has, in fact, been dying out.

The parish church, dedicated to St. Mary, was founded in the 11th century and, despite many alterations throughout the centuries, still features some 12th-century work. In 1829 the church lost its central tower which was replaced by the existing one a year later. In the earlier tower five bells were in use before 1764, which may account for the name of the **Five Bells Inn** that once stood in Church Street. In 1763 the inn was recorded as:

All that Messuage or Tenement Stable and Garden situate and being in St. Briavels aforesaid formerly in the possession of Christopher Carter and now of John Evans used as an Inn a public Alehouse or Victualling house and commonly called or known by the name or Sign of the Five Bells having the way leading from Venny Street towards the Castle, the churchyard there and a lane or way leading from Venny Street aforesaid towards Morke.

Christopher Carter's name was also recorded in the overseers accounts of 1699, when he was paid for 'keeping the sheep stealing woman', whilst Sarah Carter was paid for 'washing ye mad woman' and for supplying the madwoman with 'meat and drink while she was at St. Briavels' in 1704. This seems to indicate that the **Five Bells** was used as a poor house before the workhouse was built. It is possible that the **Five Bells** was one of the three victualling houses whose owners were presented for allowing disorderly behaviour and illegal gaming at St. Briavels in 1600. Another inn of this date may have been called the **Cross Keys**, a name that has lingered in the name of the crossroads lying to the east of the castle, where the B4228 crosses the village road.

The **Five Bells** and the **Cross Keys** are inn signs closely linked with the church. The bell has a distinctive shape that appealed to sign makers, and the number indicates those in the nearby church. The Cross Keys is a Christian sign referring to St. Peter when he was told by Christ 'I will give unto thee the keys of the kingdom of heaven'. It is interesting to note that at the Cross Keys crossroads there was a field called Church Ground in 1842.

The present **George Inn** may have been the third victualling house referred to in 1600, as the building dates from that period. It stands near the castle, only divided from the castle moat by the narrow Horsefair Lane. The cosy interior of the **George** features black beams, wall seats, stone fireplaces

The George Inn at St. Briavels in 2004

and, built into the bar, a curious stone slab dating from late Saxon or early Norman times that was discovered during alterations in the 1970s. The **George** was certainly trading as an alehouse in 1721 and would have been one of the two 'public houses which adjoin the side of the road' observed by Heath in the early 19th century. This was the time when a Friendly Society held their meetings there. From around the 1850s the Kear family kept the **George** for a lengthy period.

Charles, Lord Denton, of St. Briavels House owned the **George** in the 1890s, and when he died in 1892 he left an endowment to establish an almshouse for 'three elderly men and three elderly widows' which was later built by his heir in East Street. Denton also left a legacy for the benefit of the village and in 1924 the accrued money paid for an assembly room. This was built next to the Reading Room and Library which Denton had provided in 1854. The Kear family continued to run the **George** for some time after the death of its owner, but by 1927 William Burley had taken over as innkeeper.

More recently the **George** was known for its hospitality and in 1991 Jon Hurley added, in his updated version of the *Forest of Dean Pubs*: 'probably the best Real Ale house in the Forest'. A few years later another pub guide noted that there were 'lots of malt whiskies', and it 2004 the Free Miners beer, brewed at Cinderford, was available amongst other interesting brews and ciders.

162

The Crown Inn in 2004

At the southern end of Pystol Lane is the **Crown**, originally established as a beer house in the early 19th century when it was first occupied by William Ball and then Susanna Evans. In 1849 the 'Crown beerhouse and garden' was owned by William Peel and occupied by Samuel Palmer. The **Crown** or **Old Crown** continued as a beer house and in 1891, when it appears to have been rebuilt, the pub was owned by Messrs. Watts & Co., and tenanted to William Holmes. In 1901 the Stroud Brewery acquired the premises when Lawrence Hughes was the beer retailer. He was succeeded by Mrs. Hughes until Samuel Hobbs took over in the 1930s.

In the early 20th century the **Crown** was the headquarters of a Friendly Society called the Royal Ancient Order of Buffaloes. On the Tuesday after Whitsun its members 'paraded through the streets with their banners held high. But they were not a very strong organisation and only had a few followers' wrote Ivor Davis, who was one of the lads 'tagging on behind with no idea what it was about'. The Stroud Brewery and its licensed properties including the **Crown** were taken over by West Country Breweries in 1962 when the **Crown** became known as the 'other pub in the village'.

The only other known pub at St. Briavels was the **Plough** in the High Street. It was open in 1818 but appears to have closed in the 1870s after G. Miles had been the landlord. The largish house with its high ceilings and dairy at the back was taken over by the Davis family of builders, and in

2004 the property was called Ashfield House. After the **Plough** closed John Whittington and and William James were retailing beer at Mork and Lower Mesne, and William Whittington was licensed to sell wine and spirits in 1903.

Once the Plough at St. Briavels

As with other villages in the Forest, St. Brivels had its share of unlawful-ness which was recorded and reported in the newspapers of the time. Apart from the drunkenness associated with the Bread and Cheese Wake in the 19th century, there were cases of unruly behaviour at cockfights held on Whit Monday before they were banned by the curate around 1845. Earlier convictions were for selling ale without a license in 1790, and similar offences for selling cider in 1808. Nearly a century later Charles Harris, a farm labourer of St. Briavels, was charged for being 'drunk and disorderly'; he 'had his hat and jacket off and was challenging to fight anyone in the village'. He was fined 7s. 6d. and 8s. costs. In the same year the *Dean Forest Mercury* reported that 'Herbert Williams of Whitebrook, was summoned by P.C. Peacey for an offence at St. Briavels'. The defendant pleaded guilty for being 'drunk on the highway', and was fined 5s. with 7s. costs.

Since 1994 Hewelsfield village has been officially placed within a parish called Hewelsfield and Brockweir; the two places sharing similar links with the past.

The village derived its name in the 11th century from 'Hiwoldes stone', and its church was built a century later:

> in a churchyard which is almost a perfect circle in shape but little more that an acre in area. Undoubtedly it is the site of the pre-Christian Celtic tribal moot or meeting place where their affairs were discussed, and their dead buried.

From St. Briavels the B4228 road from Coleford to Chepstow passes west of the village centre and crosses the Tumpinhales crossroads, not named on recent Ordnance Survey maps. An earlier route — Hewelsfield Lane — led straight from St. Briavels to the church, court and former village inn at

Hewelsfield, but can now only be followed on foot. The road access to Hewelsfield was improved after 1812 when the Coleford to Chepstow road was repaired, together with the widening and improving of the half-mile length of road leading west from the church to Tumpinhales. Hewelsfield Lane, deemed to be 'impassable to carriages' was finally closed to traffic in 1837.

Tumpinhales developed as an important crossroads on the Chepstow road linking Hewelsfield to Brockweir and the river Wye. Because of the steepness of the roads, donkeys were used to carry goods unloaded from barges on the navigable Wye to the communities at Hewelsfield and St. Briavels.

To cater for the increase in passing trade at Tumpinhales an inn was established around 1830 in the north-west angle of the crossroads. It was known as the **Carpenter's Arms** and served as a welcome break for horses, drivers and riders. Its name possibly indicates the trade of its founder, in which case its sign would have depicted a carpenter's tools. Alternatively the inn could have been named after the Carpenter family of Hewelsfield. J.J. Dicker, in his *Life of Hewelsfield* published in 1950, relates a confusing tale of love and marriage set in the early 16th century. Alice Carpenter denied a marriage to William Hopkyns for she loved another whom she claimed was her husband. She was excommunicated by the church and ordered by the court to a 'public whipping', but it is not known whether this was carried out.

In 1841 the **Carpenter's Arms** was known as the **Tumpinhales** and stood opposite an unnamed beer house. From at least 1863 the name reverted to the **Carpenter's Arms** when it was kept by John Prichard. In 1897 he sold the premises to Arnold, Perrett & Co. and under the ownership of the brewery the pub was run by Thomas Keedwell during the early years of the 20th century. William Hall was the landlord in 1927 followed by Charles Vincent in the 1930s when Arnold, Perrett was taken over by Cheltenham Original Brewery in 1937.

Although the pub's name was still not resolved, it was remembered by locals as the **Carpenter's Arms** and being housed in a 'rather square plain building, nothing spectacular'. The **Carpenter's Arms** finally closed its doors around 1970 and was later demolished to make way for a small housing development and road improvements.

In the 16th century, like today, Hewelsfield was a small place with very few inhabitants. Hewelsfield Court was held by the Gough family before it was rebuilt in the 19th century; the church had been extended, but there was no record of a victualling or alehouse when, according to J.J. Dicker, 'customary drink was a small beer or cider for all including children ... The menfolk quaffed a stronger brew from the mazor bowl on special occasions', and he added that the malt was probably obtained from the former Malt House at Brockweir.

At the centre of Hewelsfield a large white house bearing a date stone of 1706 overlooks the pretty church and its circular graveyard. This house was in use as

the **Parrot Inn** in 1805 when the New Friendly and United Society held their meetings there. This unusual name for an inland pub had been a favoured sign in the Tudor period, as the natural colouring of the bird lends itself to pictorial embellishment of an attractive nature. The inn may well have had a parrot in the bar to amuse the customers with his mimicry.

Throughout the 19th century this building was the Parrot Inn at Hewelsfield

During the second half of the 19th century William Aston and John Thomas kept the **Parrot**. In 1891, when Eliza Burgham from the Redbrook Brewery had acquired the property, the new landlord, Samuel Morris, applied for an extension of opening hours for 'a house warming ceremony', which was refused. When he left, Nebemiah Moulton took the pub into the 20th century, but presumably lack of trade in this remote area led to its closure some time after 1906. The building was then converted into a private house and still stands in a picturesque setting.

From the crossroads at Tumpinhales a steeply descending lane leads down through the parish of Hewelsfield to the riverside hamlet of Brockweir. This Wyeside place was once the scene of busy activity associated with the river trade as described by Charles Heath in 1828:

> This ... small hamlet ... forms a mart for the reception of goods brought from the upper parts of the Wye, which are shipped on board vessels of about sixty tons burden, and consigned down the Severn to Bristol and other places. The village is chiefly inhabited by watermen who navigate the vessels employed in this trade.

The watermen of the early 19th century were able to refresh themselves in a number of ale houses at Brockweir including the **New Inn**, **Bristol**, **Severn Trow** and the **Ship**. By the latter half of the 20th century only the **New Inn** remained open.

It is now hard to imagine that Brockweir in the early 19th century was a place of drunkenness, cockfighting and gambling to the extent that by 1820 it was reputed to have 16 alehouses where the watermen and shipbuilders could imbibe. In 1831, in order to improve the image of Brockweir's low life, the Bristol Moravians opened a chapel beside the Wye, but it was not until 1905 that

The Brockweir Country Inn in 2004

this isolated hamlet enjoyed better communications with the Wye Valley when the iron bridge replaced the ferry crossing.

The solitary pub is now called the the **Brockweir Country Inn**, but this was known as the **George** in 1793. By 1841 it had been re-named the **New Inn**, and during the second half of the 19th century was kept by the Dibden family who also traded as butchers, shopkeepers, farmers, millers and carpenters. The **New Inn** was eventually acquired by Wintle's Forest Brewery from Mitcheldean, and in 1937, when George Blunt was the landlord, it was taken over by the Cheltenham Original Brewery.

The Brockweir malthouse

After surviving for some years as a Whitbread house, this inn emerged as the **Brockweir New Inn** in 1981 under the management of a new and energetic landlord. When Jon Hurley visited the pub in the early 1990s he wrote the following:

167

The Brock is popular with ramblers, being near the Offa's Dyke long-distance path, and locals alike. The tiled floor was a trifle cold but there was a wood-burning stove and a selection of freshly prepared dishes chalked on the board. Prints adorned the walls and with its old seats and settles it is an atmospheric little inn.

In 2004 the **Brockweir** was a cosy two-bar pub with low ceiling beams, a welcoming live fire and steps leading up to the Devil's Pulpit — a small elevated restaurant taking its name from the famous viewpoint overlooking Tintern Abbey and the Wye Valley.

Once the Royal Arms at Brockweir

On the opposite side of the road are the old stone buildings of the 14th-century malthouse used for many years as a pottery.

Unfortunately the other Brockweir pubs have long since closed. Next to the **Brockweir** was the **Bristol** of 1841, which was renamed the **Sloop** and appears to have closed after C. Williams kept the house in 1863. The **Severn Trow** of 1841 stood opposite the **Brockweir**, and the **Royal Arms**, run by the Browns in the 1870s and '80s, apparently survived until around 1960 when it was delicensed and became a private dwelling called Wyvern. The **Ship**, also run by the Browns in the 1860s and '70s, was probably adjacent to the shipyard beside the river Wye that was kept by the same family. One other beer house was recorded in 1840 as the **Spout**, but its history and whereabouts are unknown by the author.

The **George** was always a popular inn sign, either named after the patron saint or one of the Georgian kings. The **Bristol** reflects trading along the waterways with Bristol, and the **Sloop** and **Severn Trow** were named after the type of river craft used on the Wye.

CHAPTER TEN

Westbury & Littledean

*Mail coaches ran through the
Forest in 1785*

From the city of Gloucester the present A40 leads west to Highnam where a southerly turn at the roundabout becomes the busy A48, which closely follows the banks of the winding river Severn towards Chepstow. From 1726 the road 'through the parishes of Minsterworth and Westbury to a place called Hawkin's Pill' (just north of Newnham) was turnpiked by the Gloucester and Hereford Trust. Tolls were charged for the use of this road, which were set out in the 1726 Road Act. They ranged from 1s. for each coach with four or more horses to 1d. for a single horse. Cattle were 10d. per score; sheep, calves and hogs 5d. per score.

In 1785 John Phillpotts was operating a coach service from Gloucester through Minsterworth and Westbury to 'Milford Haven, Cork, Waterford, and all the south-west part of Ireland' initially in an 'elegant Post-Coach' and then across the sea in 'three well-manned Packets' which carried passengers and parcels. By 1822 John Spencer was supplying a service from Gloucester in 'Light Post Coaches' to Swansea along the same route.

169

The present A48 by-passes the original main road from Gloucester which followed very narrow lanes through Minsterworth with its interesting buildings. The only record of an inn, pub or beer house at Minsterworth has been the **Apple Tree**. This attractive building is set back from the Gloucester road at its junction with Watery Lane, and around 1960 was converted into an inn from a row of cottages (possibly called the **Bird in Hand** in 1977). So in earlier times the carriers from Littledean and Westbury, who ran their services on Mondays, Wednesdays and Saturdays, were not catered for on their return trip to Gloucester. This was cider making country where Thomas Phelps and William Pugh were listed as cider merchants in 1927, and Phelps was also manufacturing and bottling 'Malvern Hill Perry' at Minsterworth.

The Apple Tree at Minsterworth in 2003

Between Minsterworth and Westbury, the Severn widens and snakes around the tiny hamlets of Bollow, Rodley and Cleeve to form the eastern boundary of the Forest of Dean. The river Severn rises on the Plynlimon Mountains in mid-Wales close to the source of the Wye, but the Severn flows in a south-easterly direction over a distance of 220 miles to its estuary in the Bristol Channel. From time immemorial the river has been used as a waterway by coracles, trows and sloops delivering cargoes that included cider, wine, bark, coal, iron, lime, stone, timber, cloth and sugar. It is obvious from the numerous rights of way and no-through-roads that lead to the water's edge, still shown on present day Ordnance Survey maps, that there were numerous river crossings linking the east and west banks of the Severn. This activity, together with fishing of salmon, trout and elvers by net and rod, led to the establishment of various inns and beer houses at convenient places along the banks of the river. Today, the main waterfront activity is associated with the Severn Bore, a natural phenomena caused by the formation of waves that sweep upstream at the head of spring tides. At certain times during the year the Severn Bore is a spectacular event that thousands of people come to visit.

In the mid-19th century travel and trade along the meandering river Severn and by the winding turnpike road was speeded up by the more direct route chosen by the South Wales Railway which was incorporated in 1845. The line to Chepstow, which passed through Westbury to Grange Court, was opened in 1851. From Grange Court a branch line leading to Ross and Hereford was opened in 1855 by the Hereford, Ross, Gloucester Railway. Both railway companies were taken over by the Great Western Railway in 1863, and although the route to Hereford closed in 1964 the South Wales line is still open.

Minsterworth was the childhood home of the poet F.W. Harvey who was born in 1888, the son of a horse breeder and dealer. From 1890 the family lived at Minsterworth, but after his schooling he was caught up in the horrors of the First World War together with another Gloucestershire poet, Ivor Gurney. Harvey's last verse of *My Village* reads as follows:

> I love old Minsterworth. I love the men:
> The fishers and the cider-makers and
> All who laugh and labour that land
> With humour and long patience loved of God.
> I love the harmless gossips all a-nod,
> The children bird-like, and the women old
> Like wrinkled crab-apples: and I will pray —
> God save old Minsterworth, and such, for aye.

Between Minsterworth and Westbury the river, road and railway part company before rejoining west of Westbury at Broadoak. In 1863 Westbury was described as 'an extensive parish and large village containing the tithings of Adsett, Bollow, Boseley, Chaxhill, Cleeve, Elton, Lay, Northwood, Stantway, Rodley, and Westbury'. As with most places at this period Westbury village was self-sufficient, with farmers, shopkeepers, shoemakers, builders and a butcher and plumber. For the passing horse-drawn carriages and waggons there was a blacksmith, harness maker and innkeeper with a wheelwright at Northwood. In the riverside hamlets there were sloop owners, bark and timber merchants, beer retailers, fruit and cattle dealers, a pilot and even a 'boarding school for young gentlemen' at Broad Oak.

At Westbury, the National Trust has preserved the unique 17th-century Water Gardens, once associated with Westbury Court, long since demolished. Westbury church has a detached 13th-century tower that served as a place of refuge during the Civil War, when both sides in turn held the church. The spire is roofed with oak shingles, some apparently being the staves of cider casks. This seems to be confirmed in the churchwarden's accounts for 1664 which include 'casks of cider given to meet expenses of repairs to steeple, and account of nails used for same'. In the past most farms produced their own cider, and the remains of cider mills can still be seen throughout the area. In the early 18th century hops were grown in Westbury parish and a malthouse was in use between 1733 and 1808. These were the ingredients used by the local inns to brew their own ale until the larger commercial breweries took over.

The past and present inns of Westbury-on-Severn were mainly connected with the trade and transport on the river, road and rail. On the A48 the **Severn Bore** at Hartland's Hill still serves the needs of passing motorists and was originally associated with the river when it was known as the **Bird in Hand**. It dates from at least 1830 and was kept by the Vaille family of cattle dealers during the late 19th century before Arnold, Perrett acquired the premises in the early 20th century, followed by the Cheltenham Original Brewery in 1937.

The **Bird in Hand** became a Whitbread house and in 1965 Mr. A. Kinnear was the landlord catering for summer visitors and skittle players. Sometime after this date the pub was renamed the **Severn Bore** and in 1991 was offering 'Cleverly titled titbits such as Special Severn Bore Soup, Fresh Severn Salmon (when in season)'. The inn sign represents the green and turgid river flowing past.

The Severn Bore at Westbury in 2003

Nearby, amongst a row of houses at the Flat on the riverbank, was the site of the **King's Head** which was open in 1824 and from 1839 to 1843 was tenanted by John Burnett from the owner, John Vallinder. The **King's Head** was also acquired by Arnold, Perrett & Co. who closed the premises in the early 20th century. There is evidence to suggest that an earlier inn called the **Duke of Gloucester**existed at the Flat, where the manor court met in 1687. It may have been named after the duke who became Richard III.

Although not included in the area covered by this book, it is worth recording the story of a former cider house called the **Shark** lying on the opposite bank of the Severn at Elmore. Brian Waters tells the tale in his *Severn Tide* published in 1947:

> The cottage known as the 'Shark' at Elmore Back, a little above the Dinny, most probably commemorates the unrecorded taking of a shark by a long-net in these waters, since sharks have from time to time been taken in the lower Severn. The 'Shark', half hidden among orchards, was a cider house which, until it went out of business sixty years ago, lived up to its name. It was a rendezvous of smugglers, ideally situated on the river, away from any road. Bargees came here to quench their thirst and leave behind kegs of liquor finer than anything they drank at the 'Shark'. The bargees picked up their contraband of French brandy or Dutch hollands from merchantmen in the Bristol Channel, and the 'Shark' had an unquenchable thirst for unbroached casks, which looked as innocent as pickpockets where cider barrels can stand as thick as skittles in an alley without arousing comment.
>
> A local band of men found regular employment in carrying contraband from the 'Shark' to London, and when one considers the enormous popularity of Severn cider in the London of former days, their journeys can have aroused small suspicion. Their activities were, however, so well known locally that their homes, for they were all neighbours, were given the nickname of 'Rogues Row'.

Just south of the **Severn Bore** a lane follows the river to Bollow, where a signed footpath leads to an attractive riverside dwelling once known as the **Bollow House Inn** occupied by William Coldwell in 1841. The name was changed to the **Sloop** some time before 1863 when it was kept by James Baylis, a fruitier. The **Sloop** was named

The Sloop in retirement

after craft which delivered goods to a landing place there, and this name was retained by William Greening who sold the pub to the Nailsworth Brewery in the early 20th century. In 1927 Leslie Hart was the landlord and appears to have been the last one before the inn finally closed. The inn's name was one of the many nautical themes used for Severnside pubs and beer houses. Others included the Ship, Ketch, Trow, Barge, Boat, Pier, Anchor and Quay which 'adorned many a swinging inn-sign along the navigable reaches of the Severn, together with references to Severn sailors in the Jolly Waterman and Blue Boys'. This was written by F.W. Rowbottom in 1967 in his booklet *The Severn and its Bore*, where he added:

> Nearly all Severnside alehouses, whatever their name, were 'navigation' inns. Those at wharves, canal junctions and ferries had an obvious *raison d'etre,* but a great many others were in lonely positions, out in the fields, and sometimes without even a hard road access. Their only patrons were the river men, the crews of trows and barges, who called more from necessity than choice.
>
> Their existence stems from the fact that the river Severn in its natural state abounded in shallows and rock barriers over which no loaded vessel could pass without the additional depth of water provided by freshwater or, in the lower reaches, by tide. At low water there were two alternatives; either to tie up and 'wait for water' or to unload the vessel, float it over light, manhandle the cargo past the obstruction and then re-load. The latter recourse was thirsty work by any reckoning, while if it was a case of waiting for days or maybe weeks, a little hospitality ashore was a welcome change from the dreary accommodation aboard their vessels. With the elimination of the delaying factors, most of the inns were converted to private houses, though usually retaining their old names.
>
> Many of the navigation inns augmented their income with sidelines. They traded in coal, hay, bricks, groceries, hardware and general riverborne merchandise. The notorious Shark at Elmore Back ran a highly organised smuggling business, with a stable of pack-horses to convey the illicitly imported liquor post-haste to London.

At Rodley, Blue Boys Farm overlooks the Severn at the southernmost tip of Westbury parish. From at least 1824 this was the **Blue Boys Inn**, relying for trade on the Framilode Passage, an important river crossing, and on vessels moored at a nearby site. For nearly a hundred years the Butler family ran the establishment until around 1906 when it closed as an inn but remained as a working farm. Nowadays the riverside path at the former **Blue Boys** forms a section of the Severn Way, a long distance path following the Severn from 'source to sea'. Also at Rodley there was once a 'comfortable Dwelling-house, Shop, Mill-House and Cider Mill, Buildings and Productive Garden and Orchard' occupied by Thomas Roan. In 1870 the property came up for auction with other pieces of 'Freehold Accommodation Land'. This may have been one of the mills where the famous Styre Cider of Westbury was made and exported to London and Dublin for 15 and 20 guineas a hogshead until the mid-19th century, when the fashion for this extravagant tasting cider died out.

The original Junction

From Rodley the winding lane keeps company with the Severn to The Heald, where an un-named inn was recorded in the early 19th century. From Cleeve the lane leaves Severnside and heads north across the A48 to Grange Court. This was the junction of the Hereford, Ross, Gloucester Railway with the South Wales line in the mid-19th century, and although the latter railway still runs, the station has been closed. After the opening of the South Wales line a nearby grocery and tabacconist was selling 'Ale Cider and Tabacco' in 1848 and 1849. This shop eventually became the **Junction**, then lying just to the north of Grange Court station. During the second half of the 19th century the pub was kept by Philip Woodman, a local farmer, until around 1906 when Henry Jackson took over and moved the pub to its present site

The present-day Grange Court Junction

175

south of the railway. Jackson sold the **Junction** to the Stroud Brewery in 1919, and a succession of tenants served as landlords. In 1962 the Stroud Brewery was taken over by West Country Breweries, and in 1965 Mrs. F. Hill was the landlady, holding regular clay pigeon shoots, In 1984 the pub displayed railway memorabilia in its bars, but in 2004 the **Junction** appeared to be closed and looking for a future use.

From Grange Court the minor road returns to the A48 on the outskirts of Westbury-on-Severn, a small linear village with church, pub, and the formal water garden originally laid out by Maynard Colchester between 1696 and 1706. The gardens adjoined the Colchester's residence known as Westbury Court, which was rebuilt several times before being finally demolished in the early 1960s. The garden consisted of flower beds, shrubs and trees formally arranged around two long canals fed by the Westbury brook. The Gloucestershire County Council took over the neglected garden in 1964, and built a home for the elderly on the western side. The remainder of the garden with the canals was given to the National Trust who have restored the water

The Red Lion at Westbury

gardens and opened them to the public.

A passing glance at Westbury-on-Severn gives the impression of an attractive village, but on closer inspection it is a disappointing place with its church locked, buildings in need of a facelift, and a constant stream of traffic thundering through the village. The wayside cross, restored in 1887, provides a pleasing feature outside the **Red Lion**, which is the only survivor of three old village inns.

Known as the **Lion** in 1715, but recorded as the **Red Lyon** in 1728 when Maynard Colchester leased the inn to Anne Bayse, and with the spelling altered in 1748 when it was described as:

All that house wherein the said Isaac Hall now Dwells called or known by the name of the Red Lion situated lying and being in the parish of Westbury ... late in the Tenure or occupation of Thomas Carters and now of the said Isaac Hall.

In 1783 a Westbury Friendly Society met at the **Red Lion**, and was still recorded there in the mid-19th century when James Trigg, a harness maker owned and occupied the inn. From the 1890s Charles Nicholls took the inn into the 20th century, when it became tied to Godsell & Sons, a company that was eventually taken over by the ever acquisitive Stroud Brewery. That firm may have been responsible for remodelling the building with mock-timber framing in the early years of the 20th century. In the 1960s the Stroud Brewery was taken over by West Country Breweries. At this time Mr. W. Pitheran was the landlord, at a time when hounds met at the inn and National Farmer's Union meetings were held there.

The quieter Bell Lane leads to the church of St. Peter and St. Paul with its large detached tower built in the 13th century. Opposite the church is a timber-framed building called Bell House which was an 18th-century inn known as the **Bell** or **Six Bells**. Whether there were one or two inns is difficult to determine from the surviving documents. The

Bell House was at one time an inn

Bell was recorded in 1736 when Maynard Colchester leased 'All that Messuage Tenement or Dwelling house now used as a Publick house and called or known by the signe of the Bell, together with the Outhouses, Garden and Orchard therein' to Mary Wintle and Joane Handman. The **Six Bells**, however, appears in a bundle of deeds dating from 1662, including Miss Elizabeth Badger's will of 1805. She bequeathed to her sister-in-law 'All that my Messuage or Tenement Garden and Orchard called by the Name of the Six Bells situate lying and being in the parish of Westbury upon Severn aforesaid now in the occupation of James Grey'. The adjectival 'six' is somewhat confusing because only five church bells existed until a sixth was added in 1825.

The other 18th-century village inn was called the **George**, but its site and history since 1715 is unknown.

The single **Bell** was named for obvious reasons, and the **Lion** — king of beasts — is very popular, and well represented in pub names. It may have changed to the heraldic **Red Lion** by the owner who wished to be associated with courage and strength. The **George** was either named after the patron saint or King George I who came to the throne in 1714.

From Westbury-on-Severn village the A48 sweeps dramatically under the Arch Bridge of the South Wales railway, and at the next major road junction the A4151 leads west to Littledean and Cinderford.

Straight ahead, the road leads down to the Severn at Broad Oak. This riverside hamlet, in the south-west corner of Westbury parish, is where river, road and rail meet. It now provides a good place to view the Severn, but in earlier times it was a small centre of commerce and shipbuilding. Sloops and barges were built there including a 263 ton ship in 1801. This was where the Boughton family dealt in cider and bark during the latter part of the 18th century, and where stone for road building and repairs was unloaded from barges during the 19th century. In 1863 the inhabitants of Broad Oak were mainly employed in the timber, slate, bark, fruit and farming industries, and were able to enjoy a drink at either the **Broad Oak** or the **White Hart** inns.

The **Broad Oak** was the meeting place of a friendly society from 1783, and around 1841 was listed as the **Royal Oak** which may have been an

The White Hart at Broad Oak in the early 20th century

178

incorrect entry. Its name was certainly the **Broad Oak** in 1863 when a fruitier named William Butler kept the inn. In 1870 an auction was held at the inn including:

All that Messuage, Tenement, or Dwelling House, (formerly two houses), containing five rooms on the ground floor, and five rooms above, with the court, piggeries, vault, cider mill house, and cider press, loft, gardens, and pieces of Land adjoining called the Logger.

A few years later John Perks was the landlord of the **Broad Oak** which appears to have closed around 1880.

Fortunately the **White Hart** at Broadoak has managed to stay open despite its vulnerable riverside position. In 1824 the **White Hart** was important enough to be marked on Bryant's map of the county of Gloucestershire. From the mid-19th century until around 1930 the Knights followed by the Kings kept this riverside inn, which had become a Stroud Brewery house. In 1962 the brewery was taken over by West Country Breweries, and Mr. F. Sheen was recorded at the inn in 1965. Two decades later Jon Hurley wrote in his *Guide to the Forest of Dean Pubs*:

The Severn almost laps the back door of this pub but on a sunny summer's day a splendid view is guaranteed. ... The lounge is large, multi-beamed, and comfortable with a log fire, pointed stonework, and seats uniformly covered with heraldic tapestry.

The White Hart has always been an important riverside inn

By 1991, following a change of ownership, the **White Hart** had taken on a nautical character with its interior featuring boating pictures and a painted lady from the prow of an old boat. Outside a similar theme was introduced which remained visible in 2003. Today the **White Hart** does not noticeably display a pictorial sign, but since the 14th century, when it was Richard II's heraldic symbol, it became a popular inn sign. At that time tavern keepers showed their allegiance by displaying such a sign. It also had the advantage of being visually distinctive when the hart, the male deer, was probably much more common than it is today. The continued use in later centuries is explained by having become a popular name for an inn.

Returning to the crossroads and turning left on the main road towards Littledean, after a few hundred yards on the left-hand side at Elton is a cottage that once traded as the **Traveller's Rest** — a beer house open from at least 1839 to 1903.

Further along the A4151, but on the opposite side was a pub called the **Plough**, first mentioned in the Barrett family deeds dating from 1845 to 1853, and built on an encroachment of the Forest of Dean. The Barretts were followed in the 1870s by Alfred Payne who appears to have served as the last landlord before the premises were converted to a grocery and provision store

The Stroud Brewery Company advertised its ales on the Greyhound at Pope's Hill in the early 20th century

run by W.C. Cullen. Since being recorded in 1935 this store has long since closed. The **Plough** still remains one of the commonest pub names, and has been in continuous use since the 16th century. The **Plough** at Elton may have displayed a sign featuring the agricultural implement or the constellation of seven stars.

The A4151 heads west to Littledean along a route that was turnpiked from Westbury in 1768. On the north side of the road at Pope's Hill is the **Greyhound**, the only survivor of two beer houses recorded at Pope's Hill in 1841. It may have replaced the **Plough** described in 1785 as 'A Messuage at Blackmores Hall known by the Sign of the Plough with a garden Orchard' or it may have taken its name from a house called the Greyhound which had land in Flaxley and Westbury in 1693. George Baker owned and occupied the alehouse in 1891, but a year later it was acquired by the Stroud Brewery, and in turn passed to West Country Breweries in 1962. The 'Comfortable Inn situated in wooded garden' of the 1970s was 'Under the excellent Supervision of Percy Young'. Twenty years later Neil Coates in his *Pub Walks* found the **Greyhound** as:

> A substantial low, beamed old pub with a good mixture of locals and passing trade. ... The main room sports an unusual array of timepieces, recycled from old clocks and watches, dotting the walls as well as the 'traditional' brasses and prints. Continuing the unusual theme is a selection of duelling swords.

A steep walk up Pope's Hill beside Chestnut Hill woods leads past the Old Cider Press and other buildings before reaching the **Whitehouse World**,

The Greyhound in a well wooded situation in 2003

181

which offered bed and breakfast at this 'inn on the hill' with its panoramic views of the Severn and May Hill.

From Pope's Hill the A4151 ascends to Littledean where many buildings and sites are of historic interest including Littledean Hall, which dates from the 16th century and stands on a Roman site. The bleak looking building has links with the Civil War as the place where two Royalist officers were killed. The house is surrounded by ghostly tales and is reputed to have haunted rooms. The old Gaol of 1791 has since been used as a courthouse, prison, police station and depository for Gloucester Record Office; if present plans proceed the interesting old building will be conserved and open to the public. In a 1994 *Guide to the Wye Valley and Forest of Dean*, the well known local historian Mabel Beech wrote: 'Littledean still bears signs of its ancient origins. The streets, despite the attentions of modern day road builders, are still narrow and rather irregular'.

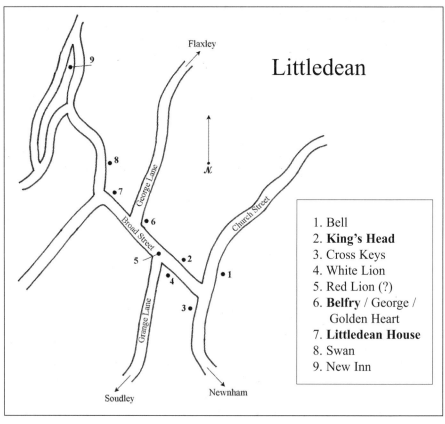

Littledean

Flaxley

N.

1. Bell
2. **King's Head**
3. Cross Keys
4. White Lion
5. Red Lion (?)
6. **Belfry** / George / Golden Heart
7. **Littledean House**
8. Swan
9. New Inn

George Lane

Broad Street

Church Street

Grange Lane

Soudley

Newnham

Littledean, showing the positions of pubs.
Those open in 2004 are shown in bold.
Those whose precise positions are uncertain are shown with (?)

182

In the past Littledean was an important ironworking centre with a market place served by a network of tracks and roads leading to Gloucester, Monmouth and Hereford. This accounts for the large number of inns and alehouses that were recorded in the parish in 1677, but despite improvements made to the roads by various turnpike trusts in the late 18th century, the number of licensed premises declined dramatically.

The former Bell in Littledean

Beyond St. Ethelbert's church, which mainly dates from the 14th century, is an attractive half- timbered building in Church Street called Ye Olde Victoria Inne, not now an inn but presumably the former **Bell** of 1779 and the meeting place of a friendly society in 1813. The **Bell** was kept by John Dalby in 1856, Frederick Roe in 1859 and Timothy Trigg for a longer period from around 1863. In 1889 an Agreement was drawn up concerning a sale of freehold properties including the inn from Mrs. S. Goold to Alfred Wintle from Bill Mills in Weston under Penyard.

Soon after this the **Bell** passed to Francis Wintle's Forest Brewery at Mitcheldean, and when the tenancy was transferred in 1898 an inventory was made of the fixtures and fittings in the four bedrooms, middle tap room, shop, front tap room, parlour, kitchen, bar, cellar and garden, all valued at £111 1s. 6d. The stock was valued at £165 16s. 6d., which included barrels and bottles of beer and cider, mineral waters and half a bottle of port. During the early 20th century there was a continual change of tenants ending with Sidney Leighton who appears to have served the last drinks in 1927.

On the opposite side of the road on the corner of Church Street and Broad Street is the **King's Head**, also dating from the late 18th century. From the records it appears that the inn was known as the **Queen's Head** in 1863, when it was kept by William Townsend, but became the **King's Head** in the 1880s under Thomas Lapington. It was later taken over by the Alton Court Brewery Company from Ross on Wye. When the license was transferred from William Glastonbury to Howard Beet in 1907 an inventory and valuation was made

The King's Head at Littledean in 2003

of the effects and stock. The inn then consisted of a club room, entrance hall, bar, commercial room, kitchen, back kitchen, sitting room, pantry, cellar, skittle alley, stable and garden. The comprehensive stock included bottles of gin, whisky, rum, brandy, ginger brandy, sherry, port and De Kuepper together with minerals, porter and beers named Golden Brown and Golden Crown.

In 1962 the Alton Court Brewery and its licensed houses were taken over by West Country Breweries, which passed to Whitbreads a year later. In 1967 the **King's Head** was run by Mr. A. Coles and the Royal Forest of Dean Licensed Victuallers Association held their monthly meeting there. In the early 1990s Jon Hurley, in his *Forest of Dean Pub Guide*, described it as a 'comfortable but unfussy two-barred corner local' with a 'nice old stone and brick fireplace which ... roars with welcoming logs in the winter. ... April, the barmaid, was friendly and comely ...'.

South-west of the Cross, a former inn was known as the **Cross Keys** in 1739, and was the meeting place of a friendly society in 1813. During the mid-19th century it was kept by Henry Clift then Hannah Parsons who may have served as the last landlady.

The 17th-century house standing on the corner of Broad Street and Grange Lane was the **White Lion** of the 18th century, and at an unknown site in Broad Street there was a **Red Lion** in 1670, a building that was used as a workhouse from 1822.

Despite its modern name and appearance the existing **Belfry** is the oldest surviving inn in Littledean, and with its buildings spread around the corner of Broad Street and George Lane it is has expanded out of all recognition since its days as the **George** and earlier the **Golden Heart** of 1785. An 18th-century estate map and a bundle of faded deeds at Gloucester Record Office confirm its age and ownership. In 1808 it was 'known by the name or sign of the Heart', and from 1813 William Wood was the innkeeper. It was he who changed the name a few years later to the **George**, perhaps to commemorate George IV taking the throne in 1820.

The one-time Cross Keys at Littledean

'All that Messuage or Dwelling House together with the several Malthouses and other Outhouses' was purchased by Joseph Bennett in 1869. Throughout his long life Bennett traded as a farmer, postmaster, grocer, draper, ironmonger, druggist, nailmaker, maltster, owner of numerous licensed premises and a long term churchwarden at Littledean church where he and his wife were buried in the 1880s. After their deaths

The George in 1910

Sale of the George Hotel in 1937

Joseph's licensed properties were purchased by Alfred Wintle of Bill Mills, and included:

> All that fully licensed Public house called the George in the town of Littledean with the garden outbuildings land occupied therewith as the same and now in the occupation of John Stone Quick and are formerly occupied by Mrs. Pitt Adams.

The **George** passed from Alfred Wintle to the family's Forest Brewery; the pub being kept by Thomas Mountjoy from the early 20th century until at least 1938. During his occupancy the 'Row of Nine Cottages' known as 'George Row' was offered for sale in 1919, and again in 1938 when the

The George has now become the Belfry

auction was held at the **George Hotel**, which by then had been taken over by the Cheltenham Original Brewery. In 1949 the brewery sold a piece of adjoining land to East Dean Rural District Council who resold it to the Littledean Parish Council in 1960 as a site for the village hall. Mr. A. Beard was the publican at the **George** when the Royal Forest of Dean Licensed Victuallers Association held their meeting there in 1967, and Mr. Beard was still there in 1980. Sometime between 1989 and 2000 the **George** was renamed and transformed into an expansive so-called 'Traditional Pub and Hotel' called the **Belfry** offering 'Bar Snacks, a Restaurant, Leisure and Games, Functions and Accommodation'.

At the northern end of Littledean's Broad Street a long line of assorted buildings forms the **Littledean House**, a licensed hotel stretching along a section of the old road. In 1838 it was occupied by Joseph Bennett, but was not converted into a boarding house until 1906. The Hallam family ran the large establishment throughout the 1920s and '30s as an 80-roomed guest house with organised games and entertainments. The same facilities were still offered after World War Two, but its image, number of rooms and acreage had changed under the proprietorship of the Evans and Feltons in the 1970s, when it was described as being capable of accommodating:

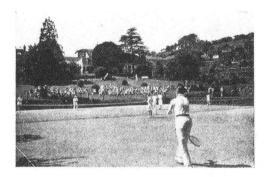

LITTLEDEAN GUEST HOUSE

LITTLEDEAN, Glos.

Telephone : Cinderford 2106.

Our own Milk and Garden Produce.
Spacious lawns amid beautiful scenery at 600 feet altitude.

80 Rooms . Grounds 12 Acres . Garage

TENNIS (2 Hard Courts) : RIDING : BOWLS
PUTTING : BILLIARDS & SNOOKER
TABLE TENNIS : DANCING : LIBRARY
An IDEAL CENTRE for the ROYAL FOREST OF
DEAN and Lower Reaches of the RIVER SEVERN
and the LOVELY WYE VALLEY. Organised Walks.
Motor Tours to all Parts.
★ Long-distance Motor Coaches stop at House ★

ORGANISED ENTERTAINMENTS

The organisation and ' House Party Atmosphere ' have
made these outstanding. There is always something
going on. Dancing, Concerts, Fancy Dress, Games,
Whist Drives, Tournaments of all kinds, wet or fine.
For those who do not wish to join in or to watch there
are many quiet spots in the House or Grounds to enjoy
a book.

TERMS : 5½ to 6 gns. SPECIAL WINTER RATES
Illustrated Brochure Free on Request.

The Littledean Guest House's 1951 brochure

187

The Littledean House Hotel in 2003

over eighty guests; all rooms have h. & c. water and either central heating or non-metered electric fires. There are Billiard and Table Tennis rooms and a T.V. lounge. The Forest Bar is a popular rendezvous in the evening or for a pre-lunch drink.

Where the A4151 bears south-west to Cinderford at the northern end of Littledean village, a lane called the Ruffitt heads north-west. It formed the original route from Newnham to the Forest, and was turnpiked in 1783. On the south side of the Ruffitt is a house called the Old Swan, a reminder of the days when it was the **Swan Inn**, occupied by Henry Wilks in the 1870s and '80s and owned by Joseph Bennett. From 1901 Joseph Phelps, a haulier, kept 'All that Beerhouse garden stable and premises known as the Swan Inn' then owned by Mrs. Susan Goold. A case of animal cruelty was reported in the *Dean Forest Mercury* on 3 May 1901:

Joseph Phelps ... was summoned by Inspector Barnes, officer of the S.P.C.A., for causing a horse to be worked while in an unfit state, on the 7th inst. Frederick Jackson, wagoner, in Phelps' employ, was also summoned by the Society's officer for working the animal whilst in that state. In another information Jackson was summoned by P.C. Newport for being drunk whilst in charge of a horse and wagon, on the 22nd inst. ... The inspector deposed that he met both defendents in charge of two horses and a wagon loaded with two tons of stone. The leader was an aged, poor old thing, but without wounds. The shaft horse was also aged and poor, and quite unfit to do any work on the road. Underneath the saddle was a terrible wound, four inches by two. Two months ago witness cautioned defendant with regard to his treatment of his horses. Jackson, in the presence of the defendant Phelps, said his master was aware of the condition the animal was in, and that Mrs. Phelps gave him two old stockings with which to protect the wound.—Defendant, examined, said he was not aware that there was a wound or that it had been padded.—Cross-examined: The horse was not 25 years old. He had had it seven years and it was the subject of a 'swop'. He certainly did not hear Jackson tell the officer that witness knew all about the condition the horse was in. Witness admitted that his wife and Jackson were cautioned with respect to another old horse.—The justices, having examined the horse, the Chairman said Phelps must pay a fine of £2, and costs 13s. 10d. Jackson must pay the costs, 4s. 9d.—Defendant suggested that it would be better to destroy the horse to avoid the penalty.—Jackson pleaded guilty to the charge of drunkenness and was fined 10s., to include costs.

This building was once the Swan Inn at Littledean

The one-time New Inn

After this incident Phelps continued for a while at the **Swan**, but the beer house appears to have closed during the early years of the 20th century.

Just within the parish of Littledean, on the outskirts of Cinderford in Littledean Hill Road, a red brick cottage standing on the east side of the road was the former **New Inn**, which traded as a beer house from the 1870s and into the 1900s. The **New Inn** was owned and occupied by Daniel then Mary Ann Meredith who was 'Licensed to Sell by Retail Beer & Cider to be Consumed on or off the Premises. Dealer in Tobacco'. Other unnamed beer houses were recorded at Littledean in the 19th century and were supplied by malt from the maltsters, Samuel Wilson in 1856, Henry James in 1863 and Joseph Bennett from 1859 from 'All that house garden stable Malthouse and premises fronting Broad Street'.

No.	Name of House.	Occupier.	Description of License.	Gross estimated Rental.	Rateable Value.	Six or Seven Days' License.	Tied or Free? If tied, to whom?	If Tenant, Nature of Tenancy.	Convictions or Endorsements during the last Five years.
	Parish of Littledean								
89	George	J. S. Quick ..	Alehouse .	23 10 0	21 10 0	7	Tied, T. Wintle	..	1 con
90	King's Head	Alfred Westbrook	Alehouse .	20 10 0	19 0 0	7	Tied Alton Court Brewery Co.,Lt.	..	..
91	Bell ..	Thomas Dee ..	Alehouse ..	23 10 0	21 10 0	7	Tied, F. Wintle	..	..
92	Swan	Henry Wilks ..	Alehouse ..	9 0 0	8 0 0	7	Free ..	..	..
93	New Inn.. ..	M. A. Meredith ..	....	10 10 0	9 10 0	7	Free ..	..	..

1891 Licensing Act — Petty Sessional Register.
List of inns in Littledean

CHAPTER ELEVEN

Newnham, Blakeney & Awre

The busy A48 from Gloucester and Westbury-on-Severn winds its way through Newnham and Blakeney on its way to Chepstow and South Wales. John Putley in his *Riverine Dean* published in 1999 described Newnham-on-Severn as:

> one of Dean's most important maritime sites. Newnham had a ford and ferry crossing that were probably in use as early as the Roman period for although there are no known Roman sites at Newnham, there are three Roman roads converging on the town ... and a Roman temple at nearby Littledean. ... its trade, most of which was with Ireland, London, Bristol and the Midlands grew rapidly reaching a peak in the late 18th and early 19th centuries. ... After the opening of the Gloucester and Sharpness canal in 1827 (which allowed ships to by-pass the port altogether) Newnham's history as a port came to an end.

On the Green, an earthwork is the only remains of Newnham's castle, said to date from the 11th century. It was visited by both Henry I and Henry II, and the site was fortified during the Civil War. On the other side of the main road is the parish church, standing on the highest point in Newnham overlooking the river Severn.

On entering Newnham today, it is immediately evident that the place enjoyed a long period of prosperity in the past. Indeed, in the 18th century it was described as an 'eligible place to live'. There was an abundance of 'Nobility, Gentry and Clergy' who required the services of the professional men who occupied many of the fine houses in the main street. With easy access to the Forest of Dean's raw materials, many trades prospered, including those associated with timber, bark, coal, iron, glass and vessels on the Severn. Newnham's merchants traded with places across the river via the Newnham / Arlingham ferry, with Bristol by trows down the Severn and by carriers on the roads. During the early years of the 19th century a tramroad was constructed by the Bullo Pill Railway Company which provided horse-

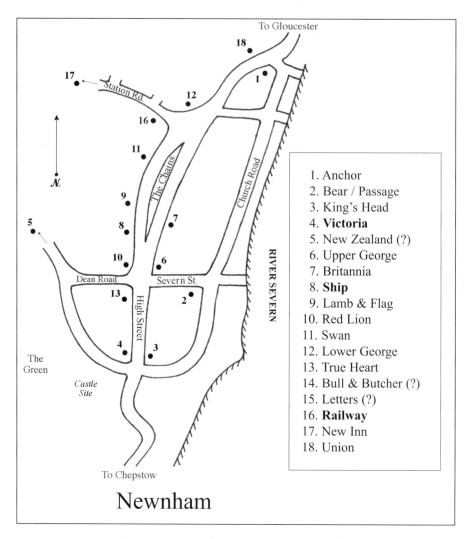

To Gloucester

18

17

Station Rd.

12

16

11

The Chains

9

8

7

5

10

6

Dean Road

Severn St.

13

2

4

3

High Street

The Green

Castle Site

Church Road

RIVER SEVERN

1. Anchor
2. Bear / Passage
3. King's Head
4. **Victoria**
5. New Zealand (?)
6. Upper George
7. Britannia
8. **Ship**
9. Lamb & Flag
10. Red Lion
11. Swan
12. Lower George
13. True Heart
14. Bull & Butcher (?)
15. Letters (?)
16. **Railway**
17. New Inn
18. Union

To Chepstow

Newnham

Newnham, showing the positions of pubs.
Those open in 2004 are shown in bold.
Those whose precise positions are uncertain are shown with (?)

powered transport from the Severn just south of Newnham to the Forest of Dean. It was taken over by the South Wales Railway Company and opened as a locomotive railway in 1854, but has since closed, although the main line from Gloucester to Chepstow is still operational.

With improved communications to and from Newnham it is not surprising to discover that at least 15 inns and two beer houses were open during the second half of the 19th century for the benefit of travellers, traders, merchants and the inhabitants of the town. The number slowly decreased to ten open in 1903, five in 1968 and only three in 2003. To visit the sites of Newnham's past and present inns and hostelries it is best to walk from the Riverside car park where the visitor can enjoy the splendid view across the Severn before starting a tour of the town. In 1982 Keith Kissack described Newnham as 'a charming town with a long main stret in which pedestrians play second fiddle to the through traffic. Yet many of the quiet lanes leading down to the river are delightful'.

In Church Road, the Police Station occupies the site of the **Anchor** which was built in 1710 to provide a licensed premises for the working men of the river. In 1828 the innkeeper was convicted for 'keeping open the Anchor Inn for purposes other than the reception of travellers', whilst during the 1830s it was used as a meeting place for one of the local Friendly Societies. John Jones kept the **Anchor** from around 1850 to at least 1863, a short while before the old inn and a row of cottages were demolished by Mr. Wintle, a solicitor in the town. He lived at Hill House, now called Unlawater, and may have carried out this demolition to improve road access and the view from his house.

Almost midway along Church Road is a prominent building called the Passage House. It stands on the corner of Severn Street and faces the lane that formerly led to the important ferry crossing to Arlingham. This was the **Bear** in the 17th century, although it was recorded as the **Passage Inn** in 1785 when it was taken over by Daniel Edmonds from Bristol. It became a busy posting-house, where the borough and manorial courts were held in 1759. Auction sales were held there including the sale of bark in 1805 as advertised in the *Gloucester Journal*:

> The Bark of 617 Oak Timber Trees, felled this season in Dean Forest, for the use of the Navy, under a warrant from the Right Hon. the Lord's Commissioners of his Majesty's Treasury.

In 1813 the inn belonged to Roynon Jones when, as the **Bear**, it was described as 'a commodious Inn for travellers situated on the West bank of the Severn'. The license was transferred from Robert Smith to William Orchard in 1833 when the **Bear's** utensils and stock were valued at the large sum of £1,348 5s. 0d. James Miles Robertson was listed as the landlord in 1842 followed by William Batem in 1852 and J. Kern who, in 1863, was possibly the last landlord before it closed as an inn.

A ceremonial sword was kept at the **Bear** when the manor court was held there in 1813. Although it was said to have been given to the town by King John, the sword was actually dated to the 15th century. In 1594 the mayor repaired the sword and supplied a scabbard. He also provided a silver mace to be carried by the mayor at fairs and festivals. When it was displayed at the

The Bear at Newnham is now a private house

The King's Head still retains its name

Bear its ownership was unknown, but when John James bought the manor in 1850 he purchased the sword some years later. After years of complications over ownership it was eventually loaned to the Gloucester City Museum in 1968. Use of the bear as an inn sign sometimes indicated that the barbaric sport of bear-baiting was held there before it was made illegal in 1849.

Church Road leads to St. Peter's and the High Street, where a building on the right is called the Old King's Head. It was only 'remembered by name' in 1975 by R.J. Mansfield as the **King's Head** Inn.

On the western side of the High Street stands the elegant **Victoria Hotel**, with its wide portico and paired columns. It was built in the early 18th century as a private residence for Thomas Crump, and probably replaced an earlier building. The name **Victoria** suggests its conversion to an inn and posting-house in 1837 when Queen Victoria ascended the throne. It was certainly open in 1842 when Jonathan Elliott was listed as the innkeeper. He was followed by several others until William King took over the 'Victoria hotel and posting house' in the 1870s and remained there until 1913. The 'Highly Important Freehold Property' was advertised for sale as 'An Old Established, First Class, Fully Licensed Hotel and Posting House, with Extensive Stabling and Garage' in 1913.

Later in the 20th century the **Victoria** changed its 'Smoking Room', 'Commercial Rooms' and 'Dining Room' to serving the 'speciality of the house' in a 'Candlelit Restaurant', with a 'Function Room catering for weddings, parties and conferences'. Since 1939 some of its original features have been lost including a central pediment and a balustraded parapet. In the 1980s the **Victoria** was described as a 'handsome old hotel with beams and a great log fire, full of ambience and very comfortable'. This continued into the 21st century, when the hotel was offering 'charm and atmosphere of bygone days'.

From the southern end of the **Victoria** a pleasant walk leads across the remains of the castle, past a fine view of the Severn and along a tree-lined path to the

Sale details of the Victoria in 1913

A 1939 advertisement for the Victoria Hotel

195

The Victoria in 2003

Dean Road which leads from Newnham to Littledean. About halfway between the two places was a beer house run by the Blewett family between 1891 and 1903. It had an unusual name — the **New Zealand** — and was remembered by R.J. Mansfield in 1975 as 'being a mile distant from both Newnham and Littledean'.

Newnham High Street was a popular site for inns, overlooking the Chains, a pleasant grassy bank, where the Market Hall, a row of market stalls and the stocks once stood. Amongst the predominately Georgian frontages of houses in the High Street is the Sanctuary, formerly the **George** or **Upper George**, standing on the corner of Severn Street. In 1785 the court leet was held at the **Upper George**, and it may have been one of the inns considered by the parish vestry when they decided to hold their meetings 'At a Convenient Public House' in 1813. There is a tradition recorded by Mabel Woods in her *Newnham* that:

> This Inn once contained a set of rooms known as Sanctuary Rooms for criminals and debtors. Legally, as it formed part of the Hundred of St. Briavels, it was out of the jurisdiction of Newnham Justices; and, as the Magistrates of St. Briavels were not likely to trouble themselves over miscreants so far from their own centre, and connected only by founderous and miry roads, it is easy to surmise that many a Newnham debtor escaped prison by this means, for violating sanctuary was a thing never dreamt of by the authorities.

AT THE GENERAL ANNUAL LICENSING MEETING of Her Majesty's Justices of the Peace acting for the *Division* of *Newnham* in the County of *Gloucester* holden at *The Bear Inn Newnham* on the *22* day of *August* in the Year One Thousand Eight Hundred and Fifty *three* for the purpose of granting Licences to Persons keeping Inns, Alehouses, and Victualling-houses, to sell exciseable Liquors by Retail, to be drunk or consumed on their Premises:

We, being *[illegible]* of Her Majesty's Justices of the Peace acting for the said *Division* and being the majority of those assembled at the said Session, do hereby authorize and empower *Drusilla Wallis* now dwelling at *Newnham* in the Parish of *Newnham* and *Keeping* an Inn, Alehouse, or Victualling-house, at the Sign of the *Upper George* in the *Parish* of *Newnham* in the *Division* and *County* aforesaid, to sell by Retail therein, and in the Premises thereunto belonging, all such exciseable Liquors as the said *Drusilla Wallis* shall be licensed and empowered to sell under the Authority and Permission of any Excise Licence, and to permit all such Liquors to be drunk or consumed in h~~is~~ her said House or in the Premises thereunto belonging: **Provided**, that h~~e~~ do not fraudulently dilute or adulterate the same, or sell the same knowing them to have been fraudulently diluted or adulterated; and do not use in selling thereof any Weights or Measures that are not of the legal Standard; and do not wilfully or knowingly permit Drunkenness or other disorderly Conduct in h~~is~~ her House or Premises; and do not knowingly suffer any unlawful Games or any Gaming whatsoever therein; and do not knowingly permit or suffer Persons of notoriously bad Character to assemble and meet together therein; and do not keep open h~~is~~ her House except for the Reception of Travellers, nor permit or suffer any Beer or other exciseable Liquor to be conveyed from or out of h~~is~~ her Premises during the usual Hours of the Morning and Afternoon Divine Service in the Church or Chapel of the Parish or place in which h~~is~~ her House is situated, on Sundays, Christmas Day, or Good Friday, but do maintain good Order and Rule therein; and this Licence shall continue in force from the Tenth Day of October~~next~~ until the Tenth Day of October then next ensuing, and no longer: **Provided**, that the said *Drusilla Wallis* shall not in the meantime become a Sheriff's Officer, or Officer executing the Process of any Court of Justice, in either of which Cases this Licence shall be void.

Given under our Hands and Seals on the Day and at the Place first above written.

Alehouses E.
Annual Licensing.
(9 Geo. 4, c. 61.)
Annual Licence, under s. 13,
endorsed for transfer, under
5 & 6 Vict. c. 44.

LONDON:
SHAW AND SONS.

The 1853 licence for the Upper George at Newnham

The Upper George in 2003

In 1853 the license of the 'George commercial inn and inland revenue office' was transferred from James Wallis to Drucilla Wallis, and from around 1860 the **Upper George** changed hands repeatedly until it became an Arnold, Perrett house at the end of the 19th century. An inventory of 1907 reveals that it contained four bedrooms, landing, sitting room, two attics, kitchen, ante room, smoke room, yard, laundry, front passage, billiard room, bar, beer cellar and spirit cellar. Thirty years later the Cheltenham Original Brewery took over.

A few doors away is Britannia House, a 17th-century timber-framed building with a gabled street frontage now all covered in roughcast, which served as the **Britannia** beer house for a short period during the 1890s and 1900s. On the west side of the High Street is the **Ship**, possibly dating from the 17th century, although W. Merrett wrote in *Pubs of the Old Stroud Brewery:* 'A pub situated on the opposite side of the road named the Rose closed in the eighteenth century, and the landlord moved himself and his business to what is now the Ship Inn'. Henry Weight kept the **Ship** in 1829

Newnham High Street with the gabled Britannia in the middle distance

Above: an early photograph of the Britannia as an inn.
Right: One gable of the inn after the render had been removed

and was licensed to sell 'excisable Liquors by retail to be drunk or consumed in the House or premises'; the license was transferred to James Wallis in 1830.

From 1863 John Mailes was the **Ship's** landlord before R.G. Taylor advertised in the *Dean Forest Mercury* the re-opening of the **Ship** in 1885 'For the Sale of Wines, Spirits, Home-brewed Beer, Bitter Ales, Burton Ale, etc.' A few years later the Stroud Brewery took over the inn and sold their 'Celebrated Ales & Stout, Wines & Spirits'. Hannah Purnell was listed as keeping the **Ship** in 1891, and was a 'Licensed Retailer of Ale, Porter, Cider, British and Foreign Wines & Spirits etc. Dealer in Tobacco'. Hannah was followed by Frederick Baghurst who ran the **Ship** from 1903 to at least 1935, and in 1962 it passed to West Country Breweries. The **Ship** eventually became a Whitbread establishment, but during the 1990s it was acquired by a very experienced innkeeper from Ross and soon gained a reputation for food and drink which has continued into the 21st century.

NOTICE.

Ship Inn, Newnham.

THE above Inn now having been thoroughly renovated, will be RE-OPENED on WED-NESDAY, 14th JANUARY, 1885, for the Sale of Wines, Spirits, Home-brewed Beer, Bitter Ales, Burton Ale, &c.

N.B.—Commercials will find a good accommodation at moderate charges.

R. G. TAYLOR, Proprietor.

Reopening of the Ship in 1885 after renovation

The landlord stands proudly outside the Ship Inn in the 1930s

Also on the west side of the High Street is a range of buildings now called Gable House, Tower Cottage and Flag House, which was once the **Lamb and Flag**. In 1807, when it was occupied by Richard Elton, this public house 'with all the Outbuildings, Yards, Gardens and the Orchard adjoining' was advertised for sale in the *Gloucester Journal*. The **Lamb and Flag** continued trading until the mid-19th century when James Dobbs appears to have been the last landlord. The Lamb and Flag inn sign usually depicts a holy lamb with a banner and suggests a connection with a church or abbey. It is also an heraldic sign referring to the Knights Templar.

Two other properties in the High Street have names suggesting they were once inns — the **Red Lion** and the **Swan**, but no documentary evidence has been found, although the former was called the Red Lion Chambers in 1884 when the premises were used as an agency for the Wilderness Stone Quarry at Mitcheldean.

The one-time Lamb and Flag in Newnham

Opposite the clock tower (erected in 1875) is a private house featuring its former name and use: 'The George Hotel Family and Commercial', which was commonly called the **Lower George** to distinguish it from the upper one. John Morgan kept the inn in 1842 before the Hobbs family took over for at least 30 years. At the end of the 19th century the **Lower George** was taken over by Arnold, Perrett & Co., and it was run by several different landlords including George Pope, who

Although the sign was still there in 2002, the Lower George no longer takes in visitors

*The Lower George by the clock tower
in the early 20th century*

upgraded the premises to an hotel. It continued until closing in 1937 when the Cheltenham Original Brewery aquired the property.

For a brief period during the 1890s and 1900s there was a **True Heart** in the High Street kept by James Page, but the **Bull and Butcher** of the 1830s, and the **Letters** of the 1890s were pubs at sites not known by the author. In other parts of the nation the sign of the Bull and Butcher dates from the early 18th century and usually indicated that the landlord was also a butcher.

From the clock tower, Station Road leads west past the **Railway Inn**, with its Carriages Restaurant, which started life as a beer house in the mid-19th century following the opening of the Gloucester to Chepstow section of the South Wales Railway. Samuel Jones was followed by other members of his family for nearly a hundred years. In 1981 Jon Hurley described the **Railway** in his *Forest of Dean Pubs* as: 'a typical front room pub with a tiny bar at one end and a friendly landlord dispensing ... to an interesting array of craggy locals. There is a piano, dartboard, quoits and an open fire'.

Station Road leads over the railway to Hyde with its Equestrian Centre. Overlooking the railway line was a former pub called the **New Inn**, originally a beer house opened by Oliver King in the early 1850s. During the last quarter of the 19th century Joseph Green kept the inn, and in 1909 'All that messuage or Public House known as the New Inn with the garden yard and outbuildings thereto belonging situated and being in Newnham in the County of Gloucestershire and for many years past in the occupation of the

202

The Railway Inn in 2003

Mortgagee' was acquired by Francis Wintle of the Forest Brewery at Mitcheldean.

In 1923 the **New Inn** contained a tap room, beer store, three sitting rooms, cider store and kitchen on the ground floor, with four bedrooms and two other rooms above. Outside was a pig cot, coal house and urinal whilst the adjoining property — the New Inn Cottage — was tenanted to Mrs. Gray. In 1937 the **New Inn** passed to the Cheltenham Original Brewery, and some time before 1954 the inn was de-licensed and became a private house called the Brambles.

ALL THAT messuage or Inn known as the New Inn situate at Newnham in the County of Gloucester and all outbuildings and appurtenances thereunto belonging comprising in rear and at side a brick and timber erection of coal house pig cot closet urinal etc. and small garden AND ALSO a piece of garden ground near to the said premises measuring about one hundred feet by thirty feet and all other outbuildings and appurtenances thereunto belonging which said premises are now in the occupation of Frederick John Miles as tenant AND ALSO ALL THAT cottage known as the New Inn Cottage adjoining the New Inn premises which said cottage is now in the occupation of Mrs. M. C. R. Carter as tenant and all outbuildings and appurtenances thereunto belonging TOGETHER with the site thereof and the land occupied therewith.

Particulars for the 1937 sale of the New Inn

Left: The one-time New Inn
Above: Once the Union Inn

From the clock tower, Newnham's High Street leads northwards past some fine houses to Old Union Cottage, formerly the **Union Inn** kept by John Hooper in 1842 and John Thomas Breen during the 1850s and '60s. He was followed by Louisa Breen who appears to have been the last innkeeper around 1880. It may have been closed due to pressure from the Temperance Movement, which was active in Newnham between 1875 and 1881. In 1876 the Temperance Society held an event where 'great fun was derived from the display by Master Playsted of a galvanic Battery from which numerous shocks were received'. The Playsteds of Newnham were grocers, drapers and wine and spirit merchants in the 1890s, but they only advertised their soft drinks in the parish magazine.

Leaving Newnham, the A48 makes a dramatic sweep away from the town and under the South Wales Railway bridge and within a couple of miles Bullo Pill is reached. According to John Putley in his *Riverine*, Bullo Pill was 'originally a small pill [a tidal creek or pool] used for shipbuilding, in 1810 the Forest of Dean Tramroad Company began to develop Bullo as a stone and coal port'. He adds 'At its height Bullo could handle over 1,000 tons of coal and stone a day, but its trade declined after 1900 and it finally closed in 1926'.

The **Railway Inn** at Bullo stood next to the tramroad which was taken over as a locomotive line by the South Wales Railway in 1851. A year later Fred Piper was recorded at the **Railway** which was later run by Mrs. Emma Birks, who was also a blacksmith. After 1906 it appears that the inn was renamed the **Bullo Cross**, where Miss Annie Birks was the landlady in the 1920s and '30s before William Middlecote took over. The Stroud Brewery purchased the **Bullo Cross** in 1947, and in 1962 the inn and outbuildings passed to West Country Breweries and has since closed.

Travelling from Gloucester on the A48 between Bullo and Blakeney, a no through road on the right leads to an isolated settlement on the Soudley brook called Two Bridges. From the 1870s there was a beer house on the side of the road not surprisingly also called the **Two Bridges** which was run for many years by the Collins family. W.H. Collins was recorded at the inn in 1939, but since then it has been converted to a private dwelling nostalgically called The Old Inn.

The A48 heads south and swings down into Blakeney, a compact and interesting village on the banks of the pretty Blackpool brook, where evidence of weirs and sluices are a reminder of Blakeney's past industries of milling, ironworking and brewing. In 1981 the local newspaper featured 'The Friendly Village of Blakeney' which revealed that

> the community is well served with business people, many of whom are long established in the area. Employment is provided by a few small firms, and there are a number of shops to meet essential needs. The only important drawback is the lack of a chemist shop, the nearest being at Lydney and Newnham.

The shops included a post office and grocers, two other grocers, a Co-op store, a butcher, two hair stylists and three inns.

On the approach to Blakeney, the A48 provides a typical example of a twisting, turnpike road designed in the 1830s to provide an easier gradient for horse-drawn vehicles. It replaced the original steep and narrow route which now only survives as a footpath known as Swan Lane, which leads past Swan House. This timber-framed building dates from the 16th century and in 1645 was recorded as the **Swan Inn**. During the latter half of the 18th century it was kept by John Jenkins before 'Thomas Cook Innholder' took over 'All that Messuage or Tenement commonly called or known by the Name of the Swanne with the Two Gardens' in 1771. A Friendly Society met there in 1791 and in 1858 a 'Ball and Tea Party' was provided by William and Ann Cadogan, who had inherited the inn from Ann's father, William Jennings.

Ann Williams was followed by James Nickoles who de-licensed the old inn and opened the Swan Temperance Hotel, which continued in use until the early 20th century. It then became Swan House and was

Swan House was once a roadside inn

205

offered for sale in 1926 as 'An Unique 15th Century Residence known as The Swan House', but the sale particulars did not mention its former life as an inn.

Near to the **Swan** in Church Square was the 18th-century **Bird in Hand**, which also served as the church house where vestry meetings were held. The building was demolished in 1819 in order to extend the chapel and by 1825 the sign of the **Bird in Hand** had been transferred to a neighbouring building on the corner of the road to Awre, and was kept by Mary Parsons in the 1870s. At the turn of the century Arnold, Perrett had acquired the inn, and when Harry Yarnton was serving behind the bar in 1937 it was taken over by the Cheltenham Original Brewery and has since closed.

Tucked away in Church Square is the **Yew Tree**, which despite being closed and for sale in 2003 was still displaying its sign. It was open in 1817, and was kept by J. Parsons in 1863. He was succeeded by several innkeepers including Maria Howelll who, on leaving the pub in 1903 advertised the auction sale in the *Dean Forest Mercury*. It appears that one Henry Thomas purchased the **Yew Tree** and it remained in his family until around 1930. It may have been during William Smith's later occupancy that the Alton Court Brewery from Ross acquired the inn with 'the skittle alley outbuildings yard gardens and land'. As with many other local inns, it passed to West Country Breweries in 1962 and then to Whitbreads.

Yew Tree Inn, Blakeney, Glo's.

Alfred E. Dykins

Has received instructions from Mrs. Maria Howell, who is leaving, to SELL BY AUCTION, on the Premises as above, on THURSDAY, OCT. 22ND, 1903, a portion of her

Household Furniture, Live Stock, Utensils, Implements, &c.,

COMPRISING—Iron frame piano, full compass, trichord, in rosewood case; old mahogany bureau, deal kitchen with table drawer, deal Pembroke table, iron French bedsteads, iron cot, folding bedstead, painted washstand, gent's arm chair, child's basket and high-back chairs, meat safe, set of shelves, capital mangle; two painted cupboards, 5ft. by 4ft. 8in.; clothes horse, end churn by Hathaway, milk bucket, tins and other dairy utensils, two pans, three scales and weights, spring balance, stone and other jars, table lamp, books, oak writing desk, sugar cutter, &c. The LIVE STOCK comprises —Brown Cow (barren), Yearling Heifer, 24 Lambs, and 17 couple fowls. The IMPLEMENTS, &c., consist of drill, root pulper, haul rake, rick poles, pulley block, ropes and fruit lugg, two 10in. lawn mowers by Ransome, hay knife; strong tip cart, suit small cob; feeding trough, three fowls, houses and runs, dog kennel, pigeon cot, three bar-frame beehives, two stocks of bees in bar-framed hives, wheelbarrow, two 28-rung ladders, two sack carts, two grindstones, six rakes and pikes, tunpail, scythe, two seakale pots, pit saws, garden and other tools, about 250ft. of matchboarding; one 25-gallon, two 18-gallon, and two 12-gallon cider casks; four large rain water butts, four wash tubbs, heavy set of pony harness, iron and stone pig troughs, boxes, bins, firewood, &c. Rick of Prime Hay, about 8 tons, to go off.

Sale to commence at One p.m. On view the day of Sale.

N.B.—Other Stock may be included in this Sale by arrangement.

Auctioneer's Office: Victoria Street, Cinderford Nat. Telephone, No. 20.

Sale of the Yew Tree's contents in 1903

206

The Yew Tree was closed in 2003 when this photograph was taken

In 1981 Bill Endley and his wife were comparative newcomers to the **Yew Tree**. They left industry to run a small country pub and thoroughly enjoyed the community life of the village. Bill 'possesses a fine tenor voice and has helped at various functions' reported a local newspaper at the time. Sadly this pub is now closed.

The **King's Head,** a late 18th-century building, stands prominently in the centre of Blakeney. It probably opened as a licensed premises during the

BLAKENEY.—THE KING'S HEAD HOTEL.

ALL THAT piece or parcel of land situate at Blakeney in the County of Gloucester on the south side of and having a frontage to the main road from Lydney to Newnham TOGETHER with the fully licensed Public House known as The King's Head Hotel with the stables sheds and all other outbuildings and appurtenances thereunto belonging TOGETHER with the right to use the W.C. drain pipe at the back of the said Hotel keeping the same free and open and in good repair and also the right to use the existing flushing cistern which is fixed over the adjoining property now or lately belonging to Sarah Ann Adams against the south wall of the said Hotel BUT RESERVING unto the said Sarah Ann Adams her heirs and assigns the right to continue the user of the well upon the land hereby conveyed in respect of the cottages adjoining the said Sarah Ann Adams her heirs and assigns and the Grantee respectively bearing one-half of the cost of keeping the said well in repair but each party respectively keeping the pipes serving their respective properties in repair access to the well for that purpose being given as required to the said Sarah Ann Adams her heirs and assigns.

The 1937 sale of the King's Head included joint use of the well

The King's Head in 2003

early to mid-19th century and, being in a more convenient position than the old **Swan**, probably took over its coaching business. It was Henry Cadogan, who also had an interest in the **Swan** before it ceased as an inn, who kept the **King's Head** in 1863. For at least 20 years Isaac Godfrey ran the inn, which had been acquired by Alfred Butler, a 'draper and grocer: and agent for W. and A. Gilbey wine and spirit merchants'. Butler traded from Sydenham House, further down the road in Blakeney. Sometime after 1903 the **King's Head** was taken over by Arnold, Perrett, and like the rest of their licensed houses passed to the Cheltenham Original Brewery in 1937 and eventually Whitbread. It was still serving the community in 2004.

At Nibley, on the main road at the southern end of Blakeney, is the existing **Cock Inn**, a building dating from the 18th century. In 1822 the *Gloucester Journal* advertised: 'to be Let by Tender, and entered upon at Lady-Day next, that old-established and well-known Inn, the Cock, at Blakeney, in this county. The South Wales Coach changes horses at this Inn every day'. The **Cock** is clearly shown on Bryant's map of 1824, and from

The Cock Inn in 2003

The Cock Inn sign features a fine 'cock' horse

the mid-19th century was run by Thomas Davis, who was there during the 1870s and '80s before it was sold in 1894 as a licensed house of the City Brewery based in Gloucester. After several other landlords, William Bush was there during the 1920s and '30s before Esther James conveyed 'the messuage or Inn known as the Cock Inn and outbuildings' to the Alton Court Brewery in 1940. The Ross based Alton Court Brewery Company was taken over by West Country Breweries in 1962, and the **Cock** probably became a Whitbread pub, and from 1955 was run by Derek and Joy Sandford. In 1981 the Cock had become 'a well known venue for many local social functions'. By the 21st century the **Cock Inn** had become a free house and was advertising that it was 'Open all Day' and that there was 'Live Music' on Saturday evenings.

*Two old photographs of the Tump House
Inn when James Reeves was landlord*

On the west side of the High Street, near Highmead House, was the site chosen for the Forest of Dean Steam Brewery, where Wilkinson Smith brewed ale and porter during the 1870s. J.H. Hands had taken over by 1885 followed by Samuel Evans in 1894. Three years later the brewery 'purchased by Messrs. Arnold, Perrett & Co. from Mr. A. Burke was closed ... the Wickwar firm having resolved to supply their local customers from their stores at Lydney'. The *Dean Forest Mercury* also reported that in future 'the building was to be devoted to the manufacture of mineral water'. This may not have happened, as Arnold, Perrett & Co. were listed as brewers at Blakeney in 1907 and production probably continued for a few more years.

Leading north from Blakeney towards the Forest of Dean is the New Road, where an alehouse called the **Traveller's Rest** was owned and occupied by William Adams in 1891. Its location is unknown to the author, but similar to other pubs in the area it was purchased by Arnold, Perrett and passed to the Cheltenham Original Brewery in 1937.

Along the road leading north-west into the Forest there is a cluster of houses and cottages standing amidst the remains of the Forest of Dean Railway and along the banks of the meandering Blackpool brook at Old Furnace Bottom. At a sharp bend in the road is the Old Tump House, formerly the **Tump House Inn**, dating from the mid-19th century. During the first quarter of the 20th century it was kept by James Reeves and was aquired by the Stroud Brewery. In 1962, it passed to West Country Breweries and remained open until around 1970.

At the **Tump House** in 1902 an enquiry was held into the 'cause of death of James James, 67, general labourer, of Blakeney Hill'. James 'was not a strong man and his eyesight was bad, he being totally blind with one eye'. James had fallen while ascending a flight of steps with a rail tied by a piece of rope. The coroner was reported in the local press as saying that 'this was a very unfortunate case. He was not surprised that it had happened, because a more miserable death trap could not have been conceived'.

The Tump House Inn in retirement

Viney Hill, lying south-west of Blakeney, can be approached from Old Furnace Bottom or from the A48. It was formed into an ecclesiastical parish in 1866 with its All Saints church consecrated a year later. In 1927 Viney Hill consisted of a post office, an elementary school, a grocer and cycle dealer, plus a beer retailer and a publican at the **Albion Inn**. Throughout its rather sketchy history, it is known that a burial club and a Blakeney Friendly Society met at the inn during the mid-19th century. It was kept by E. Thomas in 1907 and by Frederick Fowler in 1927 and became

The New Inn at Viney Hill in 2002

211

an Arnold, Perrett house before passing to the Cheltenham Original Brewery in 1937. The **Albion** was open in 1957, but has since closed.

The beer house mentioned at Viney Hill in 1927 must have been the already well-established **New Inn**, which had been acquired by the Stroud Brewery at the end of the 19th century when it was kept by Charles James. The **New Inn**, with its prominent sign to attract Forest of Dean walkers, was still open in 2004. One other beer house that existed near Blakeney is dealt with under Soudley in chapter fifteen.

From Viney Hill the road crosses the A48 at Nibley Green and leads east to Etloe and south to Purton, an isolated hamlet overlooking the Severn. As the road turns right at Purton a large white building on the right called Old Severn Bridge House was, until recently, the **Severn Bridge Hotel**. In the past the inhabitants of Purton were mainly occupied in the river trade, fishing and with the passage across the river. From medieval times a **Passage House Inn** catered for those using the river crossing. In 1726 Martin Inman operated the ferry and kept the inn, and in 1798 James Inman was recorded there and was charging the following rates for 'Pyrton Passage', which had been 'rendered more commodious and certain, by well found Boats, able and careful hands, and every attention paid to the speedy Conveyance of Passengers':

	£.	s.	d.
Man and Horse	0.	1.	0.
A Horse	0.	0.	9.
Foot Person	0.	0.	3.
Horn Calves	0.	0.	6. each
Calves	0.	0.	3. each
Pigs and Sheep	0.	2.	9. per score

By the early 19th century the Purton inn became known as the **Ship**, and was still run by the Inman family when the South Wales Railway was constructed between the cliff top hamlet and the river Severn in 1851. In 1879 the river crossing was replaced by the Severn Bridge Railway which included a footway, but the old inn's name reverted to **Purton Passage**, a hotel kept by Charles Birks, who still operated the ferry. In 1885 Arthur Fryer changed the name to the **Severn Bridge Inn**, and in 1890 another landlord, John Franklin, upgraded the inn to an hotel, which he managed until 1907, after which the license was transferred to R.A. Ansley.

In 1950 the bridge from Purton to Sharpness was described as being:

> over three-quarters of a mile long and rests on cast iron cylindrical piers filled with concrete. A whirlpool nearby is named the 'Fiddlers Pool' since here a party of Welsh fiddlers were drowned when returning from a jovial evening at Berkeley and the sound of their revels is still heard mingled with that of the waters on a stormy night.

All that Ancient and Accustomed FERRY or PASSAGE, called " Purton Ferry or Passage,"

With the Tolls, Dues, and Fees, arising and payable for or in respect thereof upon and across the River Severn, together with

TWO CAPITAL BOATS,

One for Passengers, and the other for Merchandize (the latter equal to about 10 Tons), with all requisite Gear, Chains, Anchors, &c., and also the Stone-built Approaches on both sides of the River to the said Ferry or Passage, together with all rights and appurtenances thereto belonging.

Let to Mr. Workman on a Yearly Tenancy.

LOT 5.

All that Substantially-built and pleasantly situated full-licensed FREEHOLD MESSUAGE & PREMISES,

Known as " The Purton Passage House or Ship Inn,"

Together with a Stone-built COTTAGE, and about 2½ Acres of Productive Orchard, Meadow Land, Kitchen and Pleasure Gardens, Out-buildings, &c. situate in the Tything of Purton, and Parish of LYDNEY.

The HOUSE, which stands on the Banks of the Severn, is Stone-built and Slate-roofed, in good repair, and commands extensive Views. It contains Good Entrance Hall, Bar, Large Smoking Room, Parlor, Kitchen, Back Kitchen, Pantry, Store Room, Cellars, &c., and 8 Capital Bed-rooms.

The OUT-BUILDINGS comprise Brewhouse with Furnace, Stabling for 4 Horses, and Building adjoining, which might easily be converted into Stabling for three more horses, Coach-House, Lofts, Coal-House, Fowl-House, Stone-built Cottage, &c., &c.

There is a Capital KITCHEN GARDEN, well stocked, and good bearing Orchard, and Close of Meadow Land. The whole being colored brown in the plan hereto annexed and described on the Lydney Tythe Apportionment Map and Terrier, as follows :—

NO.	DESCRIPTION.	CULTIVATION.	QUANTITY.		
789	Purton Passage ... ... ⎫ House Out-buildings ... ... ⎬ Lands and Gardens ... ... ⎭		0	3	35
790	Pasture and Orchard		1	1	33
		Total	2	1	28

Let to Mr. Workman on a Yearly Tenancy

The TIMBER on Lots 1, 2, 3 & 5, will have to be taken to by the respective Purchasers, at a Valuation in the usual way.

Lots 3 & 5, are in the immediate vicinity of the proposed Railway Bridge across the Severn, which when completed, will no doubt materially increase their value.

Sale details of the Purton Ferry and the Passage House in 1875

213

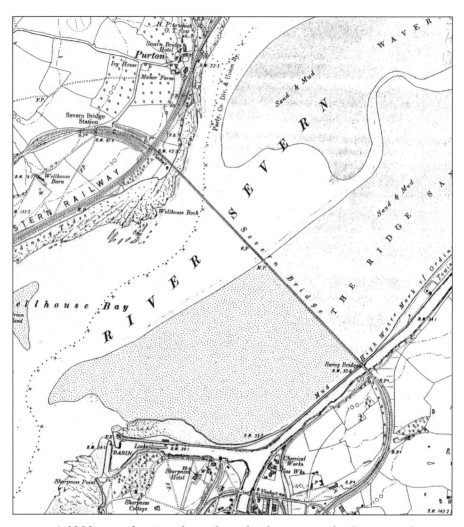

*A 1903 map showing the railway bridge across the Severn and
the Severn Bridge Hotel at Purton*

In 1960 an unfortunate accident damaged the Severn Bridge and it was
demolished between 1967 and 1970, but the **Severn Bridge Hotel** continued
to trade, and in 1981 Jon Hurley found it to be 'Splendidly situated beside a
wide expanse of darkly churning Severn ... with a wood fire and exposed
beams and stonework'. Before the **Severn Bridge** closed its door in the
1990s Neil Coates featured the hotel in his *Pub Walks in the Forest of Dean*
where he described the bar as a 'large period style drawing room ... the hugh
windows of which allow sweeping views across the great expanse of the
Severn Estuary'.

A picnic below the Severn Bridge Hotel in the 1920s

Severn Bridge House (once Hotel) in 2003

Near Severn Bridge House at Purton are the remains of a viaduct — a remnant of a failed 1830s dream to link central Forest coalfields to the Severn. The project was never completed, but in 2003 the *Forester* reported that local heritage campaigners plan to preserve the ivy clad monument.

From Etloe a narrow cul-de-sac leads down to Gatcombe, where a delightful cluster of old houses overlook the Severn flowing on the other side of the South Wales Railway. Gatcombe was once a port for shipping timber and an important fishing centre before the railway was constructed in 1851. In the past, two of the houses were inns with names associated with the river. The **Sloop**, on the east side of the inlet, is known

The one-time Sloop at Gatcombe on the right

as Drake's House because of a tradition that Sir Francis Drake visited Gatcombe. The inn was originally called the **Gatcombe Boat** when it was kept by Richard Caple in 1763. Its name was changed to the **Sloop** in the early 19th century. In 1843 the 'Well-Frequented Inn Called The Sloop' was for sale as part of the Hagloe and Poulton Court Estates, and was acquired by one of the mortgages, Nathaniel Morgan, from Ross on Wye. He resold the estate to the Crown Commissioners in 1853, and from 1863 Mrs. Maria Wiggell kept the **Sloop** until it closed as an inn around 1880.

On the west side of the Gatcombe creek in the early 19th century was another inn called the **Ship**. The manor court was held there in 1821, which gave its name to the Court House after it had closed after 1840. The **Ship Public House**, is shown on the tithe map of Awre parish but this leads to some confusion as it indicates a more southerly site.

Returning to Etloe, a twisting lane leads past Poulton Farm, a former beer house known as the **Poulton Inn,** kept by James Higgs for several decades from the last quarter of the 19th century. At Awre, a small village situated in a large loop of the river Severn, a remote country inn still survives to serve the local community. The **Red Hart** is housed in a building dating from the 17th century, and was recorded as an inn from at least 1796. It was kept by various members of the Awre family for a lengthy period, with a gap of a few years at the turn of the 19th century when Samuel Pearce was behind the bar.

In 1975 George and Roma Price advertised the **Red Hart** as a place to 'Wine and Dine in the Friendly, Quiet Atmosphere of the Old Country Inn'. In 1977, during their occupancy, members of the Gloucester Diving School investigated the stone-lined well one July evening. The local press reported that the divers 'found the old well was 29ft. 6ins. deep by 3ft. across and belled out' at its foot. At the bottom 'we got down into the silt and discovered some old coins, part of an old water pump, and some building materials'. Jon Hurley, visiting in 1981, described the building as 'an old, rambling, and nicely restored inn, with a deep well set in the middle of the bar'.

The **Red Hart** is still a thriving local pub offering a good selection of beers, good food and decent wines in a relaxing and friendly atmosphere.

On the north side of this loop of the Severn there was an inn called the **Three Doves** which existed in 1824, and a public house was open in 1840 at Hanstalls, now the Priory. Although a pub called the Two Doves has been recorded, the **Three Doves** seems to be a unique inn sign. Birds and animals were popular signs, with the majority often stemming from coats of arms associated with prominent local families.

The Red Hart at Awre

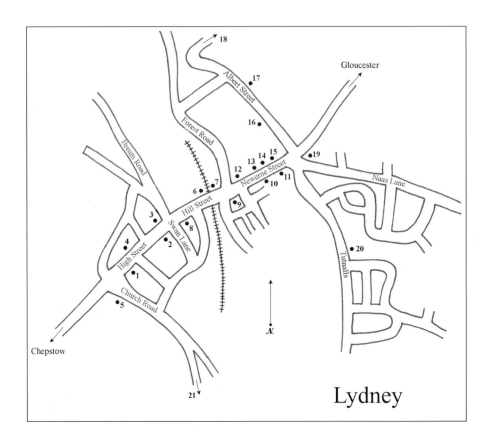

Lydney

1. Feathers / Plume of Feathers
2. Queen's Head
3. Foresters
4. King's Head
5. **Cross Keys**
6. Railway / Ship
7. Rifleman's Arms
8. **King's Bar**
9. **Swan**
10. **Harry's Bar**
11. Bridge
12. White Horse (?)

13. Fleece
14. **Annexe**
15. Royal Albert / Prince Albert
16. Step-a-side
17. Moulders Arms
18. **Severn View**
19. **Greyhound**
20. **Highland**
21. Railway Hotel
    Red Lion (?)
    True Heart (?)

Lydney, showing the positions of pubs.
Those open in 2004 are shown in bold.
Those whose precise positions are uncertain are shown with (?)

CHAPTER TWELVE

Lydney

Now that the present A48 snakes around Lydney, the visitor travelling from Gloucester to South Wales is unaware of the town which claims to be the 'southern gateway to the Royal Forest of Dean'. In 1824 Charles Heath from Monmouth was impressed with the riverside at 'Lidney':

> whose fertile and extensive shores, called the *Salt Marshes,* are particularly undistinguished for the depasturing of horses and cattle; and very extensive iron works, with a manufactory for tin plates, is carried on here, by Mr. James.
>
> Since the tram road has been laid down, through the Forest of Dean, a large BASIN has been built, and a commodious wharf formed, for the shipping of COALS, large quantities of which are sent from hence to Bristol, with other productions of the district; and trading vessels sail as regularly and as frequently from hence to that city, as from any other of the adjoining ports on this river.

A guide book of the 1930s emphasises the importance of the railways including 'The G.W.R. main line Paddington to south Wales' and the 'connection with L.M.S. main line services by the Severn and Wye Railway'. The main Gloucester to South Wales road then passed through the town centre, which was a 'quite a busy little town with one main shopping street and the rest of the town nearly all well built modern houses'. The Bathurst Park provided 'a pleasant retreat for resident and visitor' when Lydney had the reputation for being 'the smallest port in Britain', with coal and other products from the Forest 'shipped at its small dock'.

Fourteen of the older inns were splendidly summarised by John Camm:

> A man called **Albert**, who was a **Rifleman** in the **Foresters**, set off with his **Fleece** on his back and his **Greyhound** at his heels, crossed the **Bridge** over the **Railway**, and saw a young **Swan**. He made a quick **Step-a-side** and took a shot, but only made the **Feathers** fly. The **Queen**, when she heard this, was very **Cross** and with her **Keys**, locked him in a tower, where he had a perfect **Severn View**.

Despite the re-routing of the A48, a constant stream of traffic still follows the old road through the town centre, so the best way to explore Lydney is to follow a self-guided Town Walk produced in 1997 by the Forest of Dean Local History Society. Apparently Lydney and Newerne were originally two separate settlements that grew in size to form the town of Lydney. Its past industries, associated with mining and iron working, and its good communications by road, river and rail, led to a degree of prosperity in the 19th century. In the 1850s Lydney's inhabitants were mainly employed in tinplating and ironmaking, or as tradesman, craftsmen, shopkeepers, inn keepers and beer retailers. Professional men were represented together with the proprietors of collieries and trading companies, and stone and coal merchants. In 1856 there were three innkeepers and six beer retailers recorded in Lydney, a number that more than doubled throughout the remainder of the century.

In the early 18th century the Bathurst family acquired the Lydney Park estate which, according to an 1876 directory, included 'the remains of a Roman Military Station ... and old coins, ancient implements, and the fragments of tessalated pavement have been found at various times'.

The Bathursts and later Bledisloes of Lydney Park played a generous role in the development of the town during the late 19th and early 20th centuries by providing Bathurst Park in 1892, land for the Cottage Hospital in 1909 and four almshouses in 1927. Amongst other properties the Bathursts owned the principal inn which was known by the sign of the **Hand of Feathers** in 1681, the **Plume of Feathers** in the late 18th century, the **Lydney Inn** in 1839 and then the **Feathers** before it was finally demolished in 1999.

An 1885 advertisement for the Feathers

In 1754 John Norton was recorded at the **Lydney Inn**; he was followed by Thomas Holder as tenant of the 'Lydney Inn, stabling, coach house, outbuildings, garden', whilst Elizabeth Holder was living at the malthouse on the opposite side of the road. William Batten was listed at the 'Feathers hotel and posting house' in 1856, and from the mid-1860s until the end of the century the Fisher Barnards kept the inn. In 1881 Samuel Fisher Barnard was the hotel keeper, living with his brother, elderly aunt and unmarried cousin, and his staff consisted of a housekeeper, barmaid, cook, waitress, housemaid, boots, a charwoman, and no doubt others employed in the stableyard.

Between 1860 and 1890 the **Feathers** was used variously as a court house, an Inland Revenue Office, a venue for auction sales of property and a mail coach stop between Coleford and the railway station. It was also used for social and sporting occasions such as the meet of the Newnham Harriers reported in the *Forest Mercury* in March 1884:

> On Friday last these hounds met at the Feathers, Lydney, when fairly good sport was shown. The first move was made towards the low-lying meadows, which, by the by, were extremely deep and boggy, and hardly had the hounds entered the first field ere they hit upon a hare, and rattled her in the direction of Alvington at a pace which, if it had been continued, would have certainly had the effect of considerably thinning the field. However, her course were here lost, and although casts were made, they proved fruitless. A move was then made towards Woolaston Grange, and after running one large ring, the hounds threw up in a plough field, and all efforts to hit her off proved of no avail. The day drawing on a move homeward was made, and almost immediately a couple of hares jumped up in front of the hounds, who pushed one at a sharp pace towards the hills, but there she was lost, owing to the want of scent.

In 1899 the Fisher Barnards gave up the tenancy of the **Feathers**, and finding the right landlord caused some difficulty for Mr. Bathurst as this extract from a letter from the Lydney Park Estate to the agents suggests:

> Dear Sirs,
> As we have not found the class of tenant we desire for the Feathers Hotel, Mr Bathurst is not so particular as to the age of the applicant.

Eventually H.J. Smith took over the running of the hotel, and in November 1899 agreed to purchase all the 'Furniture, Fittings, Trade Fixtures and utensils, Stock-in-trade, Horses, carriages, harness, Stable and out-door effects' from Fisher Barnard. It became apparent that Smith was not a good choice because he only served for a few years. Finally, in 1914, the **Feathers Hotel** was offered for sale as 'Fully Licensed and Occupying the Most Important Position in the Town with Extensive Accommodation, Stabling, etc.'. The High Street hotel consisted of a large bar, bar parlour, private sitting room, reading room, billiard room, private dining room, commercial room, coffee room, market room, kitchen, larder, scullery and wine cellar on the ground floor with a drawing room, ten bedrooms, store room, linen room and closet above. On the second floor there was a spacious club room, a masonic room and five more bedrooms. The basement consisted of beer and wine cellars and at the rear there was an

The 1914 sale notice of the Feathers Hotel

assembly hall, stabling for 12 horses, a harness room, a storeroom formerly used as a brewhouse, four piggeries and a barn.

It appears that the **Feathers** was purchased by the Peoples Refreshment House Association and during the 1920s was managed by Archibald Snow. The Association, which had been established in 1896, was part of a temperance movement which aimed 'to carry on the Business of licensed victuallers, with a view to the encouragement of temperance by reform in the management of Licensed Inns and Canteens'.

After World War Two the **Feathers Hotel** was still 'one of the 160 Licensed Hotels and Inns controlled by the People's Refreshment House Association Ltd.' with 19 bedrooms and a dining room capable of seating a hundred. In an excellent paper on the hotel in the *New Regard,* Keith Walker quoted the notice

Police stationed at the Feathers during the 1926 General Strike
Courtesy Gloucestershire Constabulary

222

Two views of the Feathers Hotel: Top c.1930; Bottom c.1970

that 'With effect from 1st January 1962 all the Association's freehold and leasehold properties be transferred to Charrington & Co. Ltd.' Under the new owners the hotel continued to trade and in 1981 the main bar was 'large and comfortable with a good open fire and plush seating'. Despite winning a 'Welcome Good Food Award' and being 'RAC Recommended' the hotel saw a decline in business during the 1990s. After a major drug investigation and two suspicious fires the **Feathers** finally closed in February 1998, and was sold, demolished and the site redeveloped as part of the supermarket on the south side of Lydney's High Street.

LYDNEY.—THE QUEEN'S HEAD and THE FORESTER'S ARMS.

ALL THAT messuage and Beerhouse TOGETHER with the garden brew-house and premises thereto adjoining and belonging situate in High Street Lydney in the County of Gloucester and known as The Queen's Head AND ALSO ALL THAT messuage and Beerhouse garden and premises situate on the Bream Road Lydney aforesaid and known as The Forester's Arms (except and reserved the upper or northern portion or strip of garden with the shed thereon) All which premises are held for a term of twenty-one years from the twenty-ninth day of September One thousand nine hundred and nineteen at the yearly rent of One Hundred and Forty Pounds payable quarterly on the usual quarter days.

This Lease contains an option for the Lessees at any time during the term on one month's notice in writing to purchase the freehold of the demised premises at the price of Three Thousand Five Hundred Pounds.

The 21-year lease of the Queen's Head and the Forester's Arms.
The total rent was £140; both premises were beer houses

The Queen's Head in the 1970s before demolition

The buildings that once housed the **Queen's Head** and the Anglo Bavarian Brewery in the High Street were also demolished in the late 1990s. The **Queen's Head** was a beer house kept by William Walker during the 1870s and '80s. When it was owned by Joseph Taylor and occupied by Benjamin Biddle in 1903 the inn was leased by Arnold, Perrett & Co., and in 1937 the whole establishment, including 'the garden brew-house and premises' passed to the Cheltenham Original Brewery together with the lease of the **Forester's Arms**. This beer house, also owned by Joseph Taylor in 1903, had stood on the opposite side of the High Street facing Bream Road. David Camm was the tenant in 1903 and Sidney Carpenter was listed there in 1939, but at sometime after that date it was demolished to provide a private car park.

The Forester's before demolition

The **King's Head** was somewhere on the north side of the High Street during the 18th century, but apart from the name little is known of this establishment. Other beer retailers were also recorded in the High Street including Thomas Morgan in 1870 and Louisa Woolley in 1927. High Street was always very busy, and in 1907, apart from the inns, there was also a baker, a boot and shoe maker, a builder, a chemist, two drapers, a glass and china dealer, two grocers, an ironmonger, two painters and plumbers, a tailor, tobacconist, watchmaker, a blacksmith, saddler, refreshment room and the only two solicitors and solitary bank in the town. This must have been very different to the present High Street, dominated by the modern supermarket and its adjacent car parks that overlook a range of older buildings mainly in need of urgent refurbishment.

At the western end of the High Street, at its junction with Church Road, the 14th-century town cross marks the former market place. In Church Road the **Cross Keys** was originally a beer house built on a site purchased by Frederick Hathaway in 1898 and run by the James family. In 1906 the Alton Court Brewery acquired the premises, which passed to West Country Breweries in 1962 and eventually it became a Whitbread pub. It still provides an excellent service to the people of Lydney.

The Cross Keys in 2003

Church Road continues past St. Mary's church with its graceful spire, over the South Wales Railway crossing and along Harbour Road to Cookson Terrace, an unusual row of nine gabled houses built in 1859 by the Severn and Wye Railway Company, and named after Joseph Cookson the chairman of the company. The larger central building once housed the **Railway Hotel**, kept by the Ridlers for at least 60 years from the mid-19th century. Arnold, Perrett & Co. leased the hotel with its 'tap-room outbuildings yard and premises' from the London Midland & Scottish Railway Co. and the Great Western Railway Co. from 1926, at a yearly rent of £130. When Edward Green was the landlord in 1937 the lease passed to the Cheltenham Original

The Railway Hotel was the large central building in the block

Brewery, and it presumably became a Whitbread house before closing around 1970. In the 1930s the **Railway** was frequented by sailors off the Irish boats who 'would go off drinking for the evening either up at the Railway Hotel, then run by Mr. and Mrs. Green, or right into town, staggering back to the docks at 2 or 3 in the morning'.

The Railway Inn in Hill Street about 1900

By 2003 the Railway Inn had become Wong's Takeaway

Lydney High Street leads east into Hill Street, where another **Railway Inn** once existed. In 1839 it was known as the **Ship** and was owned by John Tamplin and occupied by John Smith. By 1848 it had been renamed after the adjacent railway and was for sale by auction as 'All that freehold Messuage and Public House known as the Railway Inn situate at Newerne ... with the Brewhouse Cellar Yard and Garden', and was 'let to William Close at the annual rent of £30'. The **Railway** was licensed as a beer house in 1891 when it was tied to Garton & Co., and in turn was passed to the Anglo Bavarian Brewery Co., Arnold, Perrett & Co., the Cheltenham Original Brewery and then Whitbreads. Before this **Railway Inn** closed in the early 1960s, Bill Page was the tenant offering 'Bed and Breakfast and catering for transport drivers and parties'.

Also on the same north side of Hill Street was a beer house called the **Rifleman's Arms**, presumably named after the Rifle Volunteer Corps. It was kept by Sarah Arman in the 1870s, and from the 1890s passed from the breweries of Gartons, Anglo Bavarian and Arnold, Perrett to the Cheltenham Original Brewery. The **Rifleman's Arms** was demolished in the early 1970s and redeveloped as a row of shops.

On the south side of Hill Street is a modern development that includes the **King's Bar** and a restaurant.

The main street through Lydney continues eastwards, eventually becoming Newerne Street where a number of past and present pubs are situated. On the corner of Newerne Street and Swan Lane is the oldest one, called the **Swan Inn** since at least 1777. In 1839 the 'Swan Inn, outbuildings and garden' was owned by John Eddy and occupied by Jane Hibbs, and in 1856 the maltster, George Courteen, was landlord followed by G. Jones in 1863. During the 1870s and '80s William Mallard was licensee, and the inn was taken over by Messrs. Godsell & Sons before the end of the 19th century.

At the beginning of the 20th century the **Swan** was described as a 'Family and Commercial Posting House'. It became a more formal hotel when Alfred Prosser was there in the 1920s. This was about the time that the

The Rifleman's Arms before closure in the 1950s

The King's Bar and Bistro, a modern development in Lydney

SWAN HOTEL,

.. LYDNEY ..

Family & Commercial Posting House.

Proprietor: J. FRANCIS B. SMITH,

Wine and Spirit Merchant.

Agent for Godsell and Sons' noted Bitter Ale and Stout.

GEORGE L. WOOLES,

GENERAL CONTRACTOR. & **LYDNEY, Glos.**

*Roofing, Plastering, Colouring, Painting
and Sanitary Work.*

ESTIMATES GIVEN FOR ALL BRANCHES OF THE BUILDING TRADE.

DEALER IN MATERIALS.   *All Work personally attended to.*

A 1904 advertisement for the Swan at Lydney

The Swan in 2003

Stroud Brewery took over this Godsell house which then passed to West Country Breweries in 1962. Keith and Ruth Eastwood ran the **Swan Hotel** in the 1970s, and during the Medieval Fair held in the town in 1988 the inn offered a 'Special menu served lunch time and evening'. As a free house, the **Swan** was described by Jon Hurley in 1991 as 'a bit spartan but with a large busy public bar and a couple of quieter rooms where most of the town's young ladies seem to take lunch'.

The 1995 *Town Guide* featured an advert for the **Swan Hotel** in which it was described as a '200 year old Coaching Inn which features strongly in the history of Lydney'.

Not far from the Swan, on the same side of the street, a flight of steps leads to **Harry's Bar** set in a modern block of shops.

Also on the south side of Newerne Street is an attractive row of buildings that

Harry's Bar in 2003

THE BRIDGE INN, Freehold and Fully Licensed

LYDNEY, GLOS.

Attractive Stone-built Premises with Rough Cast, occupying an important Site in this busy town, with draw up, comprising :—

FIRST FLOOR :—Four Bed Rooms, Store Room, Good Club Room with Separate Approach from Yard.

GROUND FLOOR :—Bar, Private Ditto, Smoke and Tap Room, Sitting Room, Store Cupboard, Two Beer Stores, one with Loft over, Kitchen.

IN REAR :—Small Garden, Pig Cot, Two W.C.'s, and Urinal, Two-stall Stable, etc.

The Property is of Freehold Tenure and let to Mr. A. G. Nelmes, a tenant of about 38 years' standing, on Quarterly Tenancy at

Per £80. Ann.

This Rent includes a CORRUGATED-IRON BUILT GYMNASIUM with brick foundation and match boarding interior, with Three Baths (h. and c.), Range of Eight Lavatory Basins, W.C., Boiler House, etc.

Tithe Rent Charge, 1s. 4d. per Annum. Land Tax, 21s. 10d. per Annum. Compensation Charge, £ Contribution by Brewery towards increased Licence Duty, £2 10s.

Sale details of the Bridge Inn in 1923

was formerly the **Bridge Inn**, built in 1844 and named after the bridge that crosses the river Lyd. William Saunders, who was a butcher in 1856, became the beer retailer there by 1863, and had extended his business by 1876 when he was listed as a 'butcher and haulier'. Albert Nelmes, who had taken over by the mid-1880s, was an experienced publican who had previously run the **White Horse**, an inn at the lower end of Newerne Street. During Albert's long tenure of over 50 years the **Bridge** was acquired by Wintle's Forest Brewery at Mitcheldean.

When Albert was at the **Bridge**, the rough-cast premises consisted of two bars, a smoke and tap room, a sitting room and two beer stores on the ground floor. On the first floor there were four bedrooms, a store room, and a club room with a separate entrance from the yard. Neil Parkhouse in his *Glance Back at Lydney*, published in 1998, recalled Nelmes' tenure when for decades the inn had been the headquarters of both the Lydney Rugby Club and the Football Club. Albert Nelmes also arranged charabanc outings for

The Bridge Inn in 1970

232

By 2003 the old Bridge Inn was host to several shops

his regulars and the field next to the pub was used for the annual Lydney Fair which, according to Parkhouse included:

> boxing booths, where you could win a sovereign by going three rounds with the 'champion' ... Lord Sanger's circus also used to set up the field and Harold [Albert Nelmes' son] later recalled the day his father accepted a challenge to be shaved in the lion's den.

After Albert's death in 1935 his wife Julie, took over the licence. The inn included 'a corrugated-iron built gymnasium with brick foundation and matchboarded interior with three baths range of eight lavatory basins W.C. boiler house etc.' The **Bridge** was taken over by the Cheltenham Original Brewery in 1937 and, after passing to Whitbreads, was closed as a pub in 1971.

On the north side of Newerne Street are Fleece Chambers, which once housed the **Fleece Inn**, licensed in 1863 to sell 'Beer, Ale and Porter, Cider and Perry, by retail, in order that it may be consumed in the said Dwelling-house of the said Matilda Davies'. In 1885 Emma Davies was the beer retailer and continued there into the 20th century. Tom Pollard was listed at the **Fleece** in 1927, and in 1935 Reginald Brown was the landlord. This was when Arnold, Perrett owned 'The Fleece Inn ... with the brewhouse cellars gardens and all outbuildings and appurtenances thereunto belonging'. Two

LYDNEY.—THE FLEECE INN.

ALL THAT messuage or Inn known as The Fleece Inn situate and being Numbers 27 and 29 Newerne Street in the Parish of Lydney in the County of Gloucester with the brewhouse cellars gardens and all outbuildings and appur-tenances thereunto belonging TOGETHER with the site thereof and the land occupied therewith.

Sale of the Fleece in 1937

The Fleece in the 1960s

years later it was acquired by the Cheltenham Original Brewery and in the 1970s it finally closed its doors as a licensed house and the building has since been used for other purposes, including a Red Cross Shop.

The Fleece in retirement

Next to a wine and spirit merchant in Newerne Street is the **Annexe Inn**, a modern-looking bar and restaurant with an unusual name that suggests that it was once a supplementary building attached to a main one. In 1981 Jon Hurley found the **Annexe** to be a 'place one could take that very pernickety maiden aunt,

The Annexe Inn in Newerne Street in 2003

A 3d. token from the Royal Albert c.1870

or anyone else for that matter'. The **Annexe** inn continues to serve a wide variety of customers in 2004.

The last pub known to have existed in Newerne Street was the **Royal Albert** which had stood on the corner with Albert Street before it was severely damaged by a lorry loaded with steel in the late 1960s, and never re-opened. The story is told in the *Forester* under a heading 'Lorry makes room at Inn':

> 'There's that cat again', said Mrs. Len Smith the licensee of the Royal Albert Inn, Lydney to her husband early on Monday morning when she heard a noise she described as 'like bottles smashing' from one end of the pub.
> Mr. Smith, who was about to drink a last cup of tea before going to bed, got up to see if the cat had caused the row and found a seven ton lorry instead.
> 'I tore into the bar', Mr. Smith said, 'where there was one complete fog of dust; I couldn't see anything. I switched the light on and there, jutting some feet into the room, was the tail of a lorry with its rear lights still on. The room was half filled with concrete, the fireplace had come away from the wall, chairs were crushed and a window was gone'.

*A 1904 advertisement for the Royal Albert together with one
for Mr. Jones, General Merchants, who also arranged
shipping and transport throughout the Forest and across the Severn*

Outside he found the driver of the lorry, Constantine Daniel Illidge of Newport, badly shaken but unhurt. His eight-wheeled diesel vehicle had managed to climb 50 yards up Highfield Hill before it ran back. Mr. Illidge had tried unsuccessfully to steer it into Albert Street and the seven ton 15 hundredweight lorry with its load of 13 tons of steel crashed into the corner of the Royal Albert at the junction of Albert and Newerne Streets.

The Royal Albert on the right in Newerne Street about 1920

The **Royal Albert** of 1851 was called simply the **Albert** in 1885 and the **Prince Albert** in 1907. Its long list of landlords included E. Pewtner, James Howells (a mason), John Ellaway, George Wooles, George James, Elsie Thomas, Walter Dunfold and William Gardiner. As an Alton Court Brewery pub, the 'Royal Albert Inn with the out-buildings yard and garden' passed to West Country Breweries in 1962 before it was demolished and the site redeveloped to provide shopping units.

Albert Street leads up to Primrose Hill and then into the Forest. On the west side of the street, a building displays a faded inscription confirming its former use as the **Step-Aside Inn** of the 1880s. In 1891 John Camm was the occupier of the beer house, which was owned by Mary Atkinson and leased to Samuel Barnard of the **Feathers** at Lydney. During the 1920s and '30s John Sandford kept the inn which had been acquired by Arnold, Perrett & Co. and taken over by the Cheltenham Original Brewery in 1937, and since then has closed.

On the opposite side of Albert Street in Queen Street was another beer house kept by William Halford in the 1870s. It was briefly known as the

237

Moulders Arms, named after the men who made the moulds used in iron casting.

Primrose Hill is situated high above Middle Forge, now long since dis-used and redeveloped. A footpath follows the course of an ancient hollow-way across the river Lyd where a sluice indicates the start of 'The Cut' — a very narrow canal built in the 1780s to provide a head of water for the Lower Forge which then became the tinplate

Top: The Step-Aside Inn in 1930
Below: The inn in 2003, long after closure

238

The Dean Forest Railway, 2003

works. The footpath then crosses the track of the horse-drawn tramroad of 1813, which was converted to the Severn and Wye Railway in 1868. The line closed in 1976, but was purchased by the Dean Forest Railway Company in 1983 and re-opened as 'the Friendly Forest Line — recreating the railway heritage of the Royal Forest of Dean'. Just north of Middle Forge is the Dean Forest Railway's picnic site, station, museum and cafe at Norchard. The smell and sight of steam and the sound of the train's hooter provide a pleasant and nostalgic atmosphere to Lydney on steam days.

Panoramic views of the Severn can be admired from the top of Primrose Hill, which developed into a long roadside settlement when cottages were built for industrial workers in the 1870s. To cater for the growing number of local inhabitants, John Stephens opened a beer house which became known as the **Severn View**. It was purchased by Arnold & Co. in 1887 and became

The Severn View in 2003

The Greyhound in 2003

The Greyhound sign

an Arnold, Perrett house by the end of the century. In 1903 Edwin Thomas was the tenant followed by Richard Wilkins during the 1920s and '30s until Harry Sandford took over 'All that messauge or Inn known as The Severn View Inn situate at Allaston Common ... with the cottage outbuildings and appurtenances thereunto belonging'.

The inn was taken over by the Cheltenham Original Brewery in 1937 and eventually became 'one of seven Whitbread pubs in Lydney'. In the 1980s it offered a 'cosy atmosphere'; in the 1990s it was 'worth a visit' with 'food available', and in 2004 the **Severn View** was still open for customers.

From the eastern end of Newerne Street two roads lead to Lydney's southern suburbs at Tutnalls and along Nass Lane. At the junction on Hams Road is the existing **Greyhound** which has blossomed from the mid-19th century beer house that was kept by the Wooles family and owned by Frederick Hathaway, a wine and spirit merchant. James Parry was there during the 1920s and '30s. When Arnold, Perrett & Co. acquired the property in 1937 it included the inn and also 'all those two several messuages or dwellinghouses with the gardens and all outbuildings and appurtenances thereunto belonging and adjoining ... [the] Inn and premises on the east thereof ... known as Numbers 4 and 6 Tuthill Street'.

The Highland Inn in 2003

The sign of this pub is misleading as it depicts a sailing ship, not a dog, heraldic crest or mail coach of that name, so it may represent Lydney's maritime connections. Similar to other Arnold, Perrett properties the **Greyhound** passed to Whitbread and in 1991 was 'a snug, well run little local with smoke stained ceiling, gas fire, neat tables and chairs, wood panelling [and] a couple of beams'.

Further south at Tutnalls is the **Highland Inn**, which does not appear to have been a pub until recent times. In 1988 it was offering 'Live entertainment with Gordon and his guests' and this small suburban pub was still open in 2004.

The last two pubs known to have existed in Lydney cannot be located. There was a **Red Lion**, kept by Thomas Curtis in 1879, and a **True Heart**, run by the Birks during the 1870s. Frederick Hathaway described as a chemist and druggist was also an agent for W.A. Gilbey and a wine and spirit merchant in the High Street from around 1876 to 1903.

By 2002 real ales, cider and local wines were for sale at Taurus Crafts in Lydney Park. The *Forester* reported that Freeminers, Wickwar and Wye Valley beers, Three Choirs, Compton Green and Kent's Green wines together with a range of traditional ciders were on sale at the craft centre shop called Random Shot named after an 'old coal mine of the same name, opened in 1850' near Pillowell in the Forest. In 2004 the restaurant was licensed and Forest of Dean Apple Juice and Severnside Cider were available in the shop.

There was an active temperance movement in Lydney that held a 'most successful Temperance meeting in the Alexandra Hall, Lydney in 1901, when addresses were given by the Revs. E. Davis and J. Middleton', and William Pointer provided facilities for the temperate drinker. In 1876 he ran an eating-house in the High Street and in 1879, having become a quarry owner, kept a temperance hotel which became known as a temperance refreshment house in 1885. Although Mr. Pointer was not trading in 1906, two other refreshment rooms were open in the High Street in Lydney. Despite these attempts to reduce drunkenness, many examples were reported in the local newspapers during the late 19th and early 20th centuries.

Thus in 1891 Frederick Jones, a hotel waiter at the **Feathers** was summoned for drunkenness, but he did not turn up at the court, was turned out of the hotel and charged 5s. and 9s. costs. At the same hearing in 1901 John Saunders, a drayman, was found drunk and disorderly and using bad language in the High Street, and Clara Fletcher, an old offender at Lydney, was heard for similar offences in Albert Street. She did not appear at court and was fined 20s. plus 9s. costs and one month's hard labour, whereas Saunders only paid 2s 6d. plus the same costs. Later that year Thomas Cox, a drover of no fixed abode was charged with the theft of a football suit which he had been seen with at the **Railway Inn**. When charged he replied 'I did not intend to steal it and was sober at the time', but as he had 18 previous convictions he was sent to prison for three months. Other cases in 1903 included Harry Martin of Lydney, a waterman, who was fined 20s. and costs for being 'very drunk and shouting', and William Welch, a labourer from Newport working at Lydney, who was 'charged on remand with drunkenness'. He pleaded guilty and was fined 5s. plus 7s. costs.

CHAPTER THIRTEEN

Aylburton, Alvington, Woolaston & Tidenham

From Lydbrook, the busy A48 closely follows the river Severn and skirts the southern boundary of the Forest of Dean through the parishes of Aylburton, Alvington, Woolaston and Tidenham, before crossing the river Wye into South Wales at Chepstow. This closely resembles the route turnpiked by the Cheptow Trustees in 1758 together with a branch road from Tutshill to Beachley and the Old Passage across the Severn. Since then, the main road has been widened and straightened, and the road to Beachley has become less important following the construction of the Severn road bridge in the late 1960s. The South Wales Railway from Gloucester, constructed in 1851, also follows a similar route, and again crosses the Wye at Chepstow.

Aylburton lies on the edge of Lydney Park and is an attractive village now divided by the fast-flowing A48, but in the less noisy days of the 1950s it was described in a local guide as a parish consisting of:

> A long ridge about a mile wide, separated from Lydney by the Park Brook, and from Alvington by the Ferneyley Brook, the outline of the parish bearing a striking resemblance to the map of Italy ... in the parish itself is a small factory making pipe laggings, in what was formerly a bacon factory, and a clothing factory in what was originally a malt house. Many of the village men are keen spare-time Severn fishermen ...

The chapel of ease at Aylburton originally stood at Chapel Hill on the road leading to the common, but in the mid-19th century it was dismantled and rebuilt at a 'lower and more convenient site' on the lane now known as Church Road. The 14th-century village cross was moved to its present site in the early 1960s when it was considered to be a traffic hazard. The cross was the outdoor meeting place of the Wesleyans in 1910; they then used the Malt House until their chapel was built in 1915. Overlooking the cross was one of the two pubs still open in 2004.

The Cross at Aylburton about 1950

In the High Street the **Cross Inn** is housed in a building which appears to date from an earlier period than its establishment as an inn in the 1860s. At this time it was owned and occupied by the beer retailer, John Rowland, who was followed by Robert Hoskins during the 1870s. In 1903 the **Cross** was tied to Godsell & Sons who were later taken over by the Stroud Brewery. George Nelmes served behind the bar for over 20 years at the beginning of the 20th century, and it was kept by Mr. & Mrs. Charles Edwards in 1962 when 'All that messuage or Inn in the parish of Aylburton known as the Cross Inn with the cottage outbuildings and land thereto adjoining' passed to West Country Breweries, together with 'The Almshouses High Street' adjoining

The Cross in 2003

244

the **Cross** and 'Land at High Street' which had been conveyed to the Stroud Brewery in 1950 from the Lydney Park Estate.

The other pub that still remains at Aylburton is the **George**, which claims to date from 1843 and was certainly open in 1876 and run for a long period by the Birks family. They were followed by Henry and then Mabel Davies who sold the inn to the Alton Court Brewery in 1928. The Ross based brewery was taken over by West Country Breweries in 1962 and passed onto Whitbreads. At the beginning of the 21st century it was advertised as having 'Probably the Best Real Ale in the Forest'.

The George at Aylburton in 2003

The **Cross** and the **George** emerged as pubs soon after the closure of an earlier inn called the **Hare and Hound** where a Friendly Society met in the 1790s. In 1840 the 'Hare & Hound Inn, stabling, gardens, yards' was owned by Charles Bathurst and tenanted to Richard Evans. The last innkeeper appears to have been Andrew Young, who was recorded there in 1856 and 1863, although the building was not demolished until the mid-20th century.

The **Butcher's Arms** served as a beer house for a brief period in the late 19th century. It was kept by Charles Price in 1891 and James Hopkins in 1903, and may have been the unnamed beer house run by John Hopkins in the 1870s. The only other known pub at Aylburton was the **Traveller's Rest** or **Besom**, situated on the lower common. In the 1870s and 1880s the beer retailer was Thomas James followed by William Jones, who kept the inn for Charles Garton & Co. in 1891. Gartons were taken over by the Anglo

The Besom sign c.1980

Bavarian Company which passed to Arnold, Perrett then to the Cheltenham Original Brewery in 1937 when Charles Davies was the landlord. In 2002 the *Forester* reported that 'The Besom or Traveller's Rest public house was a 19th-century hostelry where the last pint was pulled in 1989'. It was also reported that on the common 'in the autumn the mobile cider press would arrive to convert the fruit of the orchard into alcoholic beverage'. The **Besom** is named after a bunch of sticks, tied together to form a broom, and usually made by gypsies. Its alternative name, The **Traveller's Rest**, was a popular sign used in remote areas indicating an inn that could provide a resting place for travellers.

From Aylburton the present A48 by-passes an original awkward bend in the road at Sandford, and then continues to Alvington, described in 1894 as a ' village and parish on the west bank of the river Severn and on the high road from Newnham to Chepstow, two miles north from Woolaston station on the Gloucester and South Wales section of the Great Western Railway'. At that date there was a miller, wheelwright, carpenter, blacksmith, grocer, gardener, two shopkeepers, several farmers, a beer retailer at the **Blacksmith's Arms**, and a publican at the **Globe**. There was also an innkeeper at the **Swan**, which despite boundary changes made in 1935, is in Woolaston parish, but is commonly known as the **Swan** at Alvington. In 1813 there was a malthouse in Alvington, and in 1879 Taylor & Co. were brewers and beer dealers at Sandford. From the beginning of the 20th century the village was attracting tourists with guest houses, boarding houses and a tea garden.

All the above-named pubs still line the A48 and cannot be missed. The **Globe**, at the crossroads, dates from at least 1805 when a Friendly Society met there. In 1863 R. Ebbon ran the inn followed by the Wintours, who kept the inn for a lengthy period from the 1880s, and were still there in 1907 when a directory entry described it as having 'stabling, accommodation for cyclists

The Globe at Alvington in 2003

and motor'. The **Globe** is a fairly common sign, originating in Portugal on taverns selling the country's wines. The name was also used by a landlord to suggest they he was a 'man of the world' who had decided to end his days as an innkeeper. The inn continues to serve passing trade as well as locals.

A beer retailer was recorded at Alvington in 1856, who may have been trading from the beer house later known as the **Blacksmith's Arms**, which stands next to the old Smithy on the north side of the main street. Phoebe

The Blacksmith's Arms in 2003

The lofty Swan in 2003

Thorne was the beer retailer there in 1885 and in 1891, when she was recorded as the owner and occupier. Around 1927 Phoebe was followed by Albert Thorne senior who was still there in 1939. The **Blacksmith's** caught the attention of Jon Hurley, who noted in his *Pub Guide* published in 1991: 'This is a surprise, a stone terraced cottage pub filled to the beams with atmosphere and offering among other things real Indian cuisine'.

A little further south-west, standing at right angles to the main road, is the lofty **Swan** overlooking a pleasant green beside the Cone brook which in the past powered many forges, paper mills and corn mills. The **Swan** was well placed to cater for travellers on the Gloucester to South Wales road and for the local mill workers. It was well-established by 1813 and since then has been run by a number of publicans including John James in 1856, James Williams (who was also a fisherman) in 1863, and Edward Davis in 1894. In 1901 the licence was transferred to Davis's wife because 'he was killed at the front' in the Boer War. Soon afterwards William Estcourt took over and continued there until the 1930s. Throughout the 1980s and '90s the **Swan**, 'a comfortable elevated pub', enjoyed a good reputation for food and beers. With a change of tenancy in June 2003, its past reputation has been retained. The **Swan** has been in use as an inn sign since the 14th century, either referring to the majestic bird or to a local coat of arms. In this case the inn was probably named after the swans which may have been seen on the Cone brook or on the nearby ponds that once served the paper mills.

248

From Alvington the A48 proceeds in a westerly direction to Woolaston, which, apart from the business of the main road, is still similar to the description in an official guide of the 1950s:

> Woolaston is a scattered village on both sides of the main Gloucester-Chepstow road. The remains of a Roman Camp have been found at Plusterwine ... The Norman St. Andrew's Church has an impressive tower containing five bells, and was restored in 1859 and 1903.

The Netherwood Inn in 2003

Along a minor road that leads north into the Forest there are two existing pubs at Netherend and Woolaston Common. The **Netherwood Inn** is a twin-gabled stone and brick building which opened as a beer house around 1870. In 1879 Frederick Lee was the beer retailer, and at the end of the 19th century Henry Clutterbuck was the tenant of the owner, Elizabeth Harris. It appears that James Nelmes was there in 1927, which was around the time that Arnold. Perrett owned the pub before selling to the Cheltenham Original Brewery in 1937. At that time the inn garden and orchard contained altogether two acres or thereabouts.

Prettily situated at Woolaston Common is the **Rising Sun**, originally a beer house kept by James Jones in 1856 and 1863. During the 1870s John Davis ran the inn, followed by the Biddle family from around 1903 until the late 1930s. The present landlord has served the pub well during the last 25 years by serving good food and real ale. Discovered by Jon Hurley in the late 1970s for his *Forest of Dean Pub*

The sun even rises on the napkin

Jon Hurley revisiting the Rising Sun at Woolaston Common in 2003

Guide, he wrote about the 'energetic young couple who obviously know what the public want', They are still there and still energetic, running the **Rising Sun** in the 21st century.

Until around 1906 there was another beer house on the opposite side of the road, which was marked on the 1879 Ordnance Survey map as the **Carpenter's Arms**, but is now a private dwelling. It was owned and occupied by William Tudor until it closed. Another beer house was recorded on the common in the 1860s and '70s, but its name is not known.

The A48 leads through Woolaston and a small hamlet at Brookend where a number of interesting buildings are sited including the Tan House and Posssession House, both dating from the 17th century, and three former inns which share a confusing and complicated history. The least interesting is a fairly modern building set back from the main road on the north side, and indicated by an empty framed sign. This was the new **Woolaston Inn** which was opened by the Stroud Brewery in 1961, to replace an earlier inn on the opposite side of the road that they had closed, and sold to West Country Breweries a year later. In 1984 the *Guide to Real Ale in Gloucestershire* described the **Woolaston Inn** as a pub with a 'plain exterior' but with an 'accent on food'. By 1991 this had become a Whitbread pub and later, before it finally closed, Jon Hurley wrote:

A large roadside inn exulting in the new broom treatment. New management have taken the old place by the scruff of the neck and with brewery money have transformed it into an attractive pub with new furniture, carpets and a plethora of prints which now adorn spacious walls. Vivaldi provided the up-market music. A raised area one end of the large lounge has a brick built log fire and it is a cosy corner on a winter's night.

The later Woolaston Inn is now closed

All was in vain and the inn, the second of that name, is now closed.

The much earlier **Woolaston Inn**, now called Brookend House, stands on the opposite side of the main road on the corner of Station Road. It was originally called the **Duke's Head** and was owned by Edmund Woodruffe in 1800. The remaining stone gate posts bear a date of 1713 and the initials of this family. Some time between 1841 and 1856 it was renamed the **Queen's Head** by Richard Tamplin, but from 1863 it took the name of the **Woolaston Inn**. By 1903, Ind Coope & Co. had acquired the inn which was then tenanted by Henry Clutterbuck. In 1926 the old inn passed to the Stroud Brewery, and in 1935 Bert Pyne was the publican. In 1961 the old **Woolaston** was closed by the brewery but remained their property, being sold to West Country Breweries in 1962 as a 'messuage or dwellinghouse formerly an Inn known as the Woolaston Inn and the outbuildings erected thereon'.

Another old inn recorded at Brookend was housed in a late-18th-century building, now known as Lansdown House, situated on the north side of the Gloucester to Chepstow road at one time adjacent to a smithy where carriage, cart and riding horses could be conveniently shod while the drivers and riders enjoyed the hospitality of the inn. It was called the **Duke of Beaufort's Head** in 1772 and probably replaced an earlier inn of 1685 known by the sign of **Worcester's Head**. From the early 19th century it was firmly established as the more anonymous **Old Duke's Head**. It appears that the butcher, William Fletcher, kept the **Old Duke's Head** from around 1856 to 1879 when George Wintle took over. From thereon it was just known as the **Duke's Head**, as the other one of that name had been renamed. During the 1890s Thomas English ran the inn for Samuel Barnard whose company was taken over by Arnold, Perrett at the beginning of the 20th century, but it closed shortly afterwards,

The one-time Duke's Head

with Charles Madgwick serving as the last landlord in 1906.

The were many 'Duke's Head's' around the country. Most had several name changes to honour whichever hero was currently in the news. The late17th-century Worcester was almost certainly the second Marquess who sided with the king during the Civbil War. This resilted in exile in France and imprisonment in the Tower, but a portion of his vast estates was recovered at the Restoration. He was also an inventor and is accredited with the invention of the steam water pump. By the mid-18th century he was largely forgotten and replaced on the inn sign by the Duke of Beaufort. The 8th Duke was a famous sportsman, Badminton House in Gloucestershire being the family residence.

Growing apples for cider making was important in Woolaston from as far back as 1286 when it was recorded that four casks of cider were produced. Most of the larger farms and some smaller cottages had their own cider mills until the end of the 19th century, but by 1939 there was only one portable cider mill in use, based at Luggs Cross, although Dorothy Holmes wrote in her *Severn, Wye & Forest of Dean* published in 1945 that at the Grange 'The chapel has had another storey inserted, and the old crypt is now a cider store'.

According to local tradition the commonest criminal offence in Woolaston was 'selling cider without a licence'. In 1811 James Harris, a miller, was convicted, and although this was his first known offence he was fined six guineas. It was also unlawful to sell beer without a licence, as witnessed by George Davis and Lewis Jenkins in 1660 when they were both heavily fined for keeping alehouses in Woolaston without a licence; a similar case was reported in 1772.

At Tidenham, the road and rail routes from Gloucester to South Wales meet to cross the river Wye at Tutshill, and further south the rivers Wye and Severn unite at Beachley after long and very different journeys from Plynlimon in mid-Wales. Although Beachley was formed into a separate ecclesiastical parish in 1850, it is nevertheless described as included with Tidenham as an uniquely positioned parish in the 1950s *Lydney & District Guide:*

Tidenham parish forms a peninsula of the Forest of Dean, bounded on one side by the Severn, and on the other by the Wye; it is seven miles long, and five miles wide at its broadest point.

Remains of the great dyke built by Offa in the 8th century can be investigated by following the Offa's Dyke Path, which offers stunning views of the Wye Valley, whilst the Gloucestershire Way long distance path provides splendid views of the Severn.

With the growing importance of the passage across the Severn from Beachley, the turnpiking of the road from Gloucester to Chepstow in 1758, the opening of the South Wales Railway in 1851 and the Wye Valley line in 1876, it is not surprising that Tidenham with its pleasant situation grew and developed into a popular place to reside. The 1891 population of 1,736 was served by a police station, three post offices, several local and private schools and a railway station. Apart from the 'Private Residents' living in villas and picturesque dwellings, the majority of the population were farmers with others employed as blacksmiths, builders, hauliers, shopkeepers, carpenters, stone merchants, beer retailers and innkeepers.

Travelling from Woolaston along the present A48 the hamlets of Stroat and Wibdon are hardly noticeable, but at one time were were small self-contained settlements with shops, tradesmen and one inn. At Stroat the **George**, later known as the **George and Dragon**, stood on the main road opposite Stroat House. It was first recorded in 1744, was used as a meeting place by the Tidenham manor court, and served travellers and the local community until its closure around 1900. During the 1860s and '70s Abraham Turner kept the inn and James Lewis, listed there in 1891, appears to have been the last innkeeper.

About a mile-and-a-half south of Wibdon on the main road was an inn at Churchend called the **Sugar Loaf**, which dated from at least the mid-18th century. It was kept by Charles Young from around 1856 until it closed a decade later. From the A48 a narrow lane leads past Tidenham's 14th-century church and along Netherhope Lane to join the B4228 at Spital Meend. In this area there was a pub called the **Traveller's Rest**, which was open in the early 19th century at about the same time as an otherwise un-named inn at Tidenham Chase. This may have replaced an earlier inn called the **White Hart** which was present in 1584.

A Forest of Dean guide book published in 1975 describes Tidenham Chase 'which the Lords of Chepstow maintained as their as their own hunting preserve' as bearing 'woods of yew, larch and birch that clothe the steep slopes of the Wye Valley'.

From the car park at Tidenham Chase there is a pleasant footpath route leading to the legendary lookout at Devil's Pulpit and offering a memorable view of the Wye Valley and Tintern Abbey. From this scenic site the Offa's Dyke Path leads south above the river through woods, across fields and along lanes to another dramatic view of the Wye. This is known as Wintour's Leap after Sir John Wintour, a Royalist from the Forest of Dean who, it is said, escaped Parliamentary pursuit during the Civil War by riding his horse down the steep cliff and across the Wye to safety. This incredible view may also be accessed from the west side of the B4228 where it meets Donkey Lane at Woodcroft in Tidenham parish.

The Rising Sun at Woodcroft in 2003

At Woodcroft, the neat and tidy **Rising Sun** caters for walkers and visitors, but it originated as a beer house, and was kept by a mason, Francis Tyler, in the late 1880s. He was followed by the Saunders family as tenants of the Tylers by which time the **Rising Sun** was tied to Bristol United Brewery. Later it became a Courage Pub and in 1981 Jon Hurley observed that it was:

> worth a visit, that is if you can find it! Perched high up in the village of Woodcroft ... it is small, oldish and friendly. The main bar ... has an unusual ornament at one end. It is a beautiful half cask which was used by the navy to hold rum in the days 'before the Labour Government stopped it', to quote the landlady. It is inscribed in polished brass letters at least three inches high to the glory of Her Majesty.

Two other beer retailers have been recorded at Woodcroft — William Carlisle in 1859 and James Reece in 1859 and 1863. Reece may have preceded Francis Tyler at the **Rising Sun**. From around 1856 until at least 1863 there was another licensed premises in the Woodcroft area; it was called the **New Inn** and was kept by Edward Chappell. In addition, between 1879 and 1906 William Rowland traded as a beer agent from Woodcroft.

Tutshill was a small place in 1828 when the antiquarian, Charles Heath, approached 'Tuts-Hill Rocks':

> ... from [Chepstow] bridge the visitor will proceed to this eminence, on the Gloucestershire shore of the river. A public way leads to a seat, around which a magnificent Elm Tree spreads its protecting shade; and from it he will enjoy the varied view of the town, castle, river, and country ... The summit is crowned with elegant houses, the residences of persons of fortune, which give it the air of a villa near the metropolis.

From around this time Tutshill began to expand, and by 1863 it was a minor centre with two solicitors, two carpenters and wheelwrights, a butcher, a shopkeeper and a blacksmith, together with a lodging house, beer house and a public house. Tutshill continued to grow during the 20th century with rows of houses built near the railway halt and along the main and minor roads, and has effectively become a suburb of Chepstow. Since the building of a modern bridge over the Wye and the improvements made to the A48 in 1988, Tutshill and Sedbury have become more accessible to Chepstow and its links to the motorway system. In the early 21st century three pubs remain open at Tutshill and Sedbury.

The earliest known pubs in Tutshill and Sedbury appear to have been the **Cock** of 1728 and the **Hope and Anchor** of 1835 when John Kitchen was the landlord. In the 1850s the latter was taken over by Matthew Baker followed by Sarah Baker until it closed shortly after 1863. The **Cross Keys** was open in 1843 as a beer house; it was kept by Robert Loveridge during the 1850s, the Hills from the 1870s to the 1890s, the Kings in the early 20th century and George Jones and George Hutchings in the 1920s and '30s. Fifty years later the **Cross Keys** was an Ansells pub and in 2004 the free house was offering refreshment and accommodation at the junction of the B4228 with the Coleford road.

The Cross Keys at Tutshill in 2003

The Live and Let Live on the Coleford road in 2003

Also at Tutshill is the **Live and Let Live**, which was probably run as a beer house by James Price before the Prichards were listed there in 1879. This family were succeeded by the Carpenters and then the Mayos until at least 1939. As a Bristol United Brewery pub it was taken over by Courage; now as a free house on the Coleford road it provides an alternative drinking den.

It is possible that the beer retailers, James Davis and James Williams recorded in 1835, may have established the last two mentioned pubs.

At Sedbury there is the **Fisherman**, an unexpected find in the midst of a housing estate on the road to Beachley. This modern public house has only been open since 1969. Earlier in the 20th century Herbert Talbot was the proprietor of the **Sedbury Park Hotel**, which was still open in 1945, well before the Severn Bridge was built, as Dorothy Holmes commented on the two routes from Tidenham to Beachley:

> Soon after Tidenhem comes a railway bridge, and a left turn leads to Sedbury Park (now a good hotel), but for cars this is a very winding road, the better way being to keep to the main road to the 'scout' on point duty at a cross roads leading to Chepstow. Turn left here for Sedbury Park and Beachley Reach, where Wye joins Severn, and from thence the splendid little ferry boats take you, car and all, over to Aust, with its lovely red cliffs, on the Bristol side. Quite a delightful trip on a sunny day, and one that need not daunt the most nervous driver, as the sailors are competent and helpful, and a turn-table on the boats simplifies the process of embarking or the reverse.

256

The modern Fisherman at Sedbury in 2003

The crossing, known as the Old Passage, existed here from at least the 12th century and could well have been used by the Romans. By the first quarter of the 19th century steam vessels took coaches across the river, but railway competition eventually caused the ferry to close. The increasing use of the motor car lcd to the reopening of the ferry, which continued in regular use until 1966 when the suspension bridge crossing the Wye and Severn was opened.

The Old Passage about 1830 with the telegraph on the right

For the convenience of ferry passengers at least three inns existed at Beachley in the 18th century. The earliest known one is situated close to the slipway, and is now called the **Old Ferry Inn**, but was recorded as the **Green Dragon** in 1651, and the **Ostrich** in 1728. Due to an increase in travel and transport and the turnpiking of the road to Beachley in the mid-18th century, the old inn was modified and renamed the **Beachley Passage House** to cater for those using this important link in the road network. Illustrations of the late 18th century reveal a large inn, sporting arched windows, pitched roofs and many chimneys on a building standing high above the tidal Severn and reached by a long curved ramp.

In 1827 the 'Capital Posting Inn and Passage House at Beachley', the 'Improved Passage Ferry' and 'Thirty Two Acres of Land' came up for sale, and the particulars claimed that 'Seven Stage Coaches' daily used the crossing including the 'Royal Mail from Bristol and Liverpool'. A year later Charles Heath from Monmouth wrote:

> A spacious and commodious Inn, occupies an easy elevation above the shore of the river; enlivened by an extensive prospect over Gloucestershire, interspersed with towns, villages, churches, and a variety of other interesting objects. Indeed, the pleasantness of the walk, through the finest meads and pasture lands, with the splendid rivers rolling on each side their waters to the ocean, added to its easy distance from Chepstow, renders it an object worthy the stranger's attention. The House is fixed up in the most elegant manner, and visitors will meet with every accommodation, from its present occupier, Mr. Williams. To the premises are attached two gardens, parallel with the course of the Severn, with seats in each, for enjoying their beauties, in which the Church of Oldbury is a prominent feature in this fine picture.

Mr. and Mrs. Williams kept the **Beachley Inn** for many years, and in 1855 the 'state of the premises in a Lease including the outbuildings, farm buildings, ferry and cottages' was carefully examined, and it was estimated that 'the repairs now remaining to be done ... [would cost] £249'. Ann Williams continued to run the inn until at least 1863 when it was known as the **Ferry Hotel**.

With the opening of the Severn and Wye Railway Bridge in 1879 and the Severn Railway Tunnel in 1886, there was a dramatic decline in traffic using the Old Passage at Beachley, which went out of use until reopening around 1930. The old inn suffered the same changes of fortune to reopen its doors again and welcome visitors to the **Beachley Ferry Hotel** — a 'Modern and well appointed Hotel overlooking the river Severn'. During the interim period there had been a licensed **Coffee Room** kept by Ellen Mills during the 1890s and then Charles Morse in 1903. By 1906 this had presumably became the **Pier Inn**.

In 1933 the single fares of the re-established Old Passage Ferry Co. Ltd. were:

Adult passengers	1s. 0d.
Juvenile passengers	6d.
Bicycles	1s. 0d.
Motor Cycles	1s. 6d.
Motor Cycle and Sidecar	2s. 6d
Motor Cars under 8 H.P.	5s. 0d.
Motor Cars over 8 H.P.	6s. 0d.

It is interesting to compare these figures with those of 1828:

Carriage	12s. 0d.
Gig	6s. 0d.
Man and horse	1s. 6d.
Foot passenger	9d.

And later, when the Severn Bridge was opened (charges shown in old currency)

All motor vehicles	2s. 6d.
Motor cycles	1s. 0d.

By comparison, in 2004 journeys southwards across the bridge are free, but the return journey for a car is £4.60.

Throughout the transitionary period the **Beachley Ferry** continued as a 'Fully Licensed' and 'Fully Residential' hotel and in 1981 Jon Hurley wrote:

The Old Ferry Inn above the remains of the old ferry boat

To suddenly arrive at the 'Ferry', after spending a peaceful morning wandering about the Forest of Dean, is quite a shock to the system. Here, under the awe inspiring steel skeleton of the Severn bridge, with its constant stream of juggernauts traversing the sky, and fronted by the swirling murkyness of the river Severn, crouches this rather unique pub. Anyone who has ever visited an English seaside resort and who has enjoyed hearty esplanade grub will feel suddenly nostalgic for the forgotten fifties when they walk into the 'Ferry'.

The Severn Bridge rises above the Old Ferry Inn

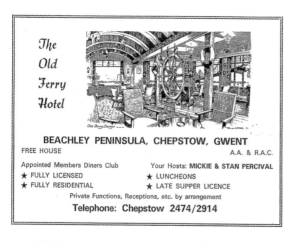

The Old Ferry Hotel

BEACHLEY PENINSULA, CHEPSTOW, GWENT

FREE HOUSE   A.A. & R.A.C.

Appointed Members Diners Club   Your Hosts: **MICKIE & STAN PERCIVAL**

★ FULLY LICENSED   ★ LUNCHEONS
★ FULLY RESIDENTIAL   ★ LATE SUPPER LICENCE
       Private Functions, Receptions, etc. by arrangement
       Telephone: Chepstow 2474/2914

A 1970s advertisement for the Old Ferry Inn at Beachley

Since the opening of the second Severn road bridge a few years ago, the noise of traffic has abated as heavy trucks and lorries tend to use the new route. The **Old Ferry Inn** now offers a quieter place to visit while exploring this ancient site, investigating the remains of the pier and viewing the abandoned *Severn Princess,* the last ferry to ply the Beachley to Aust crossing in 1966.

260

*The Salmon or Three Salmons, which closed as an inn
almost 100 years ago*

The other two known 18th-century inns recorded at Beachley in 1728
were the **George**, which had been 'late in possession of Francis Churchman',
and the **Ship**, which was described as a 'ruinous messuage'.

On the eastern side of the road between Sedbury and Beachley is a
private house called the Three Salmons, which was once an inn dating from
the 1820s. The Saunders family kept the **Salmon** or **Three Salmons** from
1850 until it closed as an inn about 60 years later. The **Salmon** was clearly
named after a stretch of the Severn called the Salmon Catch. In 1935 the
Three Salmons was a boarding house, shop and post office, and never
reopened as an inn.

There is a query over the location of an inn 'known as St. Tecla', which
was owned by the Stroud Brewery in 1962 and described as being 'in
Chepstow', but at Gloucester Record Office a 1973 listing of Whitbread
Flowers Ltd. inns places it in Tidenham.

A thorough search through past copies of the *Dean Forest Mercury* would
doubtless reveal numerous cases of drunkenness and disorderly behaviour,
but a brief glance has found the following incidents that occurred in
Aylburton, Woolaston and Tidenham at the turn of the 20th century.

In 1882 the landlord at the **Cross** was summoned and charged for permitting drunkenness, and was fined 2s. 6d. plus costs. In 1901 James Powis, a collier, was summoned for drunkenness in July. Although he had had nine previous convictions he was only fined 5s. plus 9s. costs, but was caught again in September in another parish and charged accordingly. Frank Cook, Charles Butler and Joseph Williamson, all from Woolaston, were summoned for drunkenness in 1901 and were each fined 1s. and 7s. costs. At Tidenham, in 1903, Charles Savey and William Johns, labourers, were found drunk on the highway and fined for this offence.

CHAPTER FOURTEEN

West Dean

WHITECROFT, YORKLEY & PARKEND

From Lydney, the B4234 leads north into the heart of the Forest to the **Speech House** where, just opposite the hotel, a stone pillar traditionally marks the centre of the Forest of Dean. In West Dean during the 19th century the inhabitants were chiefly employed in the numerous colleries, quarries, timber yards, and iron, tin and chemical works, which apparently were 'by no means a blot on the landscape, as it was quite easy to approach within one hundred yards of some mines without being aware that they are there, so well do the great woods enclose and conceal them'.

Many of these former industrial sites have now been landscaped to provide scenic picnic and parking places, and have taken their original names such as Speculation, Nagshead and New Fancy. Before the construction of the Lydney to Lydbrook road between 1902 and 1905, which now forms the B4234, the industries were served by a complicated network of tramroads and railways. Since the closure of these industrial activities this valuable network has been gradually converted into exciting cycleways and pleasant forest trails which attract tourists into the Forest and form a link with its past history.

At Whitecroft, there is still evidence of light industrial works at the beginning of the 21st century, but the former corn mill, station, collieries and chemical works have long since closed, together with at least one pub and several beer houses. In 1906, Whitecroft was described in a Gloucestershire *Directory* as being:

> situated in the vale betwixt rising ground covered with fine plantations of timber, and has a station on the Severn, Wye and Severn Bridge railway; the inhabitants, whose dwellings are scattered with singular irregularity, are mainly employed in the coal, chemical and quarry trades.

The New Road leads northwards from Lydney and arrives suddenly at Whitecroft around a sharp bend and over a level crossing where the whitewashed **Miners' Arms** stands at the crossroads. This former beerhouse, established in the 1840s, was kept by the Kear family for around 40 years. In 1891 it was tied to the Tewkesbury Brewery, which was later acquired by Arnold, Perrett & Co. and passed to the Cheltenham Original Brewery in 1937. It then included 'All that messuage or Inn known as The Miners' Arms ... with the yard garden stables and all other outbuildings'. The sale also included various pieces of land which, according to the description, had belonged to 'Her late Majesty's Woods and Forests'.

The Miners' Arms in 2003

In the 1980s the **Miners' Arms** was a Whitbread house and was found to be 'an immaculate and well run pub with modernised interiors, gas fires and carpeted floors'. In 1995 the hosts served food all day and the pub is still open in 2004.

From the crossroads at Whitecroft, a short walk past the old mill and up the Bream road leads to the **Royal Oak** standing in an enviable, elevated position. In the late 19th century it appears to have been kept by Thomas Hampton, and in 1919 the 'Royal Oak and the outbuildings erected thereon' were conveyed from Charles Morse to the Stroud Brewery. In 1962 the pub passed to West Country Breweries and later became a Whitbread house. It has survived as a free house into the 21st century.

Apart from several unnamed beer houses recorded from the 1870s, the only other known pub that existed at Whitecroft was on the Yorkley road. This was the **New Inn**, which is now called Kestrel House. It was kept by

The Royal Oak at Whitecroft in 2003

The New Inn at Whitecroft in its heyday

William Berry during the late 19th and early 20th centuries and was eventually purchased by the Stroud Brewery. It appears to have closed its doors around 1962 when the premises passed to West Country Breweries.

The one-time New Inn is now called Kestrel House

The road to Yorkley makes a dramatic turn at Phipps Bottom in Pillowell, where the compact **Swan** offered 'Real Ale' and 'Good Food' in 2003. From the 1890s this inn had a succession of landlords including Henry Smith, William Morgan, John James, Edwin Willetts and Queenie Williams. As with many others it was taken over by the aquisitive Arnold, Perrett & Co. and passed to the Cheltenham Original Brewery in 1937. In 1981, as a Whitbread house, it was described by Jon Hurley as 'a small and friendly "ethnic" pub with plain modernised interior and typical roaring Forest coal fire. Quoit, dart and card playing customers are made very welcome here as indeed are any passing strays in search of a snack and a pint in warm surroundings'.

The Swan at Pillowell in 2003

266

At Christmas 2002 the new landlord and his family at the **Swan** 'pulled out all the stops to put on an enlightening Christmas show' reported the *Forester*. The paper added 'Anyone following a star to Pillowell this Christmas won't necessarily find three wise men, but they will find two landlords and a landlady'.

There was one other pub at Pillowell; known as the **Royal Forester** it closed around 1958. It had been run by William Worgan before Wintle's Forest Brewery acquired the premises around 1900. From 1907 the James family kept the inn with its bar, smoke room, beer store and two kitchens, and above, on the first floor, a club room and three bedrooms. In 1937 the inn, then tenanted by Mrs.

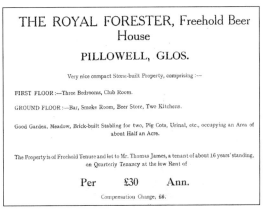

THE ROYAL FORESTER, Freehold Beer House

PILLOWELL, GLOS.

Very nice compact Stone-built Property, comprising :—

FIRST FLOOR :—Three Bedrooms, Club Room.

GROUND FLOOR :—Bar, Smoke Room, Beer Store, Two Kitchens.

Good Garden, Meadow, Brick-built Stabling for two, Pig Cots, Urinal, etc., occupying an Area of about Half an Acre.

The Property is of Freehold Tenure and let to Mr. Thomas James, a tenant of about 16 years' standing, on Quarterly Tenancy at the low Rent of

Per   £30   Ann.

Compensation Charge, £6.

Sale of the Royal Forester in 1923

Mary James, passed to West Country Breweries. Besides the inn there was 'a garden, meadow, brick built stabling for two, pig cotes, urinal etc occupying an area of about half an acre'.

From Pillowell, upper and lower roads lead through Yorkley where houses and cottages enjoy panoramic views of the Forest, and the residents are served with a well-stocked stores and post office, a school, a friendly equestrian centre offering holiday accommodation, and two pubs. Rather less licensed premises are here now than existed at the end of the 19th century, when a directory of 1894 described Yorkley as:

> a large hamlet, partly in All Saints (Viney Hill) and partly in St. Paul's (Parkend), the dwellings in which are scattered over rising ground, some parts being very steep, all the houses are detached and built in positions of grotesque irregularity; the inhabitants are chiefly employed in the coal works in the neighbourhood.

Other trades and occupations at this date included those associated with haulage, timber, building, shopkeeping and beer retailing.

At least two inns once existed along the steep lanes linking the upper and lower roads. The **Stag** on Stag Hill was kept by John Hatton in the 1870s, and in 1891 William Willicombe was running this Arnold, Perrett pub when he applied to the licensing authority for 'an extension of an hour on the occasion of a supper to the New Fancy Band'. Eliza Smith was the landlady of the

Stag in 1903 when she was summoned for selling a small amount of brandy to a lad under 14. Apparently it would not have been an offence had the quantity been greater! The incident was retold a hundred years later by John Belcher in the *Forester*:

> The officer [Superintendent Ford] said that on that day at 12.45 pm he was passing The Stag when he saw a boy named Thomas Archer leaving the Inn. He noticed a small medicine bottle in the boy's pocket. He took the boy back to the inn and found that he had sixpennyworth of brandy in the bottle.
>
> He told the defendant that the boy said she had supplied him with the brandy. She replied 'Yes, I supplied him with half a noggin but I sealed the bottle and did not know that I was doing wrong'.
>
> Supt. Ford said he had made inquiries into this case and had satisfied himself that the boy's mother was ill and that Archer's step father had met with an accident. He brought the case forward as a warning to license holders to inform them that they could not supply so small a quantity of liquour to a boy of tender years even if it was in a sealed bottle.
>
> Supt. Ford said that he brought the case forward so that the public should know that no child under 14 years of age could be supplied with less quantity than a reputed pint of liquor in a sealed bottle. There was no doubt that a technical offence had been committed but he did not want to press the case unduly.
>
> Chairman of the Bench, addressing defendant said that an offence had been committed but that there were extenuating circumstances and the case would be met by the defendant paying costs of 5s. 6d.

The Stag Inn at Yorkley is still remembered in the house name

Eliza Smith was soon replaced by John Halford, who was followed by various landlords until the **Stag** was acquired by the Cheltenham Original Brewery in 1937 as one of 'four several messuages or dwellinghouses one of which is used as an Inn known as the Stag Inn situate at Yorkley in the Forest of Dean'. The gate bearing the name 'The Old Stag Inn' is a reminder of this former pub.

At the top of Crown Lane an attractive three-storied house called 'The Old Crown Inn' was once a free house which was kept by Jane Morgan in 1891. William Robins took over around 1900, and he was followed by Elizabeth Morgan, who was the tenant

Sale details of the Crown in 1923

at the **Crown** in 1922 when Francis Wintle's Forest Brewery purchased the property. After many years service, Mrs. Morgan was still at the inn in 1927 and was possibly the last licensee. When the building was acquired by the Cheltenham Original Brewery in 1937 it was described as:

All that messuage or Inn known as the Crown Inn ... (the license for which has now been discontinued) and all outbuildings and appurtenances thereunto belonging comprising in the rear a range of stone outbuildings urinal two closets wash house coal store and small garden.

The old Crown Inn at Yorkley is now a private house

From lower Yorkley a road leads up the hill, past the present-day post office and stores, to the crossroads at Bailey Hill where the **Bailey** stands prominently on the corner. The inn was named after the Bailey Hill Colliery which had an output of 5,232 tons of coal in 1880. The **Bailey** emerged as a beer house in the 1890s and a few years later was tied to the Anglo Bavarian Brewery who kept on Edith Jones as landlady. In 1915 the brewery purchased the inn which eventually became an Arnold, Perrett house, and in turn passed to the Cheltenham Original Brewery then Whitbreads. The **Bailey** has remained open to the present day.

Before his death in 1957, F.W. Harvey, the soldier poet from the Forest of Dean, moved to Yorkley in a house near the **Bailey**. This was on the corner

YORKLEY.—THE BAILEY INN.

ALL THAT messuage or Public House known as The Bailey Inn situate at Bailey Hill Yorkley in the County of Gloucester and all outbuildings and appurtenances thereunto belonging AND ALSO ALL THAT butchers lock-up shop adjoining in the occupation of Messrs. Eastman Limited under a Lease dated the twenty-eighth day of April One thousand nine hundred and fourteen TOGETHER with the sites thereof and the land occupied therewith

Sale of the Bailey in 1937

The Bailey in 2003

of what is now Harvey Lane, named after the poet. Harvey frequented pubs, and on one occassion, while waiting several hours for a train in a village where the lord of the manor would not allow a licensed premises on the estate, wrote a verse cursing the lord 'Who grudges men their beer'.

From Bailey Hill, the road leads east to Viney Hill and at Yorkley Slade a quiet lane veers south to Oldcroft, past the picturesque **Nag's Head**. Although it dates from the late 18th century, it was extended in the mid-19th century when two cottages were added, but its interior lacks any atmosphere of the past. During the 1870s and '80s William Morse was the landlord, and was still there in the 1890s when the Stroud Brewery acquired the premises. Under the tenancy of Mary Morris a Friendly Society met at the pub, and in 1905 the following account appeared in the *Dean Forest Mercury*:

The Nag's Head at Yorkley in 2003

The annual dinner of the members of the 'Good Samaritan Lodge of Oddfellows' Yorkley, of which Mr. William Everett is the secretary, was held on Tuesday. The members assembled at the 'Nag's Head', their Headquarters, and headed by the Yorkley Excelsior Brass Band, under the conductorship of Mr. Philip Phipps, they marched to Viney Hill Parish Church where divine service was held. ... After the service, the procession was re-formed, and the district having been paraded, the members returned to their headquarters, where a capital spread, prepared by Hostess Morris, awaited them, and about 70 members and friends sat down. After the removal of the cloth, various toasts were honoured, and in response to 'Success to the Good Samaritan Lodge of Oddfellows', the Secretary said that last year 4 members left the Society through death, and non-payment of contributions, whilst one member was received, making up the roll of 55. Some £80 were paid away in sick relief last year. The Society was now worth £250.

The brewery's 'Nag's Head Inn with the cottage outbuildings and land' was taken over by West Country Breweries in 1962, and continues to serve the local community.

Further south is the small hamlet of Oldcroft where, in the 19th century, a public house known as the **Loyal Forester** was apparently trading on the north-west side of the Tuft of Beeches.

Two other brewery pubs were serving the local community in Yorkley at the turn of the 19th century. The one time **George**, 'a very sturdy looking Forest inn', was kept by Robert Wintle for a number of years. In 1927 George

An old photograph of the George at Yorkley

THE ROYAL OAK, Freehold Beer House
YORKLEY, GLOS.

Stone Building, comprising :—

FIRST FLOOR :—Two Bed Rooms, Club Room.

GROUND FLOOR :—Bar, Smoke Room, Beer Store, Kitchen, Wash-house.

IN REAR AND AT SIDE :—Garden, Pig Cots, Closet, and Stabling for two.

The Property is of Freehold Tenure and let to Mrs. Phillips a tenant of about 29 years' standing, on Quarterly Tenancy, at

Per   £26   Ann.

This Rent includes a Meadow with valuable frontage, also TWO COTTAGES adjoining, which the tenant sub-lets at a total inclusive Rent of £13 per annum.

Tithe Rent Charge, 4s. 1d. per Annum.   Compensation Charge, £3.

The 1923 sale details.
Where was the Royal Oak at Yorkley?

James was the landlord at this Stroud Brewery pub, which was taken over by West Country Breweries in 1962. Since then the site has been redeveloped and George Road is the only visible reminder of this lost pub.

There was also the **Royal Oak**, a Forest Brewery pub, which was described in 1923 as a stone building consisting of a bar, smoke room, beer store, kitchen, club room and two bedrooms. In 1927 William Ellway was the beer retailer, followed by Leonard Henry Lee in the 1930s when the Forest Brewery was taken over by the Cheltenham Original Brewery. At that time it was described as having 'in the rear and at side a garden, pig cots, closet and stabling for two and also a meadow'. The inn had two cottages adjoining which Leonard Henry Lee let out. Since then the **Royal Oak** has closed without leaving a clue to its precise whereabouts.

From the north-east edge of Yorkley the road turns west towards Parkend, but on the way a forest road is signed to the **Rising Sun** at Moseley Green.

The present road closely follows the course of a former tramroad and the Severn and Wye Valley Railway's loop line. This line opened in 1872 and served several large collieries, but after the mineral industries ceased production the line was closed in the 20th century. Since then the **Rising Sun** has stood in an isolated position in the midst of the Forest enjoying fine views of the surrounding woods. Although the inn claims to date from the early 19th century, its earlier history is scanty. However, it does appear that Thomas Guest was a beer retailer there during the 1890s when the pub was tied to the Anglo Bavarian Brewery. It later passed to Arnold, Perrett & Co. and after E.M. Seville and Thomas Allan served as publicans it was taken over by the Cheltenham Original Brewery in 1937 when it included 'the cellar club tap, garden land and all other outbuildings' and a 'triangular piece of land being a strip of frontage against the open forest to the premises ... except the mines and minerals thereunder'.

The Rising Sun at Moseley Green in 2003

The **Rising Sun's** recent history was easy to learn from the present owners, whose family, under the names of Morse and Howell, have run the pub since 1939. Old man Morse died at the age of 83 in 1967 when the Howells took over, and the **Rising Sun** became a free house in 1976. It was later renovated and extended in 1982 to provide a skittle alley/function room and a balcony. In 1984 Gloucestershire's *Real Ale Guide* reported that the 'Beautifully situated inn off the beaten track in the depths of the Forest' was a 'free house of character'.

In the 1990s the **Rising Sun** was described by Neil Coates in his *Pub Walks in the Forest of Dean* as 'A basic but welcoming pub, hugely popular with Forest recreationalists, it can have changed little since the days when half a dozen or so major coalmines and quarries were working no more than a stone's throw from the front door', and he added that 'The old industrial days are recalled by a collection of old notices and advertisements concerning sales of mines, coal, stone, etc. dotted around the walls of the pub's considerable interior'. These were still on show in 2003 together with a display of old glass beer bottles discovered in the nearby pond. The **Rising Sun** is still a popular haunt for families, walkers, cyclists, cavers and freeminers who enjoy home cooked meals, bar snacks and the delights of a well stocked bar.

From Moseley Green, the Yorkley to Parkend road leads west through the Forest and into the centre of Parkend to join the B4234 which zig-zags through the village. The village's long and interesting history has been well documented by Ralph Anstis in his *Story of Parkend*, which covers its 'fascinating industrial history, mainly of the 19th century, but also dating back much earlier'. A directory of 1880 recorded that 'The population was chiefly employed in the vast collieries, iron, tin and chemical works, and quarries in the district' and were served by an assortment of shops and tradesmen, a church and chapel and several licensed premises.

In 1882 the *Dean Forest Mercury* reported 'the number of spirit, beer and grocer licences in the district are 67 spirit houses, 49 beer houses, to be consumed on the premises, 20 off and 11 grocer licences' and the Superintendent of the Forest District was quoted as saying 'In my opinion no fresh licences are necessary'. This was probably due to the increasing number of 'drunk and disorderly' cases brought to the courts. For example in 1882 Kaziah Baker, a gypsy, was engaged in a 'general row' at midnight, disturbing 50 to 60 people from their beds. He was charged with drunkenness and fined 5s. plus costs. A few years later James James and Anthony Black who were both colliers, were charged with being 'drunk and disorderly on the highway at Yorkley'. They pleaded guilty, and as they had no previous convictions were 'let off'. A notorious drunk at Parkend was William Young, the wife of 'pious' Mary, tollkeeper at Parkend before the Dean Forest Turnpike Trust was abolished in 1888. Her husband was 'the main blot on her life', as he was as 'ardent a drunkard as she was a teetotaller', who 'took to drink and went into every public house from Blakeney to Bream', recalled George Henderson in a 2003 edition of the *Forester*.

Many other cases of drunkenness were reported in local Forest newspapers including Thomas Holder, a collier, summoned for 'being drunk on the highway' in 1901. He was found very drunk and lying on the pathway leading to a public house in Parkend, and was fined 5s. and 8s. 6d. costs. Also in 1901 another collier, James Powis from Whitecroft, and John Beeble, a tinplate worker, were charged with 'being drunk', but as it was their first appearance they only paid costs of 8s.

In 1841 two licensed premises were recorded at Parkend — one was probably a beer house at the iron works called the **British Queen**, and the other was probably the **Fountain**, which stands at the junction of the Yorkley road. In 1856 James Inman was the landlord of the latter followed by J. Griffiths in 1863 then Richard Scott until George Gunter kept the inn from around 1890 to about 1930. In 1952 it was taken over by the Stroud Brewery and passed to West Country Breweries in 1962.

The **Fountain** closed in 1976 and was converted into a guest house, but fortunately re-opened around 1990 as a free house. The original building is understood to date from the late 18th century, but it was extended after the railway arrived, and later incorporated adjoining buildings to form the present day 'Traditional Village Pub'.

Fountain Way leads west to join another road heading north past the existing **Woodman**, known as the **New Inn** in 1863 when W. Birks was the landlord. As an Arnold, Perrett house in 1903, Enos Ward was the tenant, and in 1937 the Cheltenham Original Brewery took over the inn and 'the shop adjoining and the stables coachhouse yard garden and all other outbuildings'. Although the site was only a quarter of an acre, the Crown still reserved the right to use and work 'all mines and minerals'.

The **New Inn** was kept by George Baker in 1939, when it was advertising 'Excellent Hotel Accommodation, Bed and Breakfast, Teas' and 'Buses to all

The Fountain Inn in the 1930s

The re-opened Fountain Inn in 2003

1939 advertisements for the Fountain and New Inn at Parkend

parts pass the doors'. In 1984 the *Real Ale Guide* described the pub as an
'Amazing unspoilt Forest pub'. This was a few years before it was
modernised and transformed into the **Woodman**.

The road continues past Edale House, a licensed guest house in Folly
Road, to the former **Railway**, which closed as a pub in 1959. It was suitably
named, for Parkend in the 19th century was surrounded by the railways of the
Severn and Wye and the Oakwood branch lines. There would have been a
constant sound of trains and wagons, combined with the hammering,
clanking and rattling of the iron and tin works and the nearby collieries. At
that time Parkend was a noisy and bustling place, where many hundreds of
people were employed. Remains of the railway era are very evident, and

The New Inn has become the Woodman

Sale details of the Railway in 1884

plans are afoot to extend the Dean Forest Railway from Norchard to Parkend, and restore the station where an existing footbridge leads over the old track line to join a pleasant path leading to Parkend church.

During the last quarter of the 19th century the **Railway** was known as the **Traveller's Rest** and also the **Bear**, a name that lingered on until its closure. In 1903 Arnold, Perrett owned the building and William Watkins kept the unpretentious looking pub with about one acre of ground overlooking a level crossing. In 1937 it was taken over by the Cheltenham Original Brewery.

The road leading east from Fountain Way passes Parkend House, the former home of Thomas Hedges Deakin, a 'teetotaller, non-smoker and

The one-time Railway Inn at Parkend

Methodist lay preacher' who from a modest start in life became a manager and co-owner of Parkend Colliery, and a J.P. He lived to a grand age of 85 and never relinquished his grip on his collieries. His house eventually became an hotel, but in 2003 the *Forester* reported 'the hotel building has been found to be structurally unsound, so the latest application is for demolition', and the site will probably be redeveloped despite the residents 'who objected to the loss of a building they see as part of Parkend and the Forest's history. Since then the site has been transformed into a small housing estate.

Almost opposite the hotel, set back from the road, is the Parkend Club. This is near the site of the former **British Lion**, which originated as a beer house in 1849 and was kept by C. Fox in 1863 and Mrs. Mary Fox, presumably his widow, in 1894. The pub was owned by the Cirencester Brewery before being taken over by Godsell & Sons and eventually closed during the mid-1920s.

From Parkend three very different routes lead through the heart of the scenic Forest to the **Speech House Hotel**. Motorists can drive along the B4234, called the New Road; cyclists can pedal along disused railway tracks, part of the present cycleway; and walkers can follow a section of the

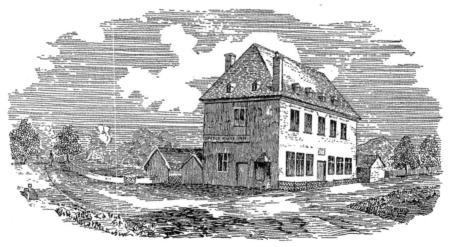

The Speech House in 1858

The Court Room at the Speech House in 1858

Gloucestershire Way. All these routes pass the delightful Cannop Ponds, which were man-made by damming the Cannop Brook to provide water power for the iron works at Parkend in the early 19th century. After the iron works closed in 1908 the ponds remained as an attractive feature and a habitat for various species of plants and animal life.

The **Speech House** stands beside the B4226 on a level plateau at 572 feet above sea level. The late 17th-century building enjoys a fascinating history since it was built to hold the Verderer's Court which deals with the management and administration of the Forest and dates from ancient times. Before 1840 it was used as a keeper's lodge and was then leased as an inn, but retaining the Verderer's Court which was held in a special room described by Cyril Hart in 1950:

> The Court Room itself is spacious, the ancient roof-beams are supported
> by curving wall-pieces, a wide and open hearth faces the western wall. At
> the south end extends a low raised gallery or dais of oak, and around the
> walls hang antlers.

In 1863 J. Coleman was the innkeeper, and from the 1870s to the 1890s John Boyce was running the establishment when the flooring of the dais gave way, and he descended into an opening filled with rubbish including old shoes, bones of deer and a 5 inch copper plate. By 1901 the hotel had become very popular, with visitors from some considerable distances as the *Dean*

279

Forest Guardian reported:

> Mr. George St. John, landlord of the Speech House Hotel, applied for and was granted occasional licenses to sell in a field near the hotel on June 1st and 3rd, on the occasion of two large parties of Birmingham excursionists visiting the house.

Even national papers took an interest and the following year this rather flowery account appeared in the *Daily Mail*:

> From the Speech House — that most sylvan of all hotels, where ancient history and modern comforts abide together — the tourist may step bareheaded into hoary holly woods or the darkly beautiful Spruce Drive, with its three miles of sentinel trees, or under the shadow of immemorial elm or beech make excursions farther afield to the wonderful scenery of the Yat or the Buckstone.
>
> Everywhere he will breathe air like that at Freshwater, estimated by Tennyson to be worth sixpence a pint, for many parts of the Forest are seven or eight hundred feet above the sea, and everywhere the botanically-minded may find rare flora and the entomologist a perfect paradise of insect life.

R. Keverne, in his *Tales of Old Inns* published in 1939, wrote:

> The Speech House has been added to through the years, but most of the

The Speech House in 2003

seventeenth-century house remains. The Court-Room where the Verderer's Court meets is used as the Dining-room. ... Of the many traditions that have grown up about this house is one which tells that an octagonal post in one of the rooms was used as a whipping-post for delinquent servants, another that a small chamber in the cellars was a cell in which prisoners were confined.

An unusual collection of four-poster beds has been accumulated in past times at the Speech House, one of them of great width. The inn keeps its dairy herd, its own pigs aand poultry, so in a way is self-supporting, and both from traditions and situation is one of the most attractive inns in England.

As a Trust House Hotel in 1970, the **Speech House** was offering 'Modern facilities and a high standard of service', and in the 1980s Jon Hurley was impressed and described it as 'a smashing place for city dwellers to slink away for a thoroughly romantic weekend' where 'one could walk off one's frustrations amid some of that soothing scenery'.

By the beginning of the 21st century the handsome **Speech House** had become a luxurious 33-bedroom hotel offering ideal facilities for conferences, business meetings, and weddings with catering ranging from simple bar meals to a full menu served in the restaurant. It is advertised in tourist guides as 'the perfect setting for a relaxing break, walking or cycling holiday'.

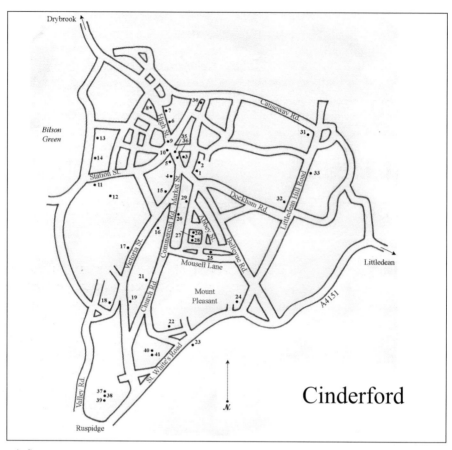

Cinderford

1. **Swan**	16. Miner's Arms	31. **Royal Forester**
2. Crown	17. Dog	32. Royal Oak
3. **Golden Lion** / Dolphin	18. **Forge Hammer**	Puddler's Arms (?)
4. Royal Union	19. Victoria	Green Dragon (?)
5. Fleece	20. Lamb	Fountain (?)
6. Collier's Arms	21. **Nag's Head**	Mason's Arms (?)
7. Globe	22. Stockwell Green	37. Albion (?)
8. Seven Stars	23. **Woodlands**	38. Lancaster (?)
9. Bell (?)	24. **Mount Pleasant**	39. Walnut Tree (?)
10. Queen's Head (?)	25. Red Lion	40. Bell (?)
11. **Railway Tavern**	26. Prince's Plume (?)	41. Lion (?)
12. Railway Inn (?)	27. Prince of Wales (?)	Ship (?)
13. **Upper Bilson**	28. Turk's Head (?)	Pheasant (?)
14. Barley Corn	29. King's Head	Woodbine (?)
15. George	30. Haywood	

Cinderford, showing the positions of pubs.
Those open in 2004 are shown in bold.
Those whose precise positions are uncertain are shown with (?)

CHAPTER FIFTEEN

East Dean

CINDERFORD, RUSPIDGE & SOUDLEY

East Dean was a township in the Forest of Dean that was divided into separate parishes during the 20th century. This eastern part of the Forest is easily accessible either from the southern A48 Gloucester to Chepstow road, or from the northern A4136 Gloucester to Monmouth road, both of which are linked by the A4151 and the B4227 leading through Cinderford, Ruspidge and Soudley. Attractive alternatives include the scenic road from the **Speech House**, in the centre of the Forest of Dean, and one along the cycleway which follows the course of former tramroads and railways from the picturesque ponds at Cannop. These two latter routes lead directly to the recently established Linear Park, a successful attempt at healing some of the worst scars left by the former industrial workings by creating a wildlife corridor and conserving industrial sites along a mile stretch of the former Great Western Railway track. The enhancement project includes footways, pools and display boards describing the history, industries and transport of the past in and around Cinderford and Ruspidge.

Cinderford has only developed as a town since the early to mid-19th century, although its name, dating from medieval times, indicates an ancient iron smelting site at the ford across the Cinder brook; the ford was replaced by a bridge in the late 17th century. In 1856 East Dean was an area where coal and iron mines were extensively worked and superior stone was quarried. In Cinderford there was a salt dealer, coal pit proprietors, iron masters, stonemasons, carriers, shopkeepers and a postmaster. The growing workforce were able to slake their thirst at five inns and four beer houses, where beer was either brewed on the premises or supplied by John Smith — brewer and wine and spirit merchant.

Cinderford rapidly grew to become an industrial town with all the trappings, including a town hall, a livestock market, railway stations, churches, chapels and schools, and in 1900 a Gloucestershire Guide described it as:

> ... this metropolis of the coal mining industries of the Dean Forest [which] stands at the centre of much of the best scenery of the Forest and Wye districts, while its importance as a commercial centre demaind due notice here. It is a market town for the surrounding country and ... the population is just over 3,000.

With the aid of a present day street map of Cinderford it is possible to locate the majority of the town's past and present pubs. Nearly 50 have been identified, including the 'thirteen Public Houses (without catering facilities) and three Hotels (licensed)' open in 1954, and the remaining eight that are still open at the time of writing. Around 1828, as the town developed north of Cinderford Bridge, a new road was constructed linking the three miles from Littledean to Nailbridge, a length of which gradually became the High Street where a host of Cinderford pubs were eventually situated.

The most prominent pub in the High Street is the existing **Swan**, apparently built in 1867 on the site of an earlier inn of the same name. In 1882, when it was described as a 'Family and Commercial Hotel' selling 'Wines and Spirits of the best quality at the lowest market price' and serving 'Pale, Bitter, and Mild Ales from 4d. per quart, in own Jugs from 3¹/₂d.', Thomas Tudge was the proprietor. In 1889, the **Swan** was purchased by Alfred Wintle from Bill Mills in Weston under Penyard, and the property passed to the Wintle's Forest Brewery at Mitcheldean. In 1901, the tenant, Edwin Knight, was involved in a fatal accident as reported in the *Dean Forest Mercury*:

> A serious accident occurred to a lad named Bullock, of the Plump, Mitcheldean, on Tuesday morning last, at Foxes Bridge Colliery. It appears that the lad was working as a 'hod' boy in the colliery, and was following his usual employment on the date named, when a fall of dirt took place, which caught the unfortunate lad, severely crushing his head and face. He was at once brought to the surface, and Dr. Macartney was soon in attendance, but his injuries were found to be so severe that it was deemed advisable to send him to Gloucetser Infirmary. Mr. Knight, of the Swan Hotel, undertook to convey the lad to Gloucheter, but the injuries are of such a character that at present there is little hope of the lad's recovery.

After the death of Thomas Wintle in 1888, it took several years to sort out his estate. This included some of his 'Freehold Properties' which were auctioned in 1906 at the **Swan Hotel**. As a fully licensed hotel, in the early part of the 20th century, the accommodation included ten bedrooms, 'a Commercial Room and two Club Rooms, a Bar, Private Bar, Ladies' Room,

The 1923 sale details of the Swan

A 1939 advert for the Swan

two Smoke Rooms and a Kitchen and Bath Room'. At the rear there was an 'Excellent Yard with Pair of Folding Gates, Bottled Beer Store, Coal House, Stabling for six, Garage for three and toilets'. In 1923 it was occupied by Mr. C.H. Pearce at a yearly rent of £72. When Sydney Bowdler was the landlord of the **Swan** in 1937 it was taken over by the Cheltenham Original Brewery and presumably passed to Whitbreads. From 1967 to 1989 it was run by Gordon Teague. The hotel continues to serve both local people and visitors to Cinderford.

The Swan in 2003

Near the corner of High Street and Heywood Road there was a 19th-century beer house known as the **Crown** which was owned and occupied by Harriett Smith in 1891 and 1903. It appears to have served as a beer house until at least 1935, when it was run by Mabel Wilce who also traded as an antique dealer in the High Street.

Lower down the High Street on the east side is the **Golden Lion** originally called just the **Lion**. It replaced an earlier inn known as the **Dolphin**, possibly kept by John Smith, the brewer, in 1856, a short while before the **Lion** was built. In 1879 Richard Smith was the landlord; he was followed by Mrs. Dianah Smith in the 1890s during which the hotel was acquired by Arnold, Perrett & Co. From its earlier distinction of being an hotel, the **Lion** reverted to a simple public house under the long-term tenancy of Arthur Fricker, who ran the pub from the 1920s to 1947, and saw its ownership change from Arnold, Perrett to the Cheltenham Original Brewery in 1937. There was apparently a flying freehold, for although the hotel included a covered carriage way, it did not include 'the room or building now standing and being over the said piece of land or carriage way and the walls on the north and south sides of such carriageway'. The property did, however, include an adjoining shop, then in the occupancy of Eastmans Ltd.

In the past the **Lion** claimed some notoriety. Thus in 1884, the *Dean Forest Mercury* reported that Mark Lucas was charged for being 'drunk and

The Golden Lion in 2003

286

incapable on the door step of the Lion Hotel, although his general character was good he was fined 5s.'. The **Lion's** publican, George Jones, was 'convicted and fined for selling out of hours' in 1920, and was again convicted in 1921 'for selling to a drunken person and permitting drunkenness'. As a result 'he was out of a job' according to the story retold by Ray Allen to Bob Smyth in the *Forest of Dean Review* in 1998.

In the 1880s several cases of drunkenness in the streets of Cinderford were reported in the local newspapers. In 1884 John Langford, a drover from Worcester, was charged with 'being drunk and disorderly', and in 1885 Thomas Davis and William Watkin were ordered to pay costs for drunkenness, and Thomas Trigg was also charged for 'drunkenness while driving a wagon without reins'.

George Beard was the **Lion's** publican in 1967, when the Forest of Dean Licensed Victuallers Association held their meetings in Cinderford. In 2002 the Freemans from Cambridge took over the **Golden Lion** — 'one of Cinderford's best-known pubs' according to the *Forester*.

On the opposite side of the High Street is a market place known as the Triangle, with a tower and two monuments. Before this was constructed in the early 1960s there were two inns on the site. Standing at the southern end was the **Royal Union**, one of Cinderford's oldest buildings with a bundle of deeds dating from 1840 to 1886 in Gloucester Record Office. Joseph Symonds was recorded as the innkeeper in 1856 followed by William Whitaker in the 1860s, when property auction sales were held at the inn. John Clements held the license in 1879 before the Forest Brewery from Mitcheldean purchased the inn, which was described in a Wintle Agreement of 1888 as being 'Fully licensed with Mark Cole tenant; Rent £40; Contains Bar, Bar parlour, Commercial room, Kitchen, Scullery, 5 bedrooms, store room and club room. Two stall stable, Coachhouse & cellars, Brewhouse or Storehouse'. A note at the bottom of the agreement suggests that the rent is high.

The Cole family were still at the **Royal Union** in 1907, offering 'Wines & Spirits of the best quality' and 'cigars of the choicest brand'. The 'Freehold and Fully Licensed' premises of 1923 was occupied by William Jones

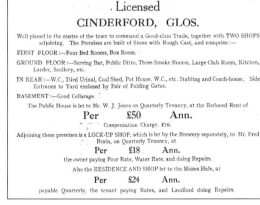

Sale details of the Royal Union in 1923

*1939 adverts for the two inns
in the Triangle —
the Royal Union and the Fleece*

The Fleece was advertising in 1884

who was still there in 1937 when the Wintle pub was taken over by the Cheltenham Original Brewery. After the Second World War the **Royal Union** was demolished and the site redeveloped.

At the northern end of the Triangle was the **Fleece**, which was demolished in 1962 after trading for a hundred years. Robert Ansley was the publican in 1879, and Mary Evans rented the inn from the Tewkesbury Brewery in 1891 before it was taken over by Arnold, Perrett & Co. During the early years of the 20th century the Taylor family ran the establishment, until Mr. F. White became the licensee around 1937 when the inn was aquired by the Cheltenham Original Brewery.

Numbers 43 to 47 High Street now comprise the offices of the *Forester*, published together with the *Citizen* by Gloucestershire Newspapers Ltd. These buildings once housed the **Collier's Arms**, a beer house occupied by Levi Wilce in 1879. Apart from being a beer retailer, Wilce had expanded his businesses to become a butcher and farmer by 1894. The *Forester* of 2002 recalls that Wilce, who died in 1912 while in his 50s, was 'at 22 stone said to be the heaviest man in Cinderford' and needed 'nine pall bearers to carry his coffin'. He left a wife and ten children, and was buried at Ruardean. The beer house was acquired by Arnold, Perrett & Co., taken over by the Cheltenham Original Brewery in 1937, and later delicensed and sold in the 1950s to the Forest builders, Collier and Brain.

On the same east side of the High Street was the former **Globe**, a building easily recognised as it still displays a Whitbread brewery sign. The **Globe** opened in the 1860s, was kept by Joseph Webb in 1879 and became a Wintle's Forest Brewery pub in 1888. It then consisted of a bar, sitting room, kitchen, back kitchen, cellar, four bedrooms, club room and a newly-built stable and coach house and was tenanted to Milson Powell for a yearly rent of £30. In 1923 Thomas Knight was the tenant until 1935 when Arthur French took over. The inn passed to the Cheltenham Original Brewery in 1937 and closed during the second half of the 20th century.

Sale details of the Globe in 1923

On the opposite side of the High Street on the corner of Seven Stars Road was the former **Seven Stars**, established as an inn in 1864. Its landlords included Milson Powell in 1879, Edward Kirby in 1891, Robert Hall in 1894 and Oliver Brain in 1903, when it had been purchased by the Alton Court Brewery. During the 1920s and '30s two women followed one another as landladies, and after passing to West Country Breweries in 1962 it appears to have closed its doors.

The old Globe Inn in 2003

It was in 1882 that the *Dean Forest Mercury* reported that a collier, John Bradley, had been charged with 'riding a horse furiously at Cinderford past the Seven Stars'. He then visited several inns and became abusive. Although he was fined,

Once the Seven Stars inn at Cinderford

he defended himself by saying he was 'riding his son-in-law's horse and told the bench he would take care that he did not ride horseback again'. A **Star Inn** was recorded in a sales particular, which appeared in the *Gloucester Journal* of 1867, but this is the only known reference and may or may not refer to the **Seven Stars**.

At least two other named beer houses existed somewhere in the High Street. The **Bell** was kept by John Briscoe in 1879, but after the deaths of its owners, Joseph and Elizabeth Bennett in 1884 and 1888, 'All that Beerhouse garden outbuilding and premises fronting the High Street, Cinderford called the Bell Inn in the occupation of John Briscoe' was purchased by Alfred Wintle from Bill Mills before passing to the Wintle's Forest Brewery at Mitcheldean. James Brain was recorded at the **Bell** in 1903 and may have been the last beer tender before it closed in 1911. The **Queen's Head** was also in the High Street and was run by Leonard Jones in 1891. It was taken over by Garton & Co. and was last recorded in 1907.

Leading west from the High Street is Station Street which, as the name suggests, leads to Cinderford Railway Station. Despite the proliferation of railways and tramways in the Forest of Dean, it was not until 1900 that Cinderford was provided with its own station, serving the Great Western Railway and the Joint Severn and Wye and Severn Bridge Railways.

THE RAILWAY HOTEL, Freehold and Fully Licensed

CINDERFORD, GLOS.

Modern Stone-built Premises outside Station, placed to command a Large and Independent Trade, comprising :—

FIRST FLOOR :—Five Bed Rooms.

HALF-LANDING :—Bed Room, Bath Room and Lavatory (h. and c.) and W.C.

GROUND FLOOR :—Serving Bar, Private Ditto, Smoke Room, Commercial Room, Kitchen, Larder, Wash-house, W.C. and Store Room.

IN THE BASEMENT :—Cellarage for Beers, Wines and Spirits.

IN REAR :—Excellent yard approached by pair of Folding Gates, W.C., Urinal and small Plot of ground.

BRICK-BUILT OUT-BUILDINGS consist of :—Garage for two, Stabling for four, Saddle Room, Two Pig Cots, &c.

The Property is of Freehold Tenure and let to Mr. Isaac Herbert, a tenant of about 10 years' standing, on Quarterly Tenancy at the Reduced Rent of

Sale details of the Railway in 1923

Opposite the station the **Railway** was established as an hotel in 1900, and was almost certainly built by Francis Wintle of the Forest Brewery to provide a 'Modern Stone-built Premises outside the station, placed to command a Large and Independent Trade'. It consisted of two bars, smoke room, commercial room, six bedrooms and cellarage for beers, wines and spirits with a yard, stabling, garaging and pig cots. During the early 20th century the **Railway Hotel** was kept by various landlords including Samuel Meredith, Isaac Herbert, Ernest Prichard and Thomas Deakins before the Cheltenham Original Brewery took over the Forest Brewery and its premises in 1937. The **Railway** eventually became a Whitbread house and in 2002 was a Pubmaster when new landlords were serving behind the 'revamped, renamed and revitalised **Railway Tavern** with its 'lounge and public bar', as reported in the *Forester*. After being closed for a brief period the tavern is being re-opened in 2004.

The purpose-built Railway Hotel in 2003

There was another **Railway Inn** kept by William Mountjoy in 1863, which must have stood near one of the earlier railway lines.

From Station Street, roads lead north through an industrialised area to Upper Bilson, where in 1841 a beer house was recorded, which may have been the forerunner of the present **Upper Bilson Inn** in Valley Road. It was a 'fully licensed' pub in 1888 when occupied by John White as a tenant of Alfred Wintle at £18 a year. The inn contained a 'Bar, Tap Room, Kitchen, Back Kitchen, Club Room and Skittle Alley combined, 3 bedrooms and small garden' together with one detached and two semi-detached cottages all 'out of repair'. White continued to trade in the neglected premises until around 1903 when John Baldwin took over. When Sidney Hale was the tenant in 1923 the property had obviously been improved. The skittle alley had become a 'Large Store Room' and outside there was a 'nice Vegetable Garden at [the] side and in [the] rear' and the whole had an increased rent of £45 a year. When the **Upper Bilson** was taken over by the Cheltenham Original Brewery in 1937 the tenant was Thomas Ellis. In the 1980s, as a Whitbread pub the **Upper**

THE UPPER BILSON INN, Freehold and Fully Licensed

UPPER BILSON, CINDERFORD, GLOS.

Substantial Stone Building, with Rough Cast, comprising :—

FIRST FLOOR :—Three Bedrooms.

GROUND FLOOR :—Bar, Tap Room, Sitting Room, Kitchen, Two Beer Stores, Pot House, Large Club Room, Large Store Room (formerly a Skittle Alley), Two Large Store Rooms over kitchen.

OUTSIDE :—Large Yard, Public Urinal, Closet, Stone erection of Stabling, Timber erection of Pig Cots, nice Vegetable Garden at side and in rear.

The Property is of Freehold Tenure and let to Mr. Sidney Hale, a tenant of nine years' standing, on Quarterly Tenancy, at the Reduced split Rent of

Per £45 Ann.

Compensation Charge, £6.

The sale details of the Upper Bilson in 1923

The Upper Bilson in 2003

Bilson was described by Jon Hurley as 'modernised and lively with space invaders, fruit machine and a few quite good oil paintings on the walls'.

The **Barley Corn** at Bilson Green was a beer house in 1888 occupied by William Reeves when it was also acquired by Alfred Wintle of Bill Mills, and in turn passed to his nephew Francis Wintle at the Forest Brewery, but was then closed around 1912. The name is remembered in a housing estate called Barley Corn Square.

From the High Street, Market Street leads south before dividing to form Victoria Street and Commercial Road. Many hostelries were located in this neighbourhood including the former **George** on the west side of Market Street. William Thomas was the landlord in 1884 when an incident of assault and drunkenness was reported in the *Dean Forest Mercury*:

> Hy. Morgan, G. Bennett, and W. Perry, were charged with drunkenness on licensed premises.—The charge was first taken against Bennett.—Wm. Thomas, landlord of the George, Cinderford, stated that at 10.40 on the 12th inst., Bennett with two others came to the Inn the worse for drink, and commenced using disorderly language. He asked them to be quiet, or leave the house. Morgan said 'We will go.' He called upon the parties to leave, and defendants declined to do so.—P.C. Curtis also gace evidence as to defendants' drunkenness while in the market place. Evidence having been given for the defence, the other charges were heard.—The several defendants were next charged with assaulting William Thomas. The

landlord stated he was knocked down, received several blows on the head, and a kick. Corroborative evidence was given—Sergt. Hawkins stated that on visiting the inn he found the landlord covered in blood.—The wife of defendant Parry gave evidence for the defence.—In the charge of drunkenness defendants were fined 5s. each; and in the assault case Morgan was fined 5s. and costs.

At one time the George in Cinderford

A few years later William Westaway was the publican at the **George**, which was then owned by Clissold & Sons. It was taken over by the Nailsworth Brewery around 1903, when Herbert Hale was the licensee. After his long-term tenancy of 20 years, he was succeeded by Ernest Parry who served an even longer period there, but it was closed in 1970. Four years later a Forest newspaper recalled: 'It is now over four years since the George Inn, Cinderford, closed its doors on the last customer; and apart from the occasional rat, the old place has remained still and empty ever since'. The piece concluded 'But if only for the appearance of the town it is to be hoped that something is done soon for there is something sad about an old building, once in daily use, standing idle and forlorn in the town centre'. These comments of 1974 seem relevant in 2004 as the building still looks neglected.

In Victoria Street, at least four pubs were open in the 1880s. The **Miner's Arms**, below the Baptist Chapel, was run by the Tingles from 1856, but towards the end of the century became an off-license. Another was recalled by the late Ray Allen in the *Forest of Dean Review* of 1998:

> On the corner of Prospect Road, the Green View Inn is recorded as being let to the Cheltenham Brewery from 1915. It was offered for sale at the end of the Great War by which time it was an off-license, known also as the Drum and Monkey.

Further down and on the opposite side of Victoria Street was the **Dog** of 1887, owned by William Jones, a grocer and retailer. In Ray's article penned by Bob Smyth, he adds 'George Morgan, landlord in 1903 was prosecuted under the 1902 Child Messenger Act for selling beer to an under 14-year old

Sale of the Forge Hammer in 1923

The Forge Hammer sign

in an inadequately sealed bottle'. Although Morgan was acquitted he 'suffered the humiliation the following year of being found guilty of being drunk on his own premises'. The **Dog** was closed in 1926.

Near the bottom of Victoria Street on a sharp bend stands the **Forge Hammer**, Cinderford's oldest surviving pub. It was established as a beer house in 1832 to cater for the workers at the revived ironworks and its early history is recorded in a bundle of deeds at Gloucester Record Office, starting with a mortgage dated 1840 of:

> All that Messuage Tenement or Dwelling House situate at Cinderford in the Hundred of St. Briavels in the county of Gloucestershire near to the Iron furnace there now used as a Beer Shop and known by the sign of the Forge Hammer with the Garden Stable Brewhouse Buildings,

all occupied by widow Wood. In 1848 Benjamin Bennett was recorded at the establishment before it was conveyed to John Baylis in 1850. The pub was occupied by his nephew of the same name who inherited the 'Public House together with the Brew House' in 1867. After Baylis died the pub was sold in 1877 for £950 to Esau Harris, a collier, and was run by the Harris family until it was acquired by the Forest Brewery at the end of the century. This was despite Joseph Harris being summoned in 1884 for 'having opened his house the Forge Hammer, Cinderford, at unlawful hours' for which he was fined 20s. plus costs.

In 1923 the **Forge Hammer** contained two bars, two sitting rooms, a smoke room, club room, kitchen, two pot houses and five bedrooms. William Leighton had been the tenant for over 40 years when the Cheltenham Original Brewery took over the premises in 1937. By the beginning of the 21st century it was a free house offering a cosy bar with

The Forge Hammer in 2003

various beers available to sip while chatting to the locals about the past 'Pit town pubs'.

Almost opposite the **Forge Hammer**, but hidden behind rows of houses, is a building that was once the **Victoria**, kept by Mrs. Elizabeth Cowmeadow in 1856, Thomas Taylor in 1863 and Mrs. Ann Tyler in 1879 before Albert Wintle from Bill Mills purchased the fully-licensed property for £350 in

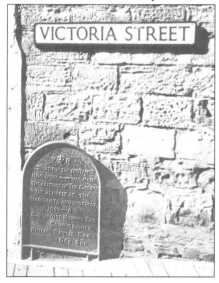

The corner of Victoria Street

1888. William Essex, the yearly tenant, paid a rent of £16 per annum for the inn which contained a 'Bar, Bar Parlour, Private Sitting Room, Kitchen, 3 Bedrooms, Club Room, Cellar'. Adjoining it was an old disused cottage and at the rear was 'a range of Outbuildings comprising a cellar and back Kitchen'. The small garden was to the front and rear of the inn and there was a detached stable and loft. There was also the note that 'Premises in good state but trade has declined'.

With the United Temperance Movement holding demonstrations and fund raising fêtes, it is surprising that one or two other licensed properties did

295

THE LAMB, Freehold Beer House
COMMERCIAL STREET, CINDERFORD,
GLOS.

Substantial Stone-built Premises, with Rough Cast Sides, comprising :—
FIRST FLOOR :—Three Bed Rooms, Club Room.
GROUND FLOOR :—Service Bar, Smoke Room, Beer Store, Kitchen, and Small Room.
IN REAR :—Yard with Roll-way for casks, Wash-house, Closet, Public Urinal, Long Strip of Garden.
The Property is of Freehold Tenure and let to Mr. H. H. Stephens, a tenant of 13 years' standing,
on Quarterly Tenancy, at the Reduced Rent of

Per   £30   Ann.

Compensation Charge, £6.

The Lamb sale details in 1923

The former Lamb in Commercial Road

not suffer the same fate as the the **Victoria** which closed as a licensed premises in 1900 and probably became the 'Victoria Temperance Hotel' by 1907. There was also Alfred Dykin's 'Commercial Temperance Hotel' of 1900 in Victoria Street.

Market Street leads south into Commercial Road, where the former **Lamb** stands on the corner of Lamb Lane. This one-time beer house is said to date from 1869, and in the 1880s was a Forest Brewery property along with three cottages all tenanted to Thomas Stephens at a rent of £25 a year. The **Lamb** consisted of a bar, smoke room, tap room, cellar, three bedrooms, club room, back kitchen and a garden, and

The Nag's Head in 2003

296

continued in the same format under the tenancies of Mary and then Howard Stephens until its closure around 1928.

Commercial Road continues south into Church Road where the existing **Nag's Head** is situated in a hollow but still offering far-reaching views from its garden. It was licensed as a beer house in the second half of the 19th century and was kept by Alice and then Henry Jenkins who sold it to the Ross based Alton Court Brewery in 1927. In 1935 the pub was tenanted to Edwin Tooze, and in 1962 the Alton Court Brewery and its pubs, including the **Nag's Head**, were taken over by West Country Breweries and then passed to Whitbreads. In 1998 Ray Allen explained that 'Whitbread sold out in 1981, it thus became one of the Forest's few free houses. Landlady Patricia Reynolds has presided since 1983' at what Ray describes as 'a friendly, lively, one bar pub of the old kind'. In 2004 the **Nag's Head** appeared to be well supported and offered a venue for watching important football matches.

From the southern end of Church Road, it is easy to access Stockwell Green and St. White's Road, where at least three past and present licensed premises are sited. Facing the green stands the former **Stockwell Greeen Inn**, one of Joseph Bennett's beer houses in the late 19th century that was purchased by Alfred Wintle in 1889 when it was occupied by Charles Tate. Apparently the 'one room pub on a bad road' was closed in 1911. On the east side of the green in St. White's Road is a building displaying the sign of the **Woodlands**, which became a hotel about 30 years ago before becoming a pub. After temporary closure it was re-opened in 2004.

Details of the Mount Pleasant in 1888

At the east end of St. White's Road, a pleasing horse and rider sign denotes the **Mount Pleasant**, a white-washed building on the corner of Mount Pleasant Road. It was recorded as a public house in 1841, and in 1888 was a Forest Brewery holding together with two cottages and land all valued at £820. At that date the 'Fully licensed' inn consisted of a 'Bar, Bar Parlour, Kitchen, Back Kitchen, pantry, two underground cellars, club room, two bedrooms, dressing room and store room, coach-house, 3 stall stable, piggeries and garden', and was occupied by Elijah Mountjoy.

Sale of the Mount Pleasant in 1923

Sometime before 1923
the **Mount Pleasant** was
altered and extended to
provide five bedrooms,
boxroom, smoke room, sitting
room, and a beer store. In
1937 the Wintle pub passed to
the Cheltenham Original
Brewery and was later taken
over by Whitbreads. Mr. W.J.
Beatty was the landlord and
member of the Royal Forest

The Mount Pleasant at Cinderford in 2003

of Dean Licensed Victuallers Association in 1967, and in 1981 the pub was
described by Jon Hurley as a 'friendly local ... with small coal fire, pine
panelled walls adorned with cheap prints of the great ex-Heavyweight
Champions of the World'.

From the Triangle in the centre of Cinderford, the Bellvue Road leads
south-east to Littledean. Lying to the west of Bellvue are the streets of
Flaxley, Abbey and Woodside which, bounded by the earlier Mousell Lane.
were developed as a residential area during the 1870s. In Flaxley Street the
former **Red Lion** stands on the corner of an alley leading to Mousell Lane.
John Milwater was the owner-occupier of this beer house in 1891, and in
1901 the 'Valuable Old Established Free Beer House and Premises Known as

the Red Lion Inn' was sold and purchased by Wintle's Forest Brewery. When Mr. S.J. Leighton was the tenant in 1923 the stone-built inn contained a bar, tap room, smoke room, sitting room, four bedrooms and a club room with stabling, pig cot and garden. A few years later

THE RED LION, Freehold Beer House
FLAXLEY STREET, CINDERFORD, GLOS.

Nicely placed to command a thriving trade. The premises are Stone Built, and comprise :—
FIRST FLOOR :—Four Rooms, Club Room.
GROUND FLOOR :—Bar, Tap Room, Smoke Room, Kitchen, Sitting Room, Larder, etc.
OUTSIDE :—Wash-house, W.C., Public Ditto, Urinal, Stone erection of Stabling, with entrance from Flaxley Lane, Brick Pig Cot, and nice Strip of Garden.

The Property is of Freehold Tenure and let to Mr. S. J. Leighton, a tenant of about four years' standing on Quarterly Tenancy, at the reduced Rent of

Per   £35   Ann.

Compensation Charge, £6.

Sale details of the Red Lion in 1923

Albert James was the tenant before it closed as a pub.

A tradition exists that in the Flaxley Street area there was 'an old coaching inn and alehouse' known as the **Prince's Plume** which may have been confused with the **Prince of Wales** in Woodside as both signs are derived from the same person. The one in Woodside only dates from the era of Queen Victoria's eldest son, who became Edward VII. The premises were owned and occupied by Thomas Burford, a shopkeeper and beer retailer in 1891, but no more recent records of this establishment have been found since Frank Dykins was running it in 1903.

The **Turk's Head** was another late 19th-century beer house in Woodside Street. It was kept by the Merediths, but closed in 1911. Woodside Street was the birth place of Jimmy Young who was born in 1921. His father and uncle were bakers and it is said that 'Jimmy was a familiar sight delivering bread around the town'. Jimmy first made his name as a crooner before becoming famous as a radio star; he was knighted in 2002.

Standing on the corner of Woodside and Abbey Streets was a prominent white-washed building which was once the **King's Head**. In 2002 the *Forester* announced that it was threatened with demolition, but the former pub still stood derelict a year later. However, in 2004 it was being demolished to make way for four bungalows. The **King's Head** was a beer house kept by a succession of landlords from the 1870s. Francis Wintle acquired it at the beginning of the 20th century, and let it to Hubert Harris when it consisted of a bar, two smoke rooms, sitting room, kitchen, a club room and three bedrooms, with a small stable and yard, store shed and strip of garden outside. In 1932 Martha Fowler took over before it followed the usual progression from Wintle

THE KING'S HEAD, Freehold Beer House
CINDERFORD, GLOS.

Occupying a good corner position for business. The Premises are Brick-built, and Rough Cast sides, comprising :—
FIRST FLOOR :—Three Bed Rooms, Club Room.
GROUND FLOOR :—Bar, Two Smoke Rooms, Sitting Room, Kitchen, Larder, etc.
IN REAR :—Small Yard, W.C., Store Shed, Coal Store, and Small Stable, Public W.C. and Urinal, Small Strip of Garden at Side.

The Property is of Freehold Tenure and let to Mr. H. E. Harris, a tenant of 17 years' standing, on Quarterly Tenancy at

Per   £35   Ann.

N.B.—This Rent includes a Brick-built Cottage adjoining, which is sub-let by the tenant at 4s. 6d. per week inclusive. Compensation Charge, £4.

Sale details of the King's Head in 1923

*A rather sad-looking King's Head in 2003 —
now demolished*

to the Cheltenham Original Brewery in 1937 and later became a Whitbread house. A story concerning the inn was related by the late Ray Allen to Bob Smyth of the *Forest Review.* It was reputedly one of the regular evening destinations of the man who was the first person in the Forest to lose his driving license under the drink-driving laws. Thereafter he took to visiting on horseback. One evening, when the man concerned, Mick Baldwin, stayed here beyond his normal leaving time, the nag shook loose its tethering and and proceeded to the next hostelry where its owner managed to catch up before it went home on its own!

*Sale of the Haywood Inn at
the Royal Union Inn in 1867*

From the Cinderford Triangle roads and lanes lead north-east to Haywood or Heywood, where the former **Haywood Inn** stands, still displaying a Whitbread plaque. In 1867 it was occupied by William Leedham, in 1882 the license was transferred to Charles Harding of Gardner Brewers, and in 1891 the beer house was kept by the curiously-named Milson Huzzy who later moved to the **Fleece**. John Russell was there in 1903 when it was owned by Ind Coope & Co. before it passed to Arnold, Perrett and thence onto the Cheltenham Original Brewery in 1937.

This may have been one of the pubs frequented by male and female gypsies as retold by Humphrey Phelps in his *Forest of Dean* published in 1982: 'One played a flute-like pipe, another a fiddle and soon their spell entered into the weary hearts of gaunt-faced miners who thumped their clumping boots upon

300

the wooden floor and beer was sent slopping'. This was despite the fact that miners were known to be 'not pleased to have a woman in their pub'. In 1984 the **Haywood** was described as 'very basic' but with a 'traditional pub atmosphere'; it closed shortly afterwards.

From Haywood, the Causeway Road leads to Littledean Hill Road where the **Royal Forester** stands on the corner of the two roads. Still open in 2004 it survives as one of Cinderford's longest remaining pubs, dating from 1838. It was kept by John Harris in the 1850s and '60s, then the Dawsons during the next two decades, and Arthur Jones in the 1890s when it was tied to the Alton Court Brewery. During the 1920s and '30s James Meek was the landlord before the inn passed to West Country Breweries in 1962. H.S. Worgan was

This rather gaunt looking building was once the Haywood Inn

Royal Forester Hotel, Littledean Hill, near Cinderford.

G. DAWSON begs to inform his sporting friends that his ANNUAL PIGEON AND SPARROW SHOOTING MATCH will take place on THURSDAY, FEB. 21, 1884, when a FAT SHEEP and other PRIZES will be Shot for. Conditions 3 birds each; handicapped from 9 to 21 yards rise. Shooting to commence at 12 o'clock sharp. A DINNER will be provided at 5 o'clock, Tickets 2/- each. ☞ A good supply of Pigeons and Sparrows on the ground.

Newspaper invitation to the Annual Pigeon and Sparrow Shoot at the Royal Forester Hotel in 1854

offering ' the finest panoramic view in Europe' from his 'Large Lounge and Spacious Bar, New Skittle Alley and Limited Accommodation', in 1973. A decade later the **Royal Forester** was described as 'a real Forest local with superb views'.

At the southern end of Littledean Hill Road there was at one time a public house called the **Royal Oak**. Herbert Williams was the landlord in 1856, Joseph Brain in 1863, and George Gwinnell in 1888, when it became a Forest Brewery premises consisting of a tap room, bar, parlour, kitchen, four bedrooms, small club room, cellar, yard, piggery, four bedroom cottage and four acres of land. George Berrows kept the inn in 1901, when a fatal and distressing gun accident took place as reported by the *Dean Forest Guardian*:

The Royal Forester in 2003

TOP OF YOUNG WOMAN'S HEAD BLOWN OFF
ONE OF KITCHENER'S HORSE CHARGED
WITH CAUSING HER DEATH

On Monday afternoon last the Eastern side of the Forest was thrown into great excitement when the alarming rumour got abroad that a young woman had been fatally shot at Littledean Hill, Cinderford. On enquiry the report turned out to be only too true, the victim being Miss Alice Berrows, sister to Mr. George Berrows, landlord of the Royal Oak Inn (the well-known old Cinderford and county Rugby forward.) The sad part of the tragedy is that the fatality appears to have been the result of a pure accident, the top of the unfortunate young woman's head being blown away by the explosion of a gun which was being carried by a young man named Mr. Ephrain Davis (a brother of Mrs. Berrows), who has recently returned from South Africa, where he was a volunteer in Kitchener's Horse. Mr. Davis, who is a man of fine physique and holds an exemplary character, has spent six years in South Africa, and since returning from the front has been staying at the home of his sister. No such a terrible occurrence is ever remembered in this neighbourhood before, and many are the expressions of sympathy for all concerned.

On Wednesday Mr. M.E. Carter, coroner, held an enquiry touching the death of Miss Berrows. The jury, who were composed entirely of tradesmen, with Mr. G. Church as foreman, met the coroner at the Royal Oak where they were sworn in and viewed the body. This presented a gastly sight, the left side of the head as far as the eye being entirely blown off, the brains having been scattered in many directions. After visiting the scene of the accident, the jury adjourned to the Police Station to hear the evidence.

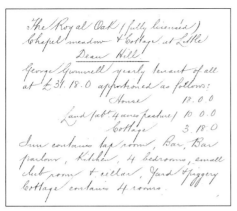

Details of the Royal Oak in 1888

The Royal Oak sale details in 1923

It was generally agreed that the tragedy was a pure accident, although it was appreciated that the gun was not in good condition and that the slightest pressure on the right hammer would force it down to the cap.

During the tenancy of William Mason the **Royal Oak** passed from Wintle's Forest Brewery to the Cheltenham Original Brewery. The 1937 conveyance included a meadow of about 3 acres and an adjoining cottage. Since then the **Royal Oak** has closed and its site has been redeveloped to provide a housing estate.

One other licensed premises once existed on Littledean Hill Road; it was known as the **Puddler's Arms**. According to an article by Ray Allen in the *Forester*, it closed in 1874. 'The circumstances were that the owner, Ernest Ryder, was about to go to trial for burglary. He had a wife who cross-dressed and went into town dressed as a man. It upset some people who had no sense of humour'.

Other pubs in Cinderford, without any known history, were listed by the late Ray Allen in his article on pub life through the centuries which appeared in the February 2002 edition of the *Forester* newspaper. Ray named the **Green Dragon**, which closed in 1867, the **Fountain** and the **Mason's Arms** in the High Street, the **Albion**, **Lancaster** and the **Walnut Tree** towards Cinderford Bridge, another **Bell** and **Lion** in St. White's, and Ray also saw references to the **Ship** of 1832, and the **Pheasant** and **Woodbine**.

Cinderford continues in a southerly direction to Ruspidge which has gradually become a suburb of the town. There does not seem to be a definite boundary, but Ruspidge is accepted to lie 'south of St. White's Road and east of Cinderford brook'. The two alehouses that were established at Cinderford Bridge are listed either at Cinderford or at Ruspidge, depending on the

Details of the Bridge Inn in 1923

period. The **Bridge** emerged in the mid-1850s and was kept by the Mountjoy family for a lengthy period; probably at this important site it would have replaced an earlier hostelry. In 1889 the trustees of Joseph and Elizabeth Bennett sold 'All that fully licensed Alehouse outbuildings and premises situated at Cinderford Bridge called the Bridge Inn in the occupation of James Hawker'. The purchaser was Alfred Wintle of Bill Mills, and he transferred the property to his nephew Francis at the Forest Brewery. In the 1920s the **Bridge**, tenanted to E. Birt, was 'believed to to be the nearest Licensed Premises to the Lightmoor Pit, where over 500 men are employed', and contained a bar, tap room, smoke room, sitting room, kitchen, five bedrooms, cellarage for 'Beers, Wines and Spirits' and stabling. The

The Bridge Inn at Ruspidge in 2003

The White Hart at Ruspidge in 2003

Cheltenham Original Brewery acquired the inn in 1937, and as a Whitbread pub in 1984 it was described as a 'Basic two bar pub on [the] outskirts of town'. Even so, it has continued trading and in 2004 was continuing to serve its customers.

Around the corner and up the hill, the extensive buildings of the **White Hart Inn** cannot be missed. This 'Country Inn & Eating House' originated as an alehouse in the 1830s, when it was owned by a local pit proprietor. It was kept by William Morse in 1863 and owned and occupied by Robert Ansley for a number of years. He was convicted in 1903 for 'permitting drunkenness on the premises', and a year later sold the inn to the Stroud Brewery. During the 20th century two different families of Jones ran the hotel as it changed from Stroud to West Country and then it fell into Whitbread hands. Before Mrs. May Jones died in 1973, the **White Hart** was used by the Cinderford Rugby Club as described in *100 Years of Cinderford Rugby*:

> It was in the summer of 1946 that a small, almost certainly dejected, band of rugby enthusiasts made their way up the White Hart Hill, still having just been told they could not use the Bridge Hotel as their headquarters for the re-formed White Rose Club. Into the White Hart Hotel they went with the request to May Jones 'Can we use the Hart to change for home games?' The immediate, almost inevitable response was 'Of course you can.' In the succeeding years, Mrs Jones gave every possible support to the club, often paying bills until finances improved.

In the late 1980s Jon Hurley described the inn in his *Forest of Dean Pub Guide* as 'a busy eccentrically shaped pub with several bars and rooms ...

The Rising Sun at Ruspidge in 2003

The New Inn at Ruspidge in 2003

The Hart is easily the best pub in this grey little town where the rain looks as if it grimly falls every day and drab shops huddle garishly'. Since then the town has had some improvements and looks considerably brighter, especially when the sun shines.

On the B4227 Ruspidge Road, there are two inns dating from the 1870s which almost face one another and are the remaining two of six beer and ale houses that were open at Ruspidge in 1894. Thomas Guest kept the **Rising Sun** in 1879 before it became a brewery-owned pub run by members of the Butt family from around 1890 to at least 1935. The **Rising Sun** was listed in the 1984 edition of *Real Ale in Gloucestershire* together with its opposite number the **New Inn**, which became an Alton Court Brewery pub in the early 20th century whe Henry Baldwin was behind the bar. By 2004 both had become free houses and the **New Inn** was offering 'Good Food and Real Ale'.

The other two pubs that were open in 1894 at Ruspidge were the **Feathers**, kept by Thomas Hall (which appears to have closed in the early 20th century) and the **George**, kept by George Evans. In 1903 the **George** was tied to the Rock Brewery and became an Arnold, Perrett property. It was taken over by the Cheltenham Original Brewery in 1937 when it was described as a beer house together 'with the existing rolling way under the cottage or dwellinghouse Number 1 adjoining with full and free right to use the same'. Since then the **George** has closed together with the two unnamed beer houses of 1894 that were run by Richard Baxter and William Morse.

From Ruspidge to Soudley, the disused track of the Forest of Dean Railway now forms the Blue Rock Trail, which takes its name from the nearby Bluerock Quarry. The trail, which opened in 2000, provides a pleasing approach to Soudley, although the road also follows a scenic stretch through the Forest, past areas where coal, iron and stone were once extensively mined and quarried. The area, which includes Blackpool Bridge, is described in a Wye Valley guide of 1951 as:

> a group of hamlets in the beautifully wooded valley through which runs the road from Cinderford to Blakeney. Ferns, bracken and a string of fish ponds help to make this a 'cool sequestered nook', especially when approached along the cobbles which once echoed to the footsteps of Roman legionaires.

Since the opening in 1983 of the Dean Heritage Museum at the former Camp Mill, Soudley has become a focal point for tourists and locals to learn about the history of the Forest. During the winter of 2002/3 the museum underwent a major refurbishment, and now tells the story of the Forest of

The White Horse at Soudley in 2003

The White Horse sign

Dean from prehistory to present-day through a series of displays. Amongst the objects on show are old bottles associated with the drink industry which are indexed in the Gage Library at the museum. The objects include beer bottles from the Alton Court Brewery at Ross, Arnold, Perrett & Co., Bill Mills at Weston under Penyard and Wintles Forest Brewery, a Guinness barrel, cider barrels, a cider jar, and mineral water bottles from the Speech House, Lydney and Cinderford. Of special interest is a beer token from Whitecroft, a half pint green-glass beer bottle from Speech House, a Royal Forest of Dean Mineral Water bottle, and a drinks crate from J. Ford & Co., Cinderford, who were wine and spirit merchants and mineral water makers in the 1890s.

In 1974 the local newspaper featured Soudley as 'Self contained, it possesses churches to satisfy the needs of most people, the local pub, club, football team, and voluntary groups to meet the requirements of all age groups'. The pub is called the **White Horse**, and originates from a modest mid-19th century beer house that stood near the chapel. It was the meeting place of a Friendly Society in 1857, and was run successively by Samuel Hewlett in 1863, James Bowen in 1879 and William Thomas in 1894. During the occupancy of the latter landlord the pub was taken over by the Alton Court Brewery and the business moved to larger premises at its present site. With a change of license from beer house to alehouse it was called the **White Horse Inn** and was taken over by West Country Breweries in 1962 when it included 'two pieces of land in Blakeney Walk adjoining ... and containing 36 perches', and another piece containing 22 perches.

At Upper Soudley, the Tramway Road leads towards the slopes of Bradley Hill where a sad looking **Comrades Club** displays a fading sign revealing a one time free house serving Whitbread beers. Other known licensed premises include the **Victoria** of the 1890s, which was another Alton Court Brewery pub, and the **Tump Inn** and the **Traveller's Rest**, both dealt with in chapter eleven. There was also a beer house run by the Collins family during the first quarter of the 20th century, a beer house at Bradley Hill in the 1840s, and another at Brains Green in the 1890s.

Sources & References

GENERAL WORKS

The Torrington Diaries, Hon. J. Byng, 1781-87
The Book of Trades, 1811
Paterson's Roads, E. Mogg, 1828
Rural Rides, W. Cobbett, 1821, 1830, 1853 editions
The Great Western Railway, P.R. Gale, 1926
The Ancient Bridges of Wales and Western England, E. Jervoise, 1936
The Local Historian's Encyclopaedia, J. Richardson, 1981
The Old Roads of South Herefordshire, H. Hurley, 1992
Victualler's Licences, J. Gibson & J. Hunter, 2000

JOURNALS & NEWSPAPERS ETC.

Gloucester Journal 1772 - 1867
Dean Forest Guardian
Dean Forest Mercury
The Forester
Wye Valley & Forest of Dean Review
Newscuttings file at Cinderford Library
B. G. S., 1884 vol viii
Gloucester Notes & Queries, vol. vi
G. S. I. A. Journal, 1974
Gloucestershire Directories 1822 - 1937
Petty Sessions Licences 1891, 1903
Deeds, Documents & Sale Particulars, G.R.O.

MAPS

Bryant's County Map of Gloucestershire, 1824
Sopwith's Map of the Forest of Dean, 1835
Tithe Maps 1838 - 1845
Ordnance Survey, 1883 - 2002

THE COUNTY

The Rural Economy of Gloucestershire, William Marshall, 1796
Excursion Down the Wye, C. Heath, 1828
Nicholls's Forest of Dean, H.G. Nicholls, 1858
The Wye Valley & the Royal Forest of Dean Guide, 1939
Severn, Wye and Forest of Dean, A.D. Holmes, 1945
Severn Tide, B. Waters, 1947
The Verderers and Speech Court, C. Hart, 1950
Lydney Guide, 1950
Wye Valley & the Royal Forest of Dean Guide, 1951
The Castle of St. Briavels, 1953
Longhope, Longhope W.I., 1953
*Littledean, c.*1960
The Changing Forest, D. Potter, 1962
The Severn & Wye Railway, H.W. Parr, 1963
Memories of Mitcheldean, B. Smith, mss. 1965
A Week's Holiday in the Forest of Dean, J. Bellows, 1965
Archaeology in Dean, C. Hart, 1967
A Village in the Forest, I. Davis, 1966
Memories of Mitcheldean, F. Boughton, *c.*1970s
Victoria County History, Gloucestershire, vol. x, 1972
*Newnham-on-Severn Guide, c.*1974
A Child in the Forest, W. Foley, 1974
Blaisdon, Blaisdon W.I., 1975
Wye Valley Guide, 1975
Gloucestershire Turnpike Roads, G.R.O., 1976
The Buildings of Gloucestershire, D. Verey, 1976
Severn Enterprise, C. Jordan, 1977
The River Wye, K. Kissack, 1978
Bream through the Ages, W. Camm, 1979
The Secret Forest, R. Wright, 1980
The Old Industries of Dean, D. Bick, 1980
Old Industrial Sites in Wyedean, A. Cross, 1982
The River Severn, K. Kissack, 1982
Coleford, C. Hart, 1983

Littledean Hall, D. Macer-Wright, 1985

Speech House Walk, Forestry Commission, 1984

Bixslade Walk, Forestry Commission, 1984

Gloucester, C. Heighway, 1985

Road, Travel & Transport in Gloucestershire, N. Herbert, 1985

Forest of Dean & Wye Valley, A.A. & O.S., 1988

F.W. Harvey, F. Townsend, 1988

Ancient Dean, B. Walters, 1992

Industrial Archaeology of Gloucestershire, Assoc for Industrial Archaeology, 1992

Water Powered Industries of the Lower Wye, S. Coates, 1992

Forest to Severn, H. Phelps, 1994

Coleford Town Walk, J. Webb, 1994

The Folklore of Gloucestershire, R. Palmer, 1994

Lydney Official Guide, 1995

The Gloucestershire Way, G. Stewart, 1996

Victoria County History, Gloucestershire, vol. v, 1996

*Dean Heritage Centre Guide, c.*1996

Lydney Town Walk, Forest of Dean Local History Society, 1997

The Story of Parkend, R. Anstis, 1998

A Glance Back at Lydney, N. Parkhouse, 1998

Riverdine Dean, J. Putley, 1998

Forest People and Places, Bob Smyth, 1998

Old Stone Crosses of West Gloucestershire, R. Hirst, 1998

Cinderford Guide, 1999

A Glance Back at Bream, R. Hirst, 1999

A Millennium Miscellany, Woolaston History Group, 2000

Newnham Millennium Heritage Walk, Newnham History Research Group, 2000

A Glance Back at Coleford, K. & J. Webb, 2000

Courtfield, C. Fox, 2000

The Story of Bill Mills, H. Hurley, 2001

A Glance Back at Mitcheldean, P. Mason, 2001

The Royal Forest of Dean Guide 2001, 2002

A Glance Back at Lydbrook, Lydbrook Historical Society, 2002

INNS, BREWERIES, CIDER & WINE

Inns, Ales and Drinking Customs, F. Hackwood, *c.*1904
Forest Steam Brewery Sale, 1923
Wintle's Brewery Sale, 1937
Arnold, Perrett's Sale, 1937
Drink, A. Simon, 1948
The Brewer's Art, B. Brown, 1949
The Old Inns of England, A. Richardson, 1952
200 Years of Brewing in the West Country, West Country Brewery, 1960
Alton Court Brewery Sale, 1962
Stroud Brewery Sale, 1962
British Inn Signs, E. Delderfield, 1965
Wine and Food, W. Younger, 1966
The Inns and Friendly Societies of Monmouth, E. Davies & K. Kissack,
    1981
Forest of Dean Pubs, J. Hurley, 1981
The English Alehouse, P. Clark, 1983
Real Ale in Gloucestershire, CAMRA, 1984
Pub Names, L. Dunkling & G. Wright, 1987
Brewing Industry, L. Richmond & A. Turton, 1990
Forest of Dean Pubs, J. Hurley, 1991
Pub Walks in the Forest of Dean, N. Coates, 1993
Quaint Signs of Olde Inns, G. Monson-Fitzjohn, 1994
Anglo-Saxon Food and Drink, A. Hagan, 1995
Paths and Pubs of the Wye Valley, H. & J. Hurley, 1998
The Good Pub Guide, 1999
Inns of the Past, Coleford Project Walk, *c.*2000
The Pubs of Ross and South Herefordshire, H. Hurley, 2001
This is Alcohol, N. Brownlee, 2002

Index of Pub Names

(Entries in italics represent illustrations)

41

44